Theodore Goodman

THE WRITING OF FICTION

An Analysis of Creative Writing

PLANTIN PUBLISHERS

Plantin Publishers
Market House, Market Place
Deddington
Oxford OX5 4SW
and
Cap de Bonne Espérance
Les Quatre Routes
24220 Saint-Cyprien

Originally published under the title *The Techniques of Fiction*
Published in Plantin Paperbacks 1990

ISBN 1 870495 08 X

Foreword

IT WAS DURING Professor Goodman's thirty years as a teacher
of narrative writing at The City College of New York that his
work and personality took on their mythical proportions; and
his long career as a teacher was undoubtedly the most important and significant aspect of his life. Indeed, for those who
knew him only at the college, it is hard to conceive of him in
other than the role of brilliant teacher, sympathetic colleague,
and inspiring mentor, in spite of the echoes of boundless
friendships and full social life which reached even into academic corridors. He was really in his element, however, dealing with the bright and talented young people who needed
and appreciated him.

For some of his students he personified knowledge and a
subtle insight into the meaning of what they were learning,
so that they could transmute their knowledge into material on
which their own creative powers might operate. To other
students he offered encouragement to use the knowledge and
ability already available to them—encouragement from one
whose own talents of articulation were prodigious, and whose
heart, quite literally, was in his mouth. And for some his
efforts were directed toward the sobering effect, the shock
treatment so beneficial (and so seldom offered nowadays) to
the gifted and cocky youngster.

Goodman's ferocious classroom remarks were famous; he
once informed a student who had read a story in class nerv-
ously and weakly, "You read that with all the clarity of a
Yugoslav with a cleft palate." Yet it was never his intention
merely to be clever at the expense of defenseless students. He
knew those who could not take the sharp reply; he knew when
to offer reserved comment, when to suggest comradeship,

when to be silent. In all that he did in his classes, a student could see that he loved good writing more than anything else in the world. And the roster of those on the literary scene today who acknowledge his impact on their development— Leonard Ehrlich, Irwin Stark, William Gibson, Paddy Chayefsky, Morris Freedman, and Eliot Wagner, to name but a few —testifies to the success of his teaching capability.

Nor did three decades of teaching writing, encountering the same problems year after year, holding conferences in the same dim office, diminish his enthusiastic and energetic approach to teaching. Heart disease may have hampered his physical agility, but it could not weaken his lectures on Joyce's short stories or his approval for a good student theme. Attaining his Ph.D. did not end his interest in scholarship; his appointment to a full professorship was less important to him than giving attention to students' needs. From first to last he maintained the youth, the spirit, and the vigor of heart and mind which kept his classes alive "with excitement, with promise, with love."

He had a theatrical personality which belied the conservative suits he always wore, complete with academically correct vest. When he spoke, there was no doubt that his audience was being treated to the musing of no ordinary academic mind. In the faculty dining room there was never a vacant seat at Teddy's table, for he entertained his companions with a gifted and limitless fund of colorful and amusing stories, emphasizing his points with appropriate gestures distinctively his.

Goodman's younger colleagues were awed by the myth, but delighted by the man. On his part, nothing was too great a burden if he thought he recognized ability or sensitivity in a new teacher. He was happy to spend many hours talking easily to, or perhaps at, the novices, whom he called "asterisks" in the departmental roster. He offered to read their graduate papers, rejoiced in the publication of their juvenile articles, sweated out each year's reappointment with them. His devotion to them was so deep that at times it proved embarrassing, as when he waved the president of the college away from the luncheon table with the offhand remark that he was saving the seat for a newly-employed tutor. Or, he might insist that the hapless and unwilling new instructor accompany him to the dean's office so that he could declare to that equally embarrassed official the merits of the neophyte.

Professor Goodman will be remembered longest by his students and colleagues as a person of extravagant personality and unique character. Nobody was neutral about him: those who did not love him, hated him. But among those who remember his words about writing, there is enthusiastic agreement that he said—and we choose the word carefully—wonderful things.

This written record of Goodman's ideas will serve as a reminder to those who were fortunate enough to hear them from Goodman himself; and we are sure that for those who read them here for the first time, they will prove as instructive and inspiring as the original lectures.

Editors' Note

AT THE TIME of his death Professor Goodman had already begun the revision of his manuscript, *The Whole Fiction,* in which he analyzed not only the techniques of narrative writing, but also the author's and the reader's experience of fiction, and the metaphysical implications of that experience. The editors, colleagues of Professor Goodman at The City College, have deleted his philosophical and psychological comments except when they are essential to Goodman's study of fiction as an art. A minimal number of verbal changes were made in this revised manuscript, *The Writing of Fiction.*

Marvin Magalaner
Brooks Wright
Julian B. Kaye
Kenneth W. Rice

Contents

Chapter 1

An Analysis of Fiction

PEOPLE WHO BRING an interest of their own to a book on fiction, who wish to compare their views with the author's, need hardly be told that ideas about art are convictions, and therefore in large measure, personal. Presumably, what any one person knows about fiction is not everything that may be known about it. Everyone will make this statement, or regard it as obvious; and having granted the obviousness, everyone will then behave as if he had never heard of it. In the course of discussing fiction, each of us has his own rate of slipping into the mood and manner of omniscience; the more circumspect hold out a little longer; the more candid confess the failing a little more readily. But everyone, sure as fate, arrives at his own convinced moment of thinking and speaking as though what he had in mind were a knowledge of every last thing there is to be known about fiction.

My own experience may be relevant here. In my thought about fiction, I make it my practice to distinguish between what I actually *know* about fiction, and the larger background of fiction as an art against which I carry on my discussion. I use the familiar term "fiction" only for my partial knowledge; and I give the total art a home-made name: "the *whole* fiction." Thus "fiction" indicates for me specific pieces of writing we all discuss; "the whole fiction" the larger study we all pursue. I have been helped in discriminating this way by a lively sense of the simple fact that the whole fiction is considerably more than the sum of human knowledge about it. Furthermore, we may make comparisons and contrasts between the parts of fiction and the whole fiction; and some of these comparisons are convenient tools for further analysis, which we come to use by second nature in our work every day.

What I am calling "the whole fiction" may be approached in several ways. In the abstract, it is imaginative narration, commonly in prose. In the concrete, it is the sum of all examples of the art; or, it is any single example regarded as representative. There is still a third way of regarding the whole fiction, but since it is somewhat unfamiliar, I must give it a little introduction.

Although the analysis of any reality into its abstract and concrete aspects is usually complete enough for any immediate purpose, I find such an analysis inadequate and unsatisfactory for the whole fiction. For, we have still to account for the process which relates the abstract art and the concrete work. Fiction involves the reading or the writing of a story. Now, either of these activities is an experience, and the two together are familiarly recognized as the experience of fiction, the *characteristic* experience for which either story-teller or reader turns to the art, and by which all of us understand it for what it is. In being experience, every instance of it is a happening, an event. No such event ever occurs twice exactly the same, so that the quality of being unique is invariably part of the experience. Therefore I call this phase of the whole fiction the *unique whole fiction*. We have only to be reminded of the peculiarly personal nature of reading and writing, to understand fully the unique quality of the whole fiction; and it is this unique experience which relates the concrete and the abstract aspects of fiction as an art.

For example, every reading of *Tom Jones* differs in some respect from every other. Among readers the differences are those of sensitivity, maturity, or, in one word, individuality. Each reader has a lifelong, periodically changing experience of fiction which is not identical with that of anyone else; and the experience of many readers, exchanged and mingled in conversation, criticism, and study, forms a socially distributed knowledge of fiction which no one would deny, or dare to inventory. If what I say is true of readers, it is certainly truer of the writer, who, in addition to being a reader himself, has an experience derived from conceiving, composing, writing, and revising story after story.

When I call anything *unique*, I do not imply that it is without resemblance to any other thing. Uniqueness is the quality by which a thing is different from anything otherwise quite like it. It is foreground difference distinguishable *because* of background resemblance. This apple is an apple, but not any other apple. This reading of "The Purloined Letter" is certainly a reading of it, but not any other reading of it, because it is my experience of it here and now. The unique whole fiction includes in itself parts of both the abstract and the concrete aspects of the whole fiction. I can express this partial identity negatively: as far as the concrete aspect is concerned, any experience of *Pride and Prejudice* is not likely to involve an experience of any character called Uncle Tom or Robinson Crusoe. And as far as the abstract idea of fiction as a *literary*

14

art is concerned, I can say that any experience of *Pride and Prejudice* is not experience of the ballet or sculpture.

Further thought will show that the three aspects of the whole fiction are not like removable parts of a machine. Although we take the abstract and the concrete for granted as constant, who can doubt that in individual personal experience the unique influences them considerably; or that the art itself periodically shows signs of change? To confuse the ease with which we separate these three parts of our analysis in our minds with their actual continuity would be to relapse into the blunder of forgetting what we all initially grant and then too carelessly take for granted: our knowledge of fiction and the reality of fiction as an art are not one and the same. Fiction has a comprehensive quality which we cannot equal fully simply by adding together its various parts, any more than we can dismember a chicken and then add up the parts into a whole (that is, a live) chicken.

If up to this moment I have made any contributions to the reader's information, they are probably the two conceptions I am calling the whole fiction and the unique. Before I turn to further explanations, I feel I must try to reduce the effect of the strangeness of a coined name. My saying "the whole fiction" is my way of making certain that in speaking about the art, our haunting sense of whatever in it continually mystifies us shall be as persistent a part of our awareness as our very proper sense of having much knowledge about it. The whole fiction, as distinct from any attempt to know or express it, is a reality that is vast, varied, and ultimately vague. It is imagination plus narration plus literature, a complex and unstable compound. It is a mixture of which one component alone—imagination—is so variable as to produce fantasy in Poe, romance in Dumas, realism in Tolstoy, and symbolism in Mann. And in certain individual works there can be a mingling of all these moods—*Gargantua, Tristram Shandy, Ulysses, The Castle.* Furthermore, though in practice we limit the literary expressions to prose, the claims of poetic novels, like *Troilus and Criseyde* and *The Ring and the Book,* and of poetic tales and romances like Crabbe's, Scott's, Tennyson's, and Longfellow's, are better proof of a helpless arbitrariness than of a true limit.

I am delighted to think that no definition of fiction could be more suitable than one which admits an irreducible element of the undefined. A chief glory of this art is the creation of novelty: the quality of whatever is inevitable the moment it occurs, but even the moment before unpredictable. So I am

15

pleased with any definition which, while sufficiently sketching the past and present, leaves the future free, and enables the public, as de Maupassant put it, "to urge young authors, as earnestly as they can, to strike out new paths." When the young authors succeed in the attempt, they amplify the art as it is achieved, and compel the revision of our idea of it. Any such change, viewed after the event, seems not an accident, but a particular fulfillment of destiny; and once we recognize change in fiction as inevitable, we are wiser in doubting our knowledge a little than in seeing it whole. Whatever we know today, we know we have come by in the course of centuries of restless realization that what we knew at any one time represented only a fragment of the truth, as the part indicates the whole.

Fiction, considered as literature, is communication through language *because of the separation of persons*. Reader or writer single-handed administers a vast mechanism for the enlargement of experience, much as a telegrapher administers some lone post in a far-flung railroad system. Fiction is society experienced in private, and shares the triumph of those arts by which mankind attains the miracle of solitary community; and the author who writes "only for himself" is simply playing Crusoe on his own little island of the mother tongue. Writer and reader, we withdraw from the world to the printed tale; with the first words we experience the lives of the characters in the privacy of our own, pass out of the confines of worldly sense and time and place, and enter upon our common humanity.

In this experience imagination is not merely a means, but an end. However we may feel about what we do before we do it or after, while we compose or read a story the great thing is the engrossment, the imagining. The fact remains that when we do experience fiction at the fullest, we have lost awareness of everything but the story, including our earlier knowledge that so far as the real world is concerned, the occurrence is, of course, imaginary. (There are people who have told me that they never lose themselves in a story. I have also been assured, and therefore have no right to doubt, that there are also people who never kiss anyone without accompanying intellectual discrimination of their role in the experience, the social significance of the act, its place in a complex chain of causality, and so on. When I am told such a thing I try hard not to show how sorry I am for those in whom love is stillborn, who cannot get from a kiss what anyone at all gets from a swift, hard, unexpected kick from behind. But when

I have sorrowed for their plight, as I do for the people who cannot so far forget themselves as to lose awareness in a story, what more can I do? Certainly I have no use for a standard of satisfaction according to which it is better to have missed than loved. The world is full of standards, some of which I prefer the other fellow to have.)

Just as, in imagining a place in which some one event is occurring, we do not lose our impression of the rest of the story simply because we are attending most closely to a specific part of it, so, too, we do not altogether discontinue our awareness of meaning and the actual print on the page. This awareness of the printed word is a habit, subordinated to the keener awareness of the illusion; but it never ceases to be part even of the swiftest and most casual performance by the accomplished reader: witness the vanishing of illusion when we come to a misprint.

If we follow this matter further, we can reach some interesting conclusions. I do not know how it is with others, but for me the very look of a poem on a page is the start of an intent interest in form, to which the metre gives pulse and continuance. I am commonly much more aware of my private monologue when I read verse than when I read prose; and knowing the near identity of fiction and poetry, I am inclined to discriminate against them by negative criteria: the one does not require metrical organization; the other does not require organization as relating of events. Although the look of a page of non-fictional prose is, from a distance, quite the same as the look of a page of fiction, in experience the two are different as night and day. One may be engrossed in either; but the engrossment differs according to what is assumed about the character of the piece and then taken for granted—that is, momentarily forgotten. In fiction, the half-forgotten assumption, easily enough remembered at need, is that the subject matter of the experience, regardless of any resemblance or lack of resemblance to what we regard as actuality, is not only being imagined by the reader, but is being imagined by him because it was imagined by an author. When, moreover, the assumption that the occurrence is an imagined one has in this sensible way been allowed to fall out of the reader's awareness, then the illusion that the narration is somehow about events in the real would may be harmlessly indulged, enjoyed, and in its turn, neglected.

Imagination of any sort in reading is determined for us by this question of what assumption concerning the nature of a piece of writing we formulate first, in order that it may be the first to be neglected. If, for example, in the experience of reading or writing a narrative, we assume that the occurrence is or was actual, then for us the experience is history or biography or some such factual account. On the other hand, if the assumption that we first lay aside is that the occurrence is an imagined one, then the experience is fiction. People so naive as not to realize that this is the true state of things will read an actual biography as a story, and a realistic novel as an account of real people. After all, we have inherited fiction from ancestors to whom myth and memory were indifferently truth. In our own more recent time, one can see that the tendency of fiction occasionally to condition itself somewhat as history, psychology, or social philosophy, or some other form of factual discourse, is made possible by a species of vagueness growing out of the basic indefinability of the whole fiction itself, and is somehow connected, too, with the ambiguous look of any page of prose.

By far the greatest contribution of the literary phase of fiction—that is, style—to the narrative phase is its ability, ideally, to disappear from view, to seem nowhere about. Then the story comes into its own, becomes "the story" we so confidently refer to when we speak of it as an object of our observation, as if it were a reality external to the mind of author and reader alike. And we behave toward it as though it were an actual occurrence in the lives of certain people at certain times and in certain places. Robinson Crusoe, cast on an uninhabited island, makes it his solitary home for more than a quarter of a century, and is then rescued. Emma Bovary attempts again and again to live a life of "romantic" love, and brings tragedy upon herself and ruin upon her family. A group of shady characters, cast out from Poker Flat in the Rockies, are overtaken by a blizzard and die in it heroically. Like a phrase in a diary, any such one-sentence outline can recall an entire action, its people, its time, and its region.

That the outline no more than indicates the action is obvious. It is not the action; it does not cause the whole experience. We have two ways of responding to a story: the one, after we have finished, when we can outline the central occurrence; the other, while we are first reading it, when we cannot. True, at any stage of our reading we feel that the part we are engrossed in is rounding toward a whole; the business of the rounding, the determination of what whole—in a word, the *form*—is somehow the essence of the experience, even if only unobtrusively. Yet the very unobtrusiveness of the role

18

of form makes it an impelling background power. What we are principally concerned with is our absorption with these people, who are doing and saying these things in this place at this time, with all the perceptibility, the vividness, of live physical bodies in physical surroundings. They come to us, therefore, with the impact of character, of feelings and thoughts, in the way that such things penetrate a notice too busy taking them in to give a thought to what they are, or whether they are. What has already happened is involved in what is happening. And now, what *will* happen?

The relationships of witnessed events in the fictional pattern are formed by the principle of conflict. The print, the monologue, the awareness of meaning as meaning, of illusion as illusion—all these are presences swallowed up in action. They have vanished from mind by vanishing into it, and are fuel to drive the fascinating events of the tale before the reader's awareness.

The experience of fiction is literary and narrative; but it is so because it is above all imaginative. Moreover, it is imaginative in all the three important meanings of the word *imagination:* the first, that so much of our experience is of things not at the moment present in the immediate environment; the second, that in reflective thought this transcending of the limits of sense operates for the discovery of things never bodily present—that is, the analyzed qualities of our own thoughts and feelings; and the third, that in art we can and do experience things never present physically or otherwise until our human creation presents them to us, in fictitious events and persons. The first is perception mimicking the senses; the second, perception identifying by reason what cannot be sensed at all; but the third is the imagination proper, the creation of new form as new presence amid the old. The creative imagination, as natural a thing as any in the world no matter how superstitiously we may react to it, is the necessity that is the mother of invention because it is the necessity that knows no law. The artist is the man who searches for the image he must have, whether it is there or not.

For the artist, the imaginative experience of the whole fiction is a Chinese puzzle, egg within egg, a complex operation dense with powers so closely affiliated as to pass one for the other—idea as value, value as need, need as feeling, feeling as desire, desire as dream and illusion, illusion as progression of events, events as audible recital, recorded script, and then print. Meaning is quick in every part of this process, often in spite of no explicitness by words, as when by the pallor of the moon the sun shines at midnight, and the familiar earth is plain and strange. The artist is a man to whom our world is but a point of departure, the whole of it no more than one land's end from which to launch lonely discovery. Yet for all his single divination, he pursues his mission by the means and at the behest of powers invisibly working within him and through him. These forces, occult only in their consort with the future, are his because they are, of course, ours; all that we lack of him is his unique specialization. Hence each of us responds to him for the humanity that all of us ceaselessly are and extend and enrich.

An examination of the processes of attention can be of help in the study of the imagination. At any rate, I feel that I ought to say something about what I mean by attention; and I observe that attention has three separate parts, each of them an action. The first is an action productive of intense awareness, which I will call *focus*. The next is an action that produces the relatively relaxed awareness of reception; this I will call *periphery*. The third, because it is an action that effects exclusion of awareness of some presences from focus and periphery, I will call disregard.*

Attention may be defined, with respect to its triple organization, as distribution of unequal awareness to presence. Thus it is one of the biases of human life, perhaps of all life. I have no doubt that the basic bias is related to our human disposition to attend to certain presences, such as flashes of light and unwonted sounds, with quite typical curiosity, whether or not we ever find out why we should do so. Also, the propensity very likely lies at the root of individual tendency to attend to this rather than to that in a given situation at a given time of life, depending upon the person's habit and regardless of whether or not he knows that he has been so accustomed. In any event, the over-all operation of attention, at one and the same moment, selects for focus, periphery, and disregard; and what is selected for each is important for what will later be selected for writing down.

The whole point about literary art, such as fiction, is that if the illusion of the author is ever to become literature, the non-linguistic portions of it must be worded. The words are first formulated within the author as private monologue, and

---

* I am using disregard, not in the more familiar meaning of no attention at all, but in the only less familiar and equally authorized meaning of neglectful or insufficient attention—not quite enough attention, *almost* none. So far as I know, what others designate as "the unconscious" has no relevance whatsoever to what I call "disregard," and therefore no relevance to my discussion of attention, the imagination, or the whole fiction.

then exported by, and away from, his body, as publicly audible or written speech, gesture, and bodily motion which others may perceive. I should like to stretch the term *publishing* to include any action which produces external notification of the author's private monologue. *Publishing,* in this sense, would be impossible, or at least fruitless, if not for an action which is its paired opposite. Unfortunately, there is no word to name this procedure, so I must coin one. The meaning I have in mind is: "to make private what is public or published." The word I offer is *to privish,* which I pronounce with the first *i* long, as in *privacy,* and of course with the accent on the first syllable. Every sensory perception is a privishing—focal and peripheral and disregardful, which may be blotted out by the one immediately following it, though not beyond the possibility of recovery.

Resolution of conflict in attention, whereby one pattern of experience is established dominantly at the expense of other patterns and sustained as "the" experience, is a resolution only for the purposes of the moment. By act of recovery the choice of focus can be unmade, can be remade into another, more inclusive resolution, for the purposes of another, later moment. Whether or not the drowning man sees his life in review, he certainly has the means to do so. No matter what the pattern of focus-periphery may know in any single privishing, disregard has absorbed into itself the complete reality, and therefore potentially holds the reproduction of the awareness of the presence attended to as a thing privished, a privishment. Privishment "has vanished," it is "forgotten," it is "nothing," when focus-periphery is busy with other presences; but when focus-periphery is trained upon privishment, then memory comes into operation; and when the specific privishment is evidently recovered, there is "a" memory.

In memory, as in sense perception, experience always *becomes,* is always new-fashioned, because it is always, inevitably, being made. Now, this making of experience in myself is what I mean by the word *imagination.* There are some varieties of experience, like sense perception or memory, in which the operation of imagination is merely instrumental, and in which it is disregarded. But in dream and reverie, imagination is lifted out of mere implementation sufficiently to make us aware of its character as a creator of experience.

The deceptive presences which the imagination of the novelist offers to our attention in a work of fiction are extraordinarily complex. His deception lies both in the process and the products of his imagination; for the slightest hint of what the novelist is doing breaks in upon and dissipates the principal function of his activity—to make us believe that his imaginary presences are real. In other words, fiction, as what is imagined, must seem not only all that appears to attentive consciousness, but all that could possibly appear. Therefore, the tale should engage all of focus and periphery, and some of disregard, in the reader's intentness upon momentary action. The phrase "art concealing art" is the witty expression of a necessity.

A story conjured up in consciousness, then, should hold us as compulsively as the most fascinating reality in the world, when we are interested beyond the slightest awareness in our interest. We must therefore not fail to note about fiction that it is profoundly a mood, the keynote of which is absorption. There is this one thing occurring, and there is nothing else anywhere, not even ourselves. Here at once we see what marks off a reading that is an imaginatively artistic experience from one that is critical. Even when the presence in imagination is that of mermaids or Lilliputians, which are not the imitation of anything in the world, my response to them is still a perfect mimicry of my response to lightning or the sea when these are full of a wonder that has replaced me with itself. The moment I ask myself whether there can or could really be mermaids or Lilliputians, I am not having an ideal imaginative experience of them. In the moment of imaginative experience, I am helpless to question. It is so for the writer as for the reader. "The personality of the artist," Joyce says, "passes into the narration itself, flowing round and round the persons and the action like a vital sea. . . . The dramatic form is reached when the vitality which has flowed and eddied round each person fills every person with such vital force that he or she assumes a proper and intangible esthetic life."*

In everyday experience, one function of consciousness is to explore the matter-of-factness of reality for ascertainment of form, value, idea, and meaning. The function of fiction, as an art, is to begin with these abstractions, and to express them secretly, implicitly, in the symbol of illusion. Thus attention, as an instrument to elicit pattern from universal conflict, is in the experience of fiction the instrument which sets the illusion free to arise with all the expanse and fascination and opacity of a dream. Fiction is therefore a mirror of reality; it reverses the process of discovery under the appearance of reproducing it, and goes, not from the awareness of being to

* A Portrait of the Artist as a Young Man. Quoted by permission of the Viking Press.

the synthesis of meaning, but from the experience of chosen illusion to the intimation of meaningfulness. It is in this cunning way that fiction reshapes reality and *creates* experience. The very time required by the operations of consciousness in reading a story is subtly transformed into the illusion of events and time *in* the story, so that the narrative organization of fiction is a characteristic form evolved from function; and the whole fiction, as what imagines together with what is imagined, is one mood in being one magic.

As imaginative experience, the whole fiction, unlike reverie or nightmare, is occurrence that we make occur, when we wish it, for whatever value that may bring us, regardless of correspondence to fact. Therefore fiction has about it something at once isolated and directive, private and public, individual, social, and racial. It is all of these things at once in the absorption of the single being who writes or reads with his thought on one presence and his body in another. He is society in its phase of solitude; and what the individual achieves in the privacy of his being, he of course achieves no less truly when he sits among hundreds of reader-writers in the hall of a library, all breathing the common quiet, each in communication with a different absence.

This, then, is the whole fiction; the purpose of this book is to analyze it into its component parts and examine them each in turn. The indispensable elements are seven: the word (as prose), imagery, character, pattern, emotion, idea, and conflict. Their intimate fusion constitutes fiction as a medium of expression, an exquisitely complex entity which may manifest its individuality as itself, or in any of the seven parts I have itemized. The presence of all of these seven elements makes fiction differ from the drama and the lyric on the one hand, and on the other, from the essay, biography, and history, regardless of what elements fiction may share with any of these. All writing, fiction included, shares the element of the word as it symbolizes literature; but in differentiating between the species of literature, I believe fiction to be the only one which must have the seven parts I have named, no fewer, and no others.

Chapter 2

Conflict

CONFLICT IS THE STRIKING of force against force. It is manifested as collision and contest. Two or more kinds of energy, or manifestations of one kind, enter into, compose, and maintain a struggle. This, while it lasts, is a conflict. Conflict is ceaselessly operative everywhere, and the dramatic arts are merely one way of expressing a necessity of existence. Even what is called a state of rest is a harmony of strains. The energies within a rock have neither been destroyed nor gone off elsewhere. The absence of visible conflict does not mean that there is none. It stands to reason, moreover, that when, of two forces engaged in opposition, one is incomparably the stronger, there may seem to be no contest at all. So the narrative of a pleasant day in the country, with no untoward occurrence, would appear to be without conflict; yet the maintenance of simply one level of contentment must of course constantly escape boredom, if only from careless little changes of activity, each an insensible heightening or at least refreshing of pleasure.

We are naturally inclined to view as conflict what is obviously so to us, overlooking subtler reality; we are most readily cognizant of conflicts that are manifest, bold, and even violent, and not of those that are hard to perceive, or mild in action, or routine in their familiarity. Furthermore, it is steadying and reassuring to believe that some achieved adjustment of our environment and of ourselves to it is absolutely a kind of cessation of hostilities, as comparatively it doubtless is. Yet all such thoughtless, habitual responses to what we consider conflict and to what we consider tranquillity are clear evidence of a curious error in believing conflict to be only violent and destructive, whereas, in reality, as a manifestation of energies in pattern, conflict is quiet often peaceful and creative. The migration of birds, the blooming of a plant, the building of a house, are instances of the emergence of purpose and order not only in interaction between cooperation and opposition, but among forces competing to establish some dominance within the group. Perhaps that is why the instances I have just given can hold our attention by arousing our suspense: the possibility of finding a pattern among things perceptibly discrete is often a fascination for thought and feeling. So the unfolding and rounding out of a story of struggle may hold our interest as compellingly as the fictitious struggle that runs through the illusion.

So true is this, that often, when the struggle is one we would hardly think of as such, in some tale by Chekhov or Katherine Mansfield, the seemingly unaccountable formation of the episode in the narration of it holds us, page by page, to the end. In fact, the distribution of conflict through all the departments of fiction makes conflict an indispensable part of the whole, whether it is ostensible or concealed, because it is first of all, as it is everywhere in the world, an inherent principle of power. The shipwreck that introduces us to the island of Robinson Crusoe is violent and destructive. Yet it is only introductory to the hero's far more engrossing struggle to establish a congenial environment in the wilderness, to subdue not only the disorder and the indifference of nature, but the sluggishness of his own resources, and the faintings of his lonely spirit. As he elicits from forces around and within him their potentialities for association in his design, and discovers in the outcome suggestions for bettering the original plan, he grows into a symbol of man evolving under new circumstances, and mastering them. Even the impressive difference between his situation and ours emphasizes the common human experience in which a conflict is known to us only in its veil of our doubt about where we are going and what we shall be when we get there—the mood in which we read of Robinson's long, slow success, and ignore the cunning victory his biographer is achieving over our mercurial attention.

It is important to understand that no reader of fiction need recognize the nature of whichever of the many conflicts in a story is the one which holds him while he reads, or need know that it is conflict, or that there is or should be any such thing as conflict. Even the writer, as we have seen, may adopt no more than a parallel technique; that is, he brings to his work a talent in which form and conflict are compounded already, while he concentrates on the story as his readers will experience it. So long as such a reader behaves as though he knew, his reaction is an action in which disregard is sufficiently complicated to hold him to his pleasure of the moment. Equally, any recognition by him of one or several of the conflicts as such, together with his running mental commentary on the details of the development, will simply convert some of the responsive into critical pleasure. He reads as long as he is interested, and is interested as long as he reads, depending on who he is—that is, on the survival of some compulsion of which, if he is lucky, he is not directly aware. The child reads of Theseus in the maze with bated breath because the hero may never get out again; but when later as a man he rereads the myth, that conflict may be simply the ground of his working out the meaning, in the course of which he may chance to relive the childish thrill to the last quiver. And with the man once again the boy, the fate of Theseus may, as if for the first time, hang on a thread.

There are many kinds of conflict. For example, there is an entire variety, to which I have referred, that is plain as the struggle which takes place between antagonists in the illusion and as part of it. This obvious contest or struggle is only part of that part of the whole fiction we are considering under the heading of conflict, yet it is commonly referred to in discussion as "the" conflict of the particular story. For instance, the restless antagonism of Saxon and Norman in *Ivanhoe* contributes to the uneasy truce of hospitable code at Cedric's castle, and rages as battle in the castle of Front-de-Boeuf. The clash of Darcy's pride and Elizabeth Bennett's prejudice is the main thread of Jane Austen's comedy. In *Remembrance of Things Past* the narrator tirelessly examines his every arresting experience for clues to its significance and therefore its place in the pattern he finally composes and presents as the form of his life—himself. Even in Chekhov's "The Chorus Girl," which reads as though it were merely a "slice of life," everything follows the line of embroilment between the wife and the prostitute, and their antagonistic codes. These, as I say, are instances of the prominent conflict running through the single piece. We are used to singling them out and talking about them without the slightest doubt of their existence. We go so far as to speak of "seeing" what the conflict is, of calling upon each other to "see" it. Our metaphor is one of habit; we forget that no conflict is directly perceived, that what we call and rightly recognize as the conflict is the power we experience in those symbols for influencing our senses, feelings, and imagination.

That is why the idea of conflict can be dispensed with by those who have not been taught to know and look for the reality, and why the instructed easily relapse into disregard of it when their awareness is consumed by the activity in the story, such as a collision in a tournament, a conversational fencing between the sexes, some mind puzzling over a problem, two women behaving as the representatives of social division without very much realization that they are little more than its unwitting weapons. Not only the conflict, then, but its processive sections, scenes, episodes, each with its very special graduation of spoken or acted opposition, are recognizable for what they are only by swift inference dependent on the intuition of the illusion, as that follows upon recognition of the meaning in the text. So it must be understood that what we recognize as the principal conflict of any story, finding it salient and not to be missed, is a prominence we safely infer from the shape it gives to what conceals it. In much the same way we say of a man that he is big-boned when we see him fully dressed. It is certainly true that there are big-boned men, and he is certainly one of them. His skeletal structure has a great deal to do with our impressions of him, but who is ever going to see it? The chain of our metaphors is such that any link becomes "the" link the moment we focus on it. When we call any of the numerous conflicts of a story the manifest one, this is what we mean. There is an illusion, and whatever in it, from start to finish, is illusion of conflict, is of course the conflict of the illusion.

In a certain whole class of stories this illusion is reinforced by the fact that the principal conflict is also the principal experience to be gained from the story, and therefore its characterizing element. Action stories, as we call them, present the illusion of people and natural forces in action—that is, physical, muscular, dynamic, violent exercise of the power of energy to re-arrange the material lay-out of things, abruptly, massively, finally. Each combatant is bent on subduing the other, by disablement or destruction or removal; so that whatever the form of things it is the aim of either side to preserve or set up, is the mark of the other to reduce, to de-form. The literature of warfare, political and economic, of nations or classes, is the archetype of such action fiction, the ancient epics, the burlier romances of chivalry, and, in modern times, Scott, Dumas, Cooper and their followers and imitators. Here, as I say, is an entire class of tales, named and widely recognized as that variety of fiction, written to present, and read to experience, some conflict and therefore conflict itself. The human combat may appropriately be set against a background of wild nature, so that the elements may join in the fray and vary it; or the battle may rage between the human and the natural, especially in those areas of earth or ocean in which cataclysm and catastrophe are part, as it were, of the local scene. Hence the importance of environment, not only to make the exotic vicariously familiar, but to enable the untraveled public to

27

follow the steps of the struggle, its ups and downs, its inevitabilities and hairbreadth escapes, with a minimum of necessary explanation in those moments when thrilling events follow each other with climactic fury. For it is these events, the moments of upheaval, peril, and clash, regardless of what matter is used incidentally, which are the high points of the narrative, and which by their frequency and the emphasis given them make such fiction what it is.

To the literature of war and natural convulsion there may accordingly be added that of arduous occupations—exploration, archaeology, anthropology, the hunt, and the handling of machinery which is new and uncertain, or which, in any case, leads men into situations known to be hazardous but unpredictable as to time or precise detail. Jules Verne, Melville, Bret Harte, Kipling, Jack London, and a host of others have created a library of this excitement. The element of gamble in such activities lends them a sporting interest; and this, by itself, is capitalized in fiction of the ring and the track, and of every sort of physical contest and race in which athletics provides the pulse of adventure. Finally, where Nature pits against man, not her aggression, not her fearful provocations of hurricane and volcano, but her stolid resistance to his will, the dead weight of enmity as mass, sterility, vast space and crawling time, we have material for the story of the farmer, the grazier, the fisherman, the miner, the empire-builder, from the pen of Tolstoy, Garland, Frank Norris, Kipling, Hardy, Mary E. Wilkins Freeman, Knut Hamsun.

That the genre varies action with descriptive and expository passages, with love interest and comic relief does not, as we have seen, lower the general tension or dissipate the general impression of maintained action, and therefore of conflict. The combatants of the illusion, whether personal or non-personal, are engaged in a struggle which we follow as the principal entertainment. Tales of this sort are for the most part tributes to strength, agility, co-ordination, and to the virtues of courage, loyalty, sacrifice. They celebrate the will to survive and conquer, a rallying of forces against emergency, for motives ranging from the noblest of human causes down to team spirit. Explicit as these aims or principles may be in the passages given to their expression, they are no less plain when, as drives of value, they impel to valor, to strategy, to utmost exertion in the climaxes of actual clash which are the great thing the story brings us. For, after all, they are what we call "story" in its obvious form, when we distinguish between that and plot or structure; indeed, what more of structure or plot has many a brave yarn needed to enthrall thousands of readers and bring them in a swarm to the next offering from the same hand?

Since the violent act, with whatever accompanies it, is the plainest form that story can take, it has been employed by authors who are not really, or are only partially or doubtfully, writers of action fiction to highlight narrative of quite other species. *The Charterhouse of Parma* and *Lord Jim* are not action stories in the sense that *The Talisman* and *The Three Musketeers* are; yet Stendhal and Conrad have certainly used action of the special sort we have been considering, for their own fuller and deeper purposes. The enrichment of the tale of physical violence with psychological study and social philosophy requires a sophisticated reader, and yet the plain story itself is not for that reason beyond those who get no more than it. We may say the same for Hemingway and Faulkner in our own century. In fact, what are called "the greatest stories of all time," meaning that their high merit has attracted and held a vast audience, are to an extraordinary extent stories in which the action has been either used for or glorified by some magnificence of feeling, or loftiness of truth, or breath-taking beauty: the Book of Job, the *Iliad, Don Quixote, Treasure Island, Huckleberry Finn, Taras Bulba.* On this basis one can understand the vogue of *Quo Vadis,* of *Anthony Adverse,* of *Gone With the Wind,* or even of such relatively better productions as *The Good Earth,* and *The Grapes of Wrath.*

Because of the obviousness of its display, the fiction of physical action provides excellent opportunity for identifying and defining the principal devices of conflict as a general phenomenon. There are first of all specific conflicts themselves, the omnipresent involvement of energy with energy, the universal catch-as-catch-can. How it comes about that the one and the many are the same, we may learn from the tongues of the fire, the whorls of the mist, the winds of the air. The combatants, in their physically perceptible materiality, are disclosed. They stand before our observation, hardly even as the embodiments of the clash, but solely in their own right as the knowable opponents. As such they fall upon each other, and the fight is on. They are two—there are others, of course—but preeminently two account for the "sides." All the others fall in line, or move back and forth across it. For this or for whatever reason, the balance shifts. Time is of the essence; the duration is stroke upon stroke; conflict appears in the event, proceeds as events, and rounds out the event at the last. I mean that climax is another ostensibility of conflict, both in the propulsive rise of furious powers interlocked, and in that event which, being the height of the upheaval, includes all the antecedent intensities in which its power to climb was successively gathered and sprung. As mountain and peak are one, climax is growth and satisfaction. In the end, one finds that it is the end, after all, that has been spurring the preceding events.

So conflict is suspense, the restless shifting of possibilities too rapid to calculate, while the issue—for there is to be finally but one—lurks now in this alignment of forces, now in that. So it is simple truth that as the embroiled forces of conflict press up and on through the stages of climax, there is carried along and held in each produced and apprehended event, the outcome—but veiled, suspended. It is unnecessary, I repeat, for the reader as for the onlooker, that in physical onslaught or contest he identify by name the aspects I have just reviewed. Better for his enjoyment, if enjoyment there is to be, that he be unaware of the rhetoric. Let him be all response, all muscular reaction. Let him fix with every ounce of perception on the movements and the changes of fortune occurring too swiftly for analysis or exposition, too swiftly and significantly for any thought that cannot be lived in a shudder or a cheer. When the cavalry charges, or the runner stumbles, or the roaring grizzly rises before the disarmed hunter, or the bomber bursts into flame, it is there—in them—that our experience is registered, instant, dense, barely supportable, but, above all, how plain!

The very plainness is, or becomes, for some readers, what is wrong with the thing. One has been beguiled in childhood and youth, let us say, with such strong magic of the imagination. In time, it no longer seems so strong, or one is grateful for some encounter that provides a change, or one simply grows up to interests more varied and complex. Perhaps the original interest is never set aside, but is carried along into and among others that develop. One discovers, or at any rate relishes without formulation, the fact that conflict aroused in the reader of a story is as much part of the experience as the mimic conflict attended to as a phase of the illusion in the story. The multiplication of interests that brings maturity or comes with it is itself so occupying that we may never dream how much of our pleasure stems from our sampling the varieties of conflict of which several kinds of fiction provide instances. This in spite of the fact that we perhaps have only the vaguest realization that our scope is expanding, or that by some means or other we escape monotony.

I must now repeat certain things I have said, to express more fully their meaning to me. When I take up a novel and begin it, the first thing to appear, literally before my nose, is the print of the text. This, presently, without in the least ceasing to be *there*, nevertheless as good as vanishes, or turns transparent. So, there stands revealed a place at a time, with people doing and saying things: technically, the illusion. With reference still to my nose as the standard, the illusion may be said to have lurked *behind* the words until it shone through and exaporated them. In much the same way, the conflict may occupy my focal attention and, without for one instant removing illusion or language, nevertheless may loosen their hold upon me, yet leave them to operate without being specially noted in the very place they filled before. This is the level of the action story, the valuation at which the author bids for our attention, and the one at which we accept or reject. So considered, the conflict is equally composed of elements which, since they do not displace it from focus, may be conceived to be lurking behind it and pressing against it: the clash of emotions as partisanship and antipathy, and further away and out of sight, the struggle of ideas as principles, let us say of courage and cowardice, fairness and treachery, good and evil. The bold prominence of the element of conflict in such a story is achieved by a deliberate selection and emphasis of this material. And it is in this way that the modulating of the fictional symbol works, on the basis of adjusted internal strains of which the conflict *in* the illusion is only one production, no matter how it tricks us into responding to it as an all-in-all. Once we grasp this principle we can see how′ in certain circumstances the action story is a fascination and in others a disappointment and why, in or out of focus—indeed, in *and* out of focus at one and the same time —conflict is a *sine qua non* of fiction. There is the reader to whom, since he never gets beyond or behind the conflict, it is the whole story; so that there is no such separate thing as the conflict. And there is, for contrast, the reader for whom the conflict within the illusion is transparent, giving immediate view of the patterning of the conflict into the plot.

I have been speaking of action with the limited meaning of an illusion of physical struggle, violent or at any rate strenuous, in which characters engage, or in which they are caught up and swept along resisting. Before I move on to a broader conception, I will say another word about a more limited use of conflict, not this time throughout stories, but periodically, at the high points of the climactic rise, or only at a certain few of them, or only at the last and highest. Dickens is a practiced hand at such change of pace. In *Oliver Twist,* for example, he alternates the pathetic episodes of Oliver, the comic ones of the beadle's courtship, and scenes of larceny, kidnapping, and brutal murder. Charlotte Brontë, in her *Shirley,* one of the best of the Victorian social novels, presents two powerful episodes of clash between employers and workers. The fantastic romances of Poe and the allegories of Hawthorne make frequent use of physical struggle, rising to a pitch of fury or anguish, and plunging to disaster. The realistic battle scenes in *War and Peace* and in *The Red Badge of Courage* match the romantic ones of Scott and Hugo. There is no mood or species of fiction, in other words, that has not in many works availed itself of the sensory appeal of strife in its manifest forms. Yet, as the high points of whatever the author is presenting by means of them, these outbursts only momentarily divide our interest with the deeper conflict they make vivid. They rise from it as from a source of might. They are the sound and fury of which it is the true force. In this light, not only the moments of physical action, but the whole of what we call the story's action may be seen as the product of the over-all conflict of narrative composition; therefore, action itself is simply one more manifestation of conflict, such as we have noted climax and suspense to be.

If we arranged fictions of various kinds in a certain order, beginning with an action story as one extreme and then moving away from that, the element of conflict would gradually lose prominence. At first it would remain noticeable in the illusion, but would change character. It would not be violently physical but only strenuously so, as in tales of athletics. Or if the tale, like *The Red Badge of Courage,* maintained the conflict of the battlefield in the illusion, it might do so to excite in us a compassionate understanding of the uncourageous soldier whose horror of war gives way to human co-operation in war, until that grows in to courage. Thus the warfare becomes part of the setting for the true conflict, which takes place in one man's spirit; and since we learn only little by little that this is so, the real conflict of the book is certainly not manifest at first. In fact, its delayed emergence into our recognition is part of the climactic rise of the action. Accordingly, the military scenes are for a long time only the cover under which the conflict has been at work. They divert us, so to speak, while the real conflict within the man is getting ready to appear. All of the introduction, then, and some of the body of the novel, which as we read seem interesting simply as a sequence of stirring episodes without formative principle beyond their coming one after the other in time, later prove to have been not merely told, but selected and planned. For the unsophisticated reader, all such management behind scenes is and remains totally unsuspected. So far as he knows, the story is always just what happens. Authors are beings who can write such things entertainingly, and that's all there is to it. Since some of these readers turn writer, with a knack for reproducing a certain kind of tale with mimetic effectiveness, the doctrine of the totally unexplainable gift has a great deal of support within the profession. Since Molière's citizen talked prose long before he learned he was doing so, he might, without the illumination, have gone on doing so to his honest deathbed, yet without causing the rhetoricians to liquidate their science. In an art that requires its practices to be concealed in the act, so much so that even certain practitioners never learn much of what it is they do, the operation of conflict may be so cunning as partially to evade the analysis even of the initiated.

The absence of conflict from the illusion, or the fact that the conflict at any moment *in* the illusion is not "the" conflict, does not mean, as we have observed in the instance of *The Red Badge of Courage,* that there is no conflict in the story. Another interesting example is E. E. Hale's "The Man Without a Country," Philip Nolan, an American officer who has cursed the United States, is condemned to live out his days on a naval vessel, never to set foot on his native land again. All this is told us briefly, at the outset. The rest seems merely a series of episodes participated in or witnessed by Nolan, each with a different set of circumstances but presenting the same theme: man has instinctive love of country. No story, apparently, could have less conflict than this succession of narrated homilies with an introduction and a conclusion. Yet conflict, of course, there is, a resurgence in Nolan of profound patriotism, struggling up against a young hothead's refusal to admit that willfullness had misled him into error. Our feeling that this is the conflict grows on us as we proceed, and casts a dreadful pathos over the ending. This is the unobtrusive, the creative role of conflict, working subtly among the elements of what it will cause to be their design, drawing them together and into arrangement, raising them out of a condition of a welter of circumstance into a clear pattern for cognition and feeling, and stamping them with a form that is finally its own.

The contrast between the action story and the story of no apparent but of actually powerful conflict may be paralleled by comparing Poe's "The Purloined Letter," in which the process of detection is itself the story, and *The Ambassadors,* by Henry James, in which it is simply machinery for presenting the central character's development in self-realization. It is true that Lambert Strether is trying to determine the facts of a matter upon which he must judge and act, but it is far more important that he is at the same time faced by the need of determining who he is and what he stands for, so that there may be no falsification of evidence or principle. The two actions proceed side by side, each with its internal strains, and each under the pressure of the other and in complication with it. Since the action involves a dozen people of marked individuality, and a clash of standards, national as well as social and psychological, and conflicts grow into a web of the utmost complexity. Since the hero is kept in the dark on questions of the greatest moment to him up to the very end, it is as though he were reading the book of his life, but in serial issue and without the recourse of turning to the last chapter for relief from the suspense. If this is Strether's case, it is no less ours. And of course this is always our case when we are in the midst of a novel. Only the frantic cannot wait until the last chapter to learn the ending. Part of the vitality of the good reader is to resist that temptation, to live out the events in their presented sequence as in life, and to learn the answer of art (life does not commonly give one) by sustaining the experience that leads up to it. The sort of conflict we are now considering is buried deep indeed, the game between author and reader, the battle of wits between the two invisible personages of the fiction, the speaking and the listening onlookers. What a happy stroke of symbolism in Browning's poem!—that the Duke should draw aside a curtain as preliminary to that revelation of the character of the Duchess which so hideously reveals his own. An artist, a very great artist like James, must be perpetually on the alert, not only against the imminent tendency of the elements of his art to strain away from each other and out of the associative design, but against that fallibility in himself that threatens at every turn to wreak upon him the transparency with which Browning damned his Duke. The artist does not always succeed in this respect—certainly James did not always succeed—but the roll of his successes is his contribution to civilized life. Indeed, even when the writer fails and succeeds in a single book, when at moments the passion of *Jane Eyre* blunders into unsophisticated ludicrousness, or the genius of Dickens sings into a passage of sentimental betrayal by emotional shallowness, even then we prize the whole achievement. But whether the conflict be in the illusion or in the technique, or in the creative fibre of the author and therefore in his tactical relation with the reader, or, as in the greatest fictions, in most or all of these together, conflict is the bloodstream of the art.

One of the commonest things said of conflict is that it takes place. This absent-minded inclusion of the idea of locality in a synonym for *occurs* brings with it a suggestion of the whereabouts of particular manifestations of energy, and therefore of their contests and collaborations. For the action story, naturally, the conflict takes place in the illusion of the region of the world, an illusion of individual objects or bodily persons, their environments as setting, and their encounters as struggle and change. This is the geography of Defoe and Smollett and Scott and Verne and Melville and Wells and London and Conrad, the public domain of energy. This geography is much more than location or extent. In addition to being the scene of conflict, it can enter into conflict as tide, blizzard, season, iceberg, earthquake, or sunshine. In stories of local color it is environment, and participates in molding character and shaping events in the guise of climate, fertility, barrenness, or jungle. It enters into the determination of such conditions of life as ease and strenuousness, of occupation and industry in some stage of development, and is therefore an influence on degrees of civilization and culture, as it is the various habitats of the races of men. Locale shares in producing the marks of race in such respects as color and stature, and also shares equally in the social customs of nakedness, clothing, ornament, tattooing, warpaint, weapons, and causes and modes of combat.

This role of the body in conflict is matched by the role of conflict in the body. The dimensions of an organism make it a place. As such, the body is the seat of forces without which our action stories could hardly have come into existence. In it, as nowhere else so literally, conflict is embodied. In it energy is specialized as impulsion and reflex and motive—hunger, sex, the will to survive. But if the body contributes to the conflicts of the world those struggles generated within its substance, that is only because the body itself teems with the adjusted and the unadjusted strains of anatomical and physiological inconsistencies. There are restraints imposed upon bodily function by tabu. There are examples of profounder oppositions in nature, such as the sleep which steals over freezing men, rivalries of hunger and indolence, decay and repair, development and degeneracy, well-being and pain, alertness and flinching. There are times when the mind seems no more than an onlooker at the play of sensations, receiving and sustaining them, rather than completely knowing them. This state of feeling or cognition may be torpor, but it need not. Coleridge and Poe and the French Symbolists practiced the literature of sensation; there are whole passages in the work of Zola and the de Goncourts, Huysmans and Proust in which a bodily state is presented, perhaps as by an observer, that is, from without, or perhaps, in its own terms, so to say, as just itself. By a kind of latter-day development in fabulism, the animal in us is made to speak.

If this art of the inarticulate has developed late and produced comparatively little, so has physiological psychology. There may be more to come—presumably there is. All the way from medieval times there comes to us an uncertain, broken line of single productions like dots far separated one from the other, but in their continuity possibly marking a direction: the debates of body and soul, Phineas Fletcher's *The Purple Island,* the *Confessions* of Rousseau, Erasmus Darwin's *Botanic Garden,* certain of Blake's Prophetic Books, Carroll's *Alice* and Lear's nonsense, the comic experiments of Gertrude Stein, and the gripping mystification of Kafka. Much of the lyricism of Meredith, of the naturism of Hardy, is a diffident, frustrated gesture toward the same end, somehow complicated by a partisanship for the body in its rebellion against social restraints; the bolder statements of George Moore, D. H. Lawrence, Frank Norris, Sherwood Anderson, Faulkner, Caldwell, and Farrell are perhaps advances only in downrightness. Certainly the conflicts of the body have not been absent from the expression of the three so often rated the highest creative powers of our age—Mann, Proust, and Joyce. It may well be that all of the relatively little of this sort of production that has appeared to date is only a breaking of barriers, perhaps a start not only negative but wrongheaded in its direction toward a fiction of world-body-consciousness as the integrated self.

When, in the course of a story, strange or startling elements are introduced, their intrusion displaces other elements or obscures them, or relegates them into disregard. Then our minds must search for whatever in our experience may help us to understand the unprecedented phenomenon we witness. For literary expression of this, the fiction of fantasy would appear the obvious type, with myths and fairy tales and *Alice in Wonderland* as examples; yet any stories that feed our craving for vicarious experience will elicit much the same impulse. The distinctions are approximately these: what fantasy is to childhood, and romance to adolescence, the probing of reality is to maturity. Of course, we may at any period of life go on to a new interest or return to a former. An American who has never been to Europe will, with or without awareness of the fact, savor the romance of travel in *Daisy Miller* as a seasoning of the realism; and the European, familiar with the geographical setting, will find a like fascination in the unaccustomed American girl as a national type. Vicariously, again, we share the experiences which are novel to the characters. David Copperfield is served by a waiter for the first time. Roderick Random goes to sea. Kim meets the Lama. Hajji Baba enters the harem. Whatever excitements, distractions, diffidences, bewilderments go with these first learnings are lived by us as well as by the characters, though perhaps differently, in spite of the fact that the circumstances are new for us, too.

We can now turn to the better known conflicts that occur within consciousness. There are struggles that arise between two of the selves of one person. In Mérimée's *Mateo Falcone* a child is torn between tribal loyalty and cupidity. In Willa Cather's *Sapphira and the Slave Girl* a loving husband conspires to spirit his wife's slave away from her by the underground route. Edwin Reardon, the hero of Gissing's *New Grub Street,* is trapped between the demands of his career as a creative writer and the demands of family support. Other conflicts arise between the social self, as this has become tyrannical in its demands, and the sense of personal integrity, or between selfishness and a dawning social consciousness; and these may be instanced by Eustacia Vye in *The Return of the Native,* Jean Valjean in *Les Miserables,* Henry Fleming in *The Red Badge of Courage,* and Silas Marner, in George Eliot's tale. Still other conflicts are those between flesh and spirit, in *Thais,* between self-assertion and alcoholism in *A Mummer's Wife,* between reason and impulse in *The Mayor of Casterbridge,* between furious love and furious pride in *Wuthering Heights,* between love and the need of security in *Diana of the Crossways,* between love and self-preservation in *Of Human Bondage.* There are tales, like *The Ambassadors,* where the single consciousness is the battleground, or certainly the chief battleground, on which the conflict is fought out. For the most part, however, the conflict in consciousness is not only generated by external pressure, but fought out in the world of the tale's illusion, in some locality and social environment of it; the human contribution affects the book's action and is affected by it. What is action is often reaction, reverberation. The forces rise now in this mimicked region, now in that. As they cross the boundaries of division, alterations take place in the mental and in the worldly scene, in heads and hearts, in facial expressions, and in postures and gestures and blows by bodies.

In conflict must take place, it must certainly take time. In fact, necessary as space and location are for action, time is of the essence. Here the traditional regions are past, present, future. Superficially, time can be a sort of setting, for historical, for contemporary, for Utopian fiction—Scott, Thackeray, or Wells. More intimately, the action of fiction is distinguishable from the doings of characters in the illusion by this: any physical movement characteristically traverses space, but dramatic action rather traverses time, and more than that, includes it and is included in it.

So far as I am concerned, an event is that outcome or production of conflict. Each blow of the axe on the tree, combined with each resistance of the tree to the axe, is an event in a series progressing toward the felling of the tree, or toward the maintained erectness of an injured tree. Many more elements enter in to this pattern than I would care to have to list. Yet I cannot help saying that since, in the history of our race, there have been comparatively few reports of men awaking from deep sleep to find themselves cutting a tree down, the element of human intent, formed and maintained, must somewhere be admitted into the picture. Nor can we omit the toppling and the crashing to earth, some time after the last blow is struck, and the effects upon the surroundings and for the human agent.

Any event, then, has antecedence and consequence in other events, and has them, not merely before itself and after, but partly *within* itself as a manifestation of what it continues. The first stroke of the axe carries on the intent that preceded it, and also carries it forward. Each stroke is characterized in part by its falling the order of events in which it takes its place in its time. When, in tracing a line of events which we have initiated or reviewed or discovered, we omit certain others, it is only because we are hewing to the line, not because the line is not there to be hewed to. When, for example, we leave out of account the development of the woodsman to the bodily state which enables him to put intent to execution, we leave it out because we know that others will, like ourselves, hardly deny it its place in the phenomenon, but will of course take all that for understood. What is excepted, so far from being denied, is on the contrary as truly granted as if it were expressly identified and mentioned.

Hence, the moment of Napoleon's birth, though we think of it as in the past, is not swallowed up by the past. That moment still persists; it will continue to be. Similarly, in drama and fiction the opening event is already charged with cross-purposes and potentialities, all of them destined to persist except one. From it there can then issue the very forces which, in their opposition, in their relentlessness of attack, give the story unity and direction. Each succeeding event therefore calls for no additional account of its predecessors, which are known, nor any inventory of its consequences, which will in their turn simply occur. Each has the accretive drive transmitted from the ones before, and the tightened power which it delivers to the next event in mounting to the climax. The last event need no more than appear in order to crown and round the whole, need be no more than an image, a gesture, a word, combining in the one ascending step left to take the peak and the panorama. In the plain presence of the last event, the antecedent drive of the beginning and the turbulence of the complication are now felt to have risen with a singleness of design. The final achievement confirms the purpose and meaning. So, an underground encounter of icy water and hot rock now looms in midair as the gleaming apparition of the geyser. In any effective climactic sweep, the final event is, etymologically and in reality, the *out-come*. It is as though an event were a triangular prism of time, bounded by past, present and future, so that, from a certain view, one face might seem to be the whole figure, but a shift would disclose the truth.

The fact that every event is charged with the three kinds of time makes possible a variety of narrative devices. A character, for example, may make a remark revealing a past event or pointing to a future one, and may thus heighten dramatic interest. There is an interesting example in Meredith's "The House on the Beach." Fellingham has been unsuccessful in wooing Annette Van Diemen. He goes out by moonlight to brood on the beach, and is found there by the girl's father.

"There you are," said Van Diemen's voice; "I smelt your pipe. You're a rum fellow to be lying out on the beach on a cold night. Lord! I don't like you the worse for it. I was for the romance of the moon in my young days."

"Where is Annette?" said Fellingham, jumping to his feet.

"My daughter? She is taking leave of her intended."

"What's that?" Fellingham gasped. "Good heavens . . . what do you mean?"

"Pick up your pipe, my lad. Girls choose as they please, I suppose."

"Her *intended,* did you say, sir? What can that mean?"

The way Fellingham is surprised by the news, and the insight we gain into the violence of his surprise by Meredith's manner of handling the business of the pipe, are two tricks out of the one box.

Another instance of the same general sort, but much more complex in what is revealed, is to be found in Joyce's "Counterparts." This is the story of a clerk of whom circumstances have made a confirmed alcoholic. During a morning of petty upsets and humiliations at the office, he is suddenly gripped by thirst. He must get out to the pub. If he takes his hat from the rack, the chief clerk will miss it, and report him. Without it, then, he leaves the room. At this point occurs the single sentence: "As soon as he was out on the landing the man pulled a shepherd's plaid cap out of his pocket, put it on his head and ran quickly down the stairs." The act, performed before our eyes, lights up in a flash the whole sordid little series of events in which the man planned the manoeuver and turned it into a practice. It also, of course, advances the possibility of his getting to the pub, as he does.

The use of an event that plainly radiates in all three directions of time at once, for purposes of introduction, is of such antiquity that Horace was able to turn one of his most famous phrases on it. The opening scene of *Hamlet* is a familiar example. There is also Poe's

"True!—nervous—very, very dreadfully nervous I had been and am; but why *will* you say that I am mad?"

the first words of "The Tell-Tale Heart." As for the use of the same principle in springing the so-called "surprise ending," the work of de Maupassant and O. Henry is too well known to call for any but general reference. And there is Stockton's inspiration that turns the end of "The Lady, or the Tiger?" into a beginning.

The way the author uses divisions of time throughout a story will contribute to determining its character. Narratives in which the simple chronological treatment obtains are generally regarded as more remarkable for story than for plot.

40

This in spite of the introduction of one or more episodes, themselves narrated chronologically, or some single thread of mystery running through the weave and accounted for at the end. In such tales each event is in the present as it occurs, and thereafter in the past. This, as I say, is the art of story, and a very great art indeed. If I deal with it briefly here, it is only because the temporal disposal of the conflict requires me to make only passing statement, more as a reminder to the reader than as an exposition. The simplicity of the form has lent itself to many of the deathless fictions of our race—Arthurian Romance, the Robin Hood ballads, many great fairly tales, and, in modern times, to the work of Bunyan, Defoe, Smollett, Scott, Irving, Cooper, Dickens, Dumas, and Mark Twain. Its single flow from present to future gives it great appeal to most readers and provides enormous freedom for a genius of copious, swift improvisation.

In addition to being the simplest ordering of events, it is, as such, indispensable to the complexity of any more elaborate pattern. In combination, simple chronology and rearranged chronology produce what is called *plot*. There is one sequence, as I say, that proceeds, with more or less interruption, from present to future, much as the text itself advances. This is the time-order, for example, in which Jim Hawkins and Dr. Livesey *tell* the events of *Treasure Island*, as distinct from the time-order of the events in the larger imagined occurrence with which the book deals. Thus the former is the time-order of *recital*; and each of *its* events, in its turn, is present time in and to that time-order. The events *narrated* by this order may be themselves given chronologically, with interruptions by the recital-order, as in Conrad's *Lord Jim*; or they may be given in an order generally the reverse of their presumable order, as in Edith Wharton's *Ethan Frome*; or in no apparent order save that of capricious mental association, as in *Tristram Shandy* or *Ulysses*. Since I will deal with this subject at some length in the chapter on pattern, I do no more than outline it here. I think that the implications for conflict are obvious. The conflict is not at all dispensed with, but greatly complicated by elaborate techniques. One can see what the procedure means for the detective story, where the story of the detection is avowedly set against the story of the mystery. In *The Ambassadors*, the narrative of Strether's experiences is the chronological matrix into which many antecedent matters concerning other people are introduced, not in the order of their occurrence, but of his enlightenment about them.

There are other respects in which manipulation of time is

important to plot, especially in relation to change in character. Such change is broadly of two kinds, the one being moment-to-moment adjustment by character to environment, including, of course, other characters; the other a deep-seated alteration, whether of maturity, improvement, or degeneracy. Either way, the fact that the event is charged with its past and its future as well as its present makes possible the depiction of character as a consistent identity undergoing perpetual adjustment, or as a persistent identity with considerable permanent adjustment. The former would be the emergence of this or that trait in responses; the latter would be the accretion of experience resulting in a broad, enduring change in personality. Metaphorically, the contrast would be that of the disarrangements and rearrangements of furniture in the course of a day's living, as against a complete redecoration, or the addition of a wing. In both instances the character of the house would be considerably changed and yet recognizably the same. I am not concerned with those responses of consciousness that are ignored in the performance of a bodily act, or in the mere bodily experiencing of a blow or a handclasp. Nor have I in mind the sort of passing reference to thought or feeling which Defoe, for one example, found so convenient for verisimilitude, without halting the pace of other events: the "reader-you-can-imagine-my-feelings-upon-hearing" sort of aside. To these exceptions I add the kind of dialogue (as in Peacock or Gissing) which serves the needs of the story without varying our sense of the personalities acting upon each other by means of spoken sentences or paragraphs. What I do have in mind is the play and variation of individuality itself, consciousness exhibited by act and glance and speech with such manipulation of the factor of time as to create illusion of a living spirit responsively various.

For change of the long view, the kind which provides the major conflict of the story, I suppose that George Eliot is the writer who would come first to mind. Silas Marner, from being virtually a nonentity, grows to spiritual nobility as a result of adopting and rearing Eppie. As the child grows, there is in him a laying up of experiences, an accumulation of relations with neighbors, an emotional richness, contentment, beauty. Time and again the mans' native gregariousness is warmed back to new life, his youthful principles re-invigorated. In the course of the same action, Eppie's rightful father, Godfrey Cass, who abandoned her, goes empty and dry. This contrast of ascent and descent is a familiar pattern in George Eliot's plots—Adam Bede and Arthur Donnithorne, Romola and Melemma, Dorothea and Lydgate. Of a somewhat different sort is simple growth out of childhood into maturity. This is not the same as the biographical or autobiographical fact: *Moll Flanders,* which Defoe wrote as from the point of view of an old woman, has the chronological plausibility of a lifetime, but is stamped in every part by the reminiscence of age. Dickens, who had nothing less than genius for the recapture of childhood, was not so good at the transition into manhood. David Copperfield is a boy, and then a man; but in *Great Expectations* the gradation is wholly worked out with the most admirable plausibility. Somehow or other, Louisa May Alcott, in her series of juvenile novels about the Marches, managed very well in bringing her little women and men up to be big ones. Willa Cather did excellent studies in *Song of the Lark, O Pioneers!,* and *My Antonia.* Although not the whole of *The Way of All Flesh* is devoted to Ernest, Butler gives him the bulk of the story, and presents a remarkable combination of the themes both of development into manhood and achievement of personal liberation from the tyranny of convention. Thomas Mann's *Buddenbrooks* is a magnificent illusion of the passage of time and the passing of institutions. In Galsworthy's two Forsyte sagas the central character, Soames, is not so much changed as mellowed and weathered, like a strong old house. When novels of alteration of character are successful, they show how innate traits are affected, now one, now another, as time and circumstance challenge and elicit them, or defeat and crush. What I have said about *The Ambassadors* I will now simply ask the reader to recall; and James' exploration of the expanding mind was worked with the same power in *The Portrait of a Lady, The Golden Bowl,* and in almost all of his finest work. May Sinclair's *The Life and Death of Harriet Frean* is an uncanny rendition, in a very short novel, of aging infantilism. For brief statement of a boy's maturity into heartbroken disillusion, Joyce's *Portrait of the Artist as a Young Man* is matchless. His *Ulysses* gives the same time-depth to the three principal persons, but with the effect of its having been achieved in the past, so that it now emerges from privishment with fragmentary appositeness. The most thoroughgoing treatment of time in fiction, of course, is the superb monument of Marcel Proust—*Remembrance of Things Past.*

Where Joyce and Proust differ from Mann, I think, in this regard, is in their complication of the long-view alteration of personality by the application of the moment-to-moment variation. Yet the Frenchman and the Irishman are of course not at all alike, even here. The reminiscent, analytical discursiveness of Proust has not been equalled for slow building up of total massive attainment; but the reccurent brochure style, although it spins out certain realities with a strength and an exquisiteness beyond envy or praise, thins the illusion of observed contemporaneousness. Here Joyce is not alone the master, but the creator and the prophet. His power to present the living moment of the character's consciousness, an illusion of teeming disorder, utterly unmixed with auctorial participation, is a fact without precedent, even in Sterne. *Tristram Shandy* is a work of the first brilliance, and, for its time, nothing short of a miracle. The illusion of delivery of every mad shift in the thought of the characters is a triumph of impressionistic momentaneity; but, though it would be inaccurate to say that the impression is everywhere of the author alone, it would be quite accurate to say that it is not everywhere of the characters alone, that it is certainly nowhere theirs alone. Sterne was Fielding's contemporary after all: the author is not only in the book, he is in every part, and therefore in every person, of it. Like Joyce, Sterne presents the illusion of a character, not just as an individual, but in his uniqueness in every moment and breath. Because of the newness of his technique, designed to snatch the whole complexity of immediacy, perplexity included, Joyce has permanently alienated most contemporary readers, and the spread of his public has been slow. On the other hand, bright high school sophomores are now reading *Ulysses* with enjoyment; in another generation, their successors will want to know what all the fuss was about. People will be quite accustomed to the exploitation of conflict in presenting the moment of experience, and in linking moment to moment, and in intertwining the impressions of the moment with their past and future relevances as memories and anticipations. If Joyce had failed in *Ulysses,* if he had not produced out of his welter a great city full of living, individual people, the tale of his reputation would already be told.

Although the fullness of Joyce's achievement had no precedent, it had anticipations in part. There are passages in Madame de Lafayette's *La Princesse de Clèves* and in Richardson's *Pamela* and *Clarissa* in which the heat and strife of the moment's passion seem to plunge us into the very heart of the character's unique existence. There are quite different passages in Jane Austen's pages, where the comedy of the dialogue, playing over some little scene of morning visit or afternoon stroll, lights up the mind and mood of every member of the group in every reaction, however guarded the visible and audible behavior. Her *Emma* is a gem and a joy of this kind, quivering and alert constantly beneath its demure surface; and it is a model, too, of the union of character and action, in the long view, by reason of the author's superb ease in effecting the heroine's development in self-knowledge. To go off in quite another direction, there are passages of imagistic selection and vividness in certain French works by Stendhal and Balzac, Flaubert, de Maupassant, and Huysmans, wherein the mute declaration of the present as appearance and panorama lends a piercing quality to the reflections and remarks of characters, with the double effect of colorful painting and solid sculpture. There have been Russian, English, and American writers who have studied and practiced this art—Turgenev, Chekhov, Stevenson, Conrad, Bennett, Willa Cather—whose rounded work conveys the same effect of restless, vivacious reality, moved within itself as it moves forward in time. Here the depth and the propulsion of life are intensified in the symbols of its sensorily perceptible surface. A graphic and colorful economy, a seizure, too, of sounds and tastes and all those pluckings by the world that stir our sense with the promise of enlightening as they arouse—these unite, all of them together, in presenting the many-dimensional, polymodal substance of the things we know to be our environment. As we have seen, there is no fiction without conflict, for then there is neither story nor plot. But conflict, however it may characterize the art, is never the whole of it. Indeed, since art always involves concealment of art, what is concealed in some fictions may be the conflict. For example, in *A Rebours,* the luxurious interior with which the recluse has surrounded himself is not only the wall he has built to keep out the world, but the sign of his neurotic struggle to resist the world's ceaseless demands upon him. But conflict, whether ostensible or relegated into disregard, is that element that makes a story a story, a plot a plot, and generates the power of climax, suspense, and action. It is certainly not all that there is of the imagined presence of the illusion. That, as in lyric or any form of imaginative letters, is the appearance of a presence in consciousness as it mimics, not necessarily worldly objects, but the sensory perceptibility of objects in a world.

Chapter 3

Image

By IMAGE I MEAN any presence in consciousness experienced as though by the senses. There are other conceptions and definitions of the term, but for the sake of accuracy I will adhere to the specification I have just now stated. Imagery or any instance of it, so far as I am concerned as a student of fiction, is perceived as though by an organ of sense. Such a phenomenon might be the memory of a sailboat race in a sunny bay. In not being of my environment of the moment, or any part of it included by means of such an instrument as the spyglass, it is a presence in consciousness only. The principal differences between the sort of presence I have instanced, and the presence of a boat race in my environment, are two. The latter presence occurs in the region of the world. It is experienced not *as though* by, but *actually* by the senses. The second difference is like the first. In the yacht races of the world, my unassisted will or purpose cannot alter the position of the contestants, nor dry up the bay. In yacht races that are presences in consciousness only, I can often perform such magic. I say "often" and no more, because the image—in a dream, for example—may willfully resist my will, to the extent of turning into nightmare.

In every other important respect, I find the two kinds of experience notable for resemblance. Although it is said that the image is faint by comparison with the worldly object, I have not found it so in my own observation or in the report of many others. The power of daydream to relegate our surroundings out of awareness, even to the extreme of blotting it out, so that, for example, we go past our destination without noticing it, is too familiar to dilate on. How many little boys—and big ones—have been so deafened by the yells of Cooper's Indians as not instantly to hear a call to dinner? Furthermore, the presence of objects in the world is no guarantee of our sensing them plainly. There are such hindrances as darkness, fog, haze, and distance. Who knows what are the parallels of these in the mind? If, for example, waning or fickle interest is a kind of night or cloud of consciousness, then equivalent conditions of frustration operate in both regions. Certainly not every one is able to see equally well; the sort of vividness we ascribe to our perception of physical objects, so far from being the average lot, is most exceptional. In the same way, some people imagine more vividly than others. Our contrast between the intensity of an image and its environmental counterpart takes too much for granted. In terms of duration, the distinction seems no better founded. If my train carries me past a narrow gap in the mountain, the scene I glimpse is of an instant's duration. As presence by power of memory it may remain in consciousness for minutes, that is, more than a hundred times as long. A reader of *Typhoon* may witness the storied tempest for the greater part of an evening. There can be no doubt that the persistence of this image is fueled by physically notable words on material paper; but what recourse of such sort did Conrad have, not alone for the imagining, but for the writing?

People have a way of speaking of the endurance of worldly objects as though there were no such things as seasons, or moving objects, or our own movements, as though water, fire, and air were stiff as stone; as though there were no such comings and going as twilight and tide and tonality—as though no one ever turned inward from the world to review what it and he once were, or to conjecture by image how things may become. The most I will grant about the differences between the two sorts of presence we are considering is that many human beings so neglect the image, so disregard and disvalue its occurrence as a reality for them, that historically and for "practical" purposes, the experience of it *has been* faint and brief by comparison with their experience of the world. Yet against this allowance there must be set the massive evidence of the arts, from the most primitive to the most civilized, in every known medium, in every known epoch, in every race, in every quarter of the globe.

Finally, although it has been urged upon me that there are people who do not form images, especially the visual, and who therefore exist mentally by what is called "imageless thought"—frankly, what am *I* supposed to do about *that*? If the blind do not begrudge such people the blessing of a sight of the world, or ask that human experience be characterized, standardized, by the handicap of the relatively few, on what stronger plea of human solidarity are we who rejoice in the reality of the imagination to deny the sensed presence within? Shall the deaf, too, be asked to give up the clairaudience of dialogue in stories (incidentally, what do the imageless thinkers do about that?) in company with composers and other musicians? The more I grant—and how much against common sense, I simply cannot express—that there are people in whose lives the image is an utter nonentity of experience, the less can I see of what earthly concern that can be for me in my attempt to set out whatever it is I know about the *whole* fiction. Such books as this are of course written for people with the amplest powers or potentialities for entertaining the subject. If books were to be limited to the least achieved ability of any member of the race, not even a Rousseau would ever write a book, because not a minority, but the overwhelming majority of men have never read one. Then, for the public I address I repeat that the distinction I note in the two sorts of presence we have been considering is the difference of the region in which each sort occurs. The imaginary knife cannot slice a real loaf, nor a real knife the bread in the Lord's Prayer. Yet they have their link in bodily experience.

Perhaps that is why, once the true difference is determined, the two categories of presence often seem to be strikingly similar. At any rate, the image may be that of any of the senses, or of several or all in concert. It may be of an entire environment, a curtained room, a crowded street, the countryside of Lilliput, or the belly of Jonah's whale. Whether of this world or not, it will be complete, unbroken, and possible to think of as continuous beyond the limits of sense, and so of being only a locality within a vaster extent. Time will pass in it, events occur. There will be people in it with life, both as a community and as individuals. What I have here so far indicated would be the larger image, the localizing illusion of some episode of a story, like a stage set, or better, a movie shot, with the characters going about their affairs of the moment. A simple image might be a close-up: a face with a hand shading the eyes, a vase of lilac with a bug on one leaf, a ring too large for the finger, a slipper left overturned on a bath mat, the chime of a distant bell, the sizzle of bacon, a calling card, a beer glass underslung by a confident lip, a stain of coffee on a cube of sugar. Each such detail would be not only itself in the general scene, but an additional plausibility, a magical reconstituting of the environment of which it is one point. It might possibly set the tone of the occasion, give to the illusory environment some unifying pervasion of quality. In *The Spoils of Poynton* Fleda Vetch feels at a certain time invaded by the luxurious beauty of Mrs. Gereth's possessions: ". . . the very fingers of her glove, resting on the seat of the sofa, had thrilled at the touch of an old velvet brocade, a wondrous texture that . . . she would have recognized among a thousand, without dropping her eyes on it." Sometimes the single image, repeated like a motif in music, is the constant center of radiating portent, like the great fissure in the wall of the house of Usher, or the frightful baying of the hound of the Baskervilles. For the image, like the phenomenon in the world, has the dual character of signifying not only that a thing exists, but also what it is, and is therefore inextricably part of the dense relation among distinguishable identities. The insight of the artist is his sensibility for appearances as the revelation of what lies behind them; and since the image is a thing of consciousness, since it may, like an iceberg or a rainbow, be all of the otherwise unapparent that appears, its use as a symbol needs only recognition of the fact that of course it *is* one, that in its mere naive presence it represents the consciousness which is so much more besides.

Every image, then, has a secret passage leading into sensation, and thence into feeling and ideation and language. The secrecy arises from the condition which the image shares with its equivalent in the world, that is, its seeming to be so utterly an object. When I eat an orange, I regard the taste as itself wholly, and not as in part my tasting it, my adaptation in singling out, from all flavors, this one. I behave as though I know that orange-taste is subject-object, but of course I need not give the matter the recognition of a thought. Should I do so, however, I may react in a manner which I have indicated by means of the hyphen, so that now the image stands accompanied by the sensation. Nor need that be all: there may in addition be a fine pleasurableness, a sweet-and-acrid oscillation, a relief after dryness of the throat, a quite active little joy. The greater the accretion of these individualizings of sensation and feeling, and even the ideas of these and their names, the more they seem to be myself; while the taste of orange as the taste in the orange persists—this simply as an image, mind you—in remaining "objectively" itself. Not until, not unless, I recollect the imaginative nature of the experience does the image then truly join with the other sorts of presence in consciousness and in being consciousness.

Complex and unreliable as this process of domesticating the image in its region is with relation to taste, smell, and touch, it is child's play by comparison with doing so in relation to hearing and sight. One of the commonest synonyms for *understanding* is *seeing*. Talking face to face with a man, we express a wish to "see" him for five minutes; we say that we "see" his reason for doing so and so; all that we ask is that he "see" our position. It is no wonder that the fictional image, of environment or person or detail or symbol, is most often visual, and secondarily auditory. Perhaps that is why the fact of the image in fiction is disregarded, depreciated, even denied. By the same token, the less rarely used imagery of taste, touch, or smell, especially when it is sharply individualized, seems not only vivid, but an exceptional experience.

Before I quit the subject of the fictional image as a mental phenomenon, I would like to say something about the peculiar relation of image and idea. Occasionally, in a discussion of thoughts as contrasted with things, one hears it said that a thing may be brown, like earth, or sharp, like a knife; and that we may have an idea of what is brown or sharp; but that there is no such thing as a brown idea or a sharp idea. I cannot agree. A clod or a knife is made up of energy and matter, but our senses perceive them as matter only. An energy they are known only intellectually, that is, by ideas. The image of the knife, however, includes more than sense perceptions; it includes our ideas of its function, its activity, and the forces that operate in it. What then would be the difficulty in regarding the image as a sensed idea? If we accept this notion, then Coleridge's

> Brown skeletons of leaves that lag
> My forest brook along

would seem to include a brown idea; while Goethe's *Werther* and Thackeray's parody of it would seem to present a sharp idea in the form of the imagined knife with which Charlotte is seen "cutting bread and butter."

The separate identities of image, idea, sensation, emotion, are the subtly interwoven figures of one tapestry. Consciousness, in its interrelations with the body and the world, may be considered the region of things as ideas, and the world the region of ideas as things; so that the body may be thought of as the region which transforms ideas as things into things as ideas, or things as ideas into ideas as things. Hence, symbolism may be inevitable in art because the process of symbolization is inherent within ourselves. Hence, moreover, the meeting of consciousness and the world in the images of painting and sculpture, whether as detailed realism, or symbolic convention, or as non-objective and abstract art. The last, in not being direct imitation of the appearance of anything, resembles the visible text of fiction, the written or printed page in comparison with the illusion it suggests. Yet a curious exploitation of the visibility of the text as a "thing" in the world, as fictional imagery, occurs when the image itself is of words: lettering on doors and maps, road and station and shop signs, engraved cards and announcements, ticker flashes, newspaper headlines and stories, telegrams, letters, manuscript, and excerpts, of factual or fictional matter, from imagined books, magazines, or reviews. One recalls Pamela's mention of her handwriting, tear blots, and so on. In *Finnegans Wake* one passage deals with a letter dug up out of a midden by a hen, and another passage comments on the penmanship, obliterations, and stains. In such evocation of fancied writing or print, the text has a direct relation to the image in giving the order of letters, words, and punctuation; and an indirect relation in mentioning or suggesting script, font, size, materials, or colors.

The exploitation of the private monologue of reading or writing is the principal source for the auditory image of the speech of characters, the dialogue. It has also been used for monologue narratives, such as those by Defoe, Poe, Browning, or Ring Lardner. The most recent developments are Dujardin's interior monologue, or verbalized recital in the head of the character, and the stream-of-consciousness technique, best known in Joyce's three longest fictions. As for customary dialogue as imagery of hearing, there is indirect stimulation by mention or suggestion of volume, pitch, or quality; and for this, as for any sound, or indeed for imagery of any sense, there may be used denotative description or figurative comparison. Mention of the sex and age of the speaker earlier in the story, or at the time of speaking, will be enough to create vocal illusion of approximately the right sort, and most authors do little more than this. For the speeches themselves there are quotation marks, single or double, or opening and closing dashes, or merely the indentation of the paragraph for each new speech.

There is also the "he said" in various locutions and in various positions in the sentence. Indirect discourse, an ancient device of classic literature, is now uncharacteristic. Defoe used it a very great deal; a striking instance in the present century is Frances Newman's *The Hardboiled Virgin*, to which, as satire, the rhetorical formalism gives an additional mockery of quaint, cross-stitch pattern. Because of this rhetorical formality in presenting speech, indirect discourse generally quarrels with the illusion of life. It lacks vividness because it summarizes speech, or reports it, instead of rendering it as imagery. On the other hand, the device may be used very naturally in tales in the fictional first person, since in our conversation we often report the remarks of people that way. Further, in stories of incident, where dialogue is of lesser importance, it gives action free play; and for the same reason it is adequate in conveying necessary brief remarks, especially of minor characters. After all allowance has been made, however, the fact remains that direct discourse is the practice, so much so that many readers will on inspection reject a novel in which dialogue appears to be scanty.

Speech has become a principal symbol of life. To be plausible, the character must talk for himself. In fact, in the most advanced mode of the times, he must in his private inwardness talk *to* himself. At any rate, we want to hear him, in his very idiom, vocabulary, pronunciation, dialect, grammar, rhetoric, and rhythm. Whether or not we recognize these matters as such, we want them as oral evidences of his thought, feeling, education, breeding, and general personality—they represent his responses and motives, the acts of his consciousness in reaction and in contribution to the conflict as it involves him at the moment of his life to which we are attending. For the rest, dialogue relieves the monotony of the appearance of the text, and complicates our private monologue into many-voiced society. To the reader as a shut-in, even as a voluntary one, it brings greater illusion of company; in the alternation between it and the rest of the text he is kept too busy with adjustment to pay undue attention to the fact that he is reading, so that the illusion all the more readily holds to its place in focus once it has taken it. Dialogue is not, of course, synonymous with drama, any more than it is in a talkative play. The dramatic is the function of conflict, for which speech is an armory of weapons and a terrain of tactics. As mimesis of spoken thought and emotion and will, dialogue provides, like imagery of any sort, the possibility of the indication and reception of such drama as is enacted in the perceived illusion.

Though imagery is not the life of the illusion, it is certainly its manifest body. Now, in any discussion with my friend, I concentrate on the issue between us. As to his material presence, I neither attend focally to that nor fail to be aware of it; I take it in, in taking it for granted. Should he grow pale and press his hand to his heart, even without interrupting the cogent flow of expression, or if he should merely yawn while I am speaking, I should find myself taking him much more into account physically. But if in the midst of his sentence, and while still talking, he were simply to vanish, I should find myself, possibly, incredulous about the evidence of my ears, and staring very intently at the dented and disarrayed upholstery of his chair. His body is like background imagery. There can be no doubt that the imagery of a story plays only a contributive part to the action; but without the image, where would the action *be?* This is like saying that if I do not remember what my dream was, I cannot be sure what it was about. I may have a recollection of the fact of dreaming, an idea of the experience, and perhaps a vestige of the emotional quality, but more of its nature I cannot communicate; that is gone with the apparition. It may be true that only the unusual reader is concerned with the imaged illusion, but since few have any trouble recovering the general character of it or recalling details when these are mentioned, the majority plainly have had the experience. There are not many tales in which, as in *Shadows on the Rock,* the picture is perpetually in focus. There are not many artists to whom, as to Willa Cather, the picture is by intent a boldly beautiful presence. The fact that pictorial vividness is a mark that distinguishes many of the celebrated names in fiction is a fact that speaks for itself: Stendhal, Scott, Flaubert, Melville, Mark Twain, Hardy, Conrad, and Katherine Mansfield.

What I am arguing is not that the mimicry of the painter's art is an indispensable sign of excellence in the story-teller, but that the necessary image may be made more than a powerful auxiliary, be one of the central features of the art; claiming and winning an admiration second only to that of the occurrence, often vying with it, and occasionally, for a bright interval, forcing the events to labor in support of it. I am not at the moment speaking exclusively of so-called local colorists, such as G. W. Cable and Sarah Orne Jewett, who do indeed present the physical scene as a means of featuring the social scene, in what used to be called "fiction of manners." I am speaking more particularly of writers who, having a special gift for *imaging,* delight in expressing it, as Scott and Hugo did, or who aim to make their fictions works of rounded art without omission of any opportunity for the creation of beauty, as perfect in the imagistic aspect as in others, as Charlotte Brontë and Chekhov and Proust did. When one considers these last three writers, with the contrasts of their personalities and of the things they limned, it is evident at once how vast a reality the delineative rendition of the illusion has been, and can be made.

Once more let me approach the matter negatively by saying that by the designed prominence of the image in fiction I do not mean, or rather do not mean exclusively, the kind of discourse known as description. The formal, set descriptive

53

passage has its place in the delineation I am referring to, but even so, its chief merit there would always be the economy which jealously holds it to its function. The description of the rhetorics, the familiar scheme of the one effect aimed at, the chosen point of view, the selection and the ordering of details, the mingling of familiar and unfamiliar, of concrete and unique, all these and the other rules of formulated procedure are practiced by writers, including those who no longer remember that they ever learned them. Since the memory of readers is even shorter, such passages are ideally experienced and absorbed as part of what is going on in the illusion, with little or no notice of their nature or their technique, or of the fact that the illusion is an illusion. When, as in a Scott introduction, the depiction of the scene delays the start of the action, or when, as in *Death Comes for the Archbishop,* Miss Cather seems so often to substitute the relatively static delights of the senses for the movement of the action, some readers lose patience. That others relish the pictorial effectiveness, just as others of a different sort relish George Eliot's expositions of psychological analysis and generalization, is a fact that serves to highlight the reality of the unique whole fiction. Further, although such passages may be read for themselves, they may additionally contribute to interest in the action when that is resumed, so that afterward it is difficult to conceive of the action without them. In this service to narrative operation, the patterned description provides another good example of the omnipresent influence of conflict, and so of the elusiveness of the whole fiction, and its actuality.

There is, then, such a modulation of the medium as will present the image with so shaped and detailed an appearance, with such evident approximation to the author's view of it, as to make us believe that we in our consciousness seem to sense what he has sensed in his, precisely and identically. This closeness, this tightness of his control may be sustained by us either as an attraction or as a burden. Some of us are all eyes and ears for the particularity of the experience, for the change it gives from reading what is not so particularly descriptive, with the result that, if we think of it at all, we are grateful for the effectiveness of the writer, appreciative of the skill. Others, again, feel only the grip of the discipline; if they do not shake it off, they cannot wait for it to relax. What they want is the story; and what they want in that—whether or not they are analytical about the preference—is the freedom to image what they can out of their own resources, since doing it means so little to them anyhow. It is curious to see how inconsistent authors themselves can be about this matter of loose or tight control of the reader. Scott and Dickens, who relish a large leeway in the matter of story, may particularize most carefully in some imaged effect. George Eliot and Henry James, on the other hand, will work out a plot to the most minute causal relation in character, yet may spend only the least possible energy on delivering certain physical appearances. In *Middlemarch* Lydgate is not described to the extent of a syllable; and in *The Sacred Fount,* although person after person is said to have changed in appearance so astoundingly as to be almost unrecognizable, no one is pictured! Whatever Lydgate I visualize is a matter of indifference, since the conflict in its reference to him does not hinge on his physical appearance; but in the James novel the point often involves something about the physical appearance of certain people, and this the author simply does not give me. Scott and Conrad and Cather represent an extreme of the prominence of intentional guidance about the illusion as though it were physical; and it is this prominence of the image in the experience that I have been aiming to convey, certainly not from a contention that it is invariable and therefore indispensable as a development, but simply to show that such development is incontestably one actual way to present an element which *is* invariable, whether writers put it in, as we see some of them do, or leave it to the reader to put in by himself.

There are some curious sidelights on all this. A conventionalized, stock description, such as one of the heroine as an innocent slip of a girl, blue-eyed and golden-ringleted, will be quite proper for one reader, but will make another wonder what sort of ass the writer is, or takes him to be. Some description does not describe. As a result, some writers rely on the reader's visualization, knowing that they can count on it to improvise, at the least, some picture, of some appropriateness. A hint is enough. Of Moll Flanders' beauty in her girlhood, Defoe has her say only this by way of comparing herself with others: "I was apparently handsomer than any of them." The "apparently" reminds one of Homer's device of having the old men turn from their talk to stare after Helen, and of Marlowe's

Was this the face that launched a thousand ships . . .

Hawthorne, to whom the image was a symbol rather than a likeness, contents himself with introducing Beatrice Rappaccini so: "a young girl arrayed with as much richness of taste as the most splendid of the flowers, beautiful as the day." Also, of course, there is Sterne's trick about the Widow Wadman's allure for Uncle Toby. This, he declares, is beyond conveyance; the reader must picture her for himself. "Sit down, Sir, paint her to your own mind . . ." The next page of the novel is accordingly left blank; and at the top of the very next the author cries out "—Was ever anything in Nature so sweet—so exquisite!" Other novelists may have known more than he about imaginative creation, but none was ever so knowing about it. It is much to our present purpose that among the pranks Sterne played with the materials of fiction, he should have given such spatial blankness of display to this one. If we are to have his Widow Wadman in our mind's eye at all, she must be ours; so that she is additionally an illustration of the share of the unique whole fiction in the setting up of the illusion, and of the impossibility, do as one may, of dispensing with the image.

Familiar things, familiarly regarded, do not generally call for description. If it is enough for the writer's purpose to say "the street," or "a kitchen," or "a nurse went by the door," then the picture—any suitable picture—comes with the denotation. So long as a thing is no more than one of a class, it may even be quite unfamiliar, and yet may need only a brief comparison with something we know; for example, a shaddock and a grapefruit are similar, but the former is somewhat pear-shaped, while the latter is globular, like a big grape. If I am told that a certain flower on a distant planet resembles our talisman rose, but that the petals have outer indigo and inner turquoise faces; or if the warriors there are said to carry a saw-toothed dagger, thick and heavy, but otherwise like a certain kind of our bread-knives, my picture is likely to be adequate. On the other hand, even what is familiar may call for description if it changes, or if it takes on new importance from a change of circumstance, or if it is presented, though as one of a class, in its uniqueness. It is therefore not surprising to find formal description somewhere in the introduction of a story. Either at the very start, or after the first bit of action or dialogue, the setting and the people are at their newest and possibly strangest. In our everyday lives, when we first arrive at a place or meet a person, we look at what we are encountering. As a rule, writers take this into account in introducing a character, a locality, or anything that is likely to arouse attention; set description is here a provision against the likelihood of the reader's impulse to "take a look." Similarly, there may later be additional description, after an event that alters things notably, or calls for perceptible evidence of a novel reaction on the part of a character we already know. The reader takes another look, to follow up the metaphor, at a woman whose pride has been suddenly wounded, at a man who is hearing unbelievably good news, at the sea when the storm comes up, at the barroom with its main lights shot out.

What I am saying about description will, I believe, hold good for exposition. In tales of mystery and detection, the opening frequently contains both together; the image is clearer than the explanation of the scene of the crime only because of a cunning deception, an adept omission or understatement which fools us into oversight, into believing that the evidence of our senses may be relied on as our sense of the evidence. The image and the explanation may be united, again, in a part of the story that introduces a diagram, a map, the analysis of a code, with elucidation or other comment. In fiction dealing with human activities that are presumably not familiar to the general public, there will be passages of enlightenment, with a degree of formal description: some one tours an industrial plant; an apprentice learns his duties, is lectured on what to avoid, perhaps even witnesses a type of mishap which will afterward be repeated with much more significance for him or for the action. In such writing, the descriptive-explanatory function is conveyed in narrative form. In this way bits of information are produced at moments when the reader may be supposed to need them in order to follow the occurrence. So far from boring him, they may heighten the interest with an illusion of vicarious experience; or if he knows the material, he may be alertly checking its accuracy. Such dispersed or distributed description, its parts, as one might say, studding the narrative with gleams of sensory perception, is no longer quite the formal description we were considering a little way back; it is far less obvious compared with that. We are less aware of it as a distinct mode of literary composition; we may note it, but as a barely sensible force, a more flashing current, in the movement of the action.

When this sort of imaging is thinned out a little further; when it is no more than a sentence, a phrase, an adjective conveying a color, a scent, a tone, a texture, a flavor; and when the touch so administered is a rare and unobtrusive aside, I find myself disinclined to call it description at all. Description it possibly is, but in a way so fragmentary and diffuse as hardly to require the formal name. I have grown accustomed to think and speak of it as "indication of the physical"; and people who have heard me call it that have seemed to accept the designation as apt. Such touches of indication, occurring as naturally as they do briefly in the stream of the action, periodically include the illusion of the physical and refresh it unobtrusively, in the way that, on the stage, an actor's taking a cigar from his pocket, or running his hand over the back of a couch, revivifies our awareness of the whole setting. What is done by an adjective or an adverb in this way may be accomplished even more subtly by a proper or a common noun, by a verb of exquisite adequacy, by a metaphor or an epigram which, arousing our appreciation of witty penetration, causes us to disregard the accompanying picturesqueness. Indication of such sort, granular, imbedded, pervasive in the action, one might almost say ground up in and with it, gives us the image in the most intimately fictional manner, since the illusion and the conflict are so hard to distinguish that they come to us as one unanalyzed experience. This is the true narrative way. The imagery in the usual sense of the word, as we conveniently contrast it with dialogue, is then like effective dialogue in operating as the story's self.

As I have already said, this is the manner in which Defoe transmits to us the illusory world and people of *Moll Flanders* and *Roxana*. One must not take it for granted, though, that the maintenance of our sensory perception of the illusion continues inevitably from the fact of conflict, or even (beyond the auditory transformation of the private monologue) from the use of dialogue. There are long stretches in the pages of Gissing's books, where characters are debating or thinking out an issue, that are as white as a desert of abstraction under the glare of relentless intellectuality, passages bleached of color and tone and fragrance, and in no small measure, I feel sure, responsible for the neglect of his otherwise superior powers. In certain works of Henry James, oddly enough in those two that deal with collections of *objets d'art*—*The Spoils of Poynton* and *The Outcry*—there is such a preponderance of this same chalky quality of abstract noun and latinist proposition as to give one's private monologue the crackle and rustle of speech gone dry. On the other hand, *The Portrait of a Lady, The Turn of the Screw, The Ambassadors,* and the earlier *Washington Square,* all have the complexion of life, fed by the inner, the true corpuscular flow. It is my suspicion that the neglect of Gissing, and the complaint by readers that Henry James in certain works is dry, can be laid in part to the comparative absence of imagery, or at least to its anemic pal-

58

lor; if I am right, then here again is negative evidence of a positive need.

We have been following a scheme, throughout this chapter, of degrees of imaging ranging from downright, descriptive explicitness, as in Scott or Flaubert, to a diffuse kind of fragmentary description, a scheme varying in degree only. The kind is still one: the perceptible surface of illusion, whether composed and still for portrayal, or witnessed in the flash of movement, or laboriously supplied by the irritated reader for himself, since the author has failed to provide it at all. We have seen how, because of our excitement over the action, the actually sensed illusion may be relegated, as background, to the periphery of our attention by the incidental naming of objects involved in the recital—tools, weapons, furniture. Possibly, such sleight-of-hand comes under the heading of "suggestion." This word, as people use it, is vague enough to mean almost anything not announced with a flourish. At any rate, an image is presented unobtrusively; and the fact that no one especially heeds it, or heeds the fact that its presence is brought about by subdued explicitness, is perhaps the negative factor which causes us to say that it has been suggested. In the same way, I suppose, the lay observer of a Rembrandt portrait hardly heeds the obscure background, and so never realizes that what is to him altogether peripheral was at some time very much the focus of the artist's attention. That the weave of the canvas nowhere appears is a simple truth that goes unnoted. A thin layer of pigment gives the image an opacity to screen away its very materiality, to say nothing of the hidden substance of the physical world behind it. So with water-color, ink, shadows on a screen, and the meanings of language. So long as the conveying medium is not the concern of focus, there is suggestion, because there is dominance by illusion, the fancied presence. Then, for any unaccountable presence there must be something which *is* present, but which is left out of the account from the point of view of focus at the moment. This feat is achieved too commonly to aruse comment, when the senses pool their impotences as well as their powers in perceiving things in the world. A presence, for example, is noted by the ear, though nothing of it comes to the eye, for the simple reason that sound is never visible anyway. To see a ringing bell is not to see the bell's ringing. With a spyglass one may have clear sight of a ship's bell swinging far away. Amid the sounds close about one, the silence of that bell will mark the experience of it almost with identification. Yet the imagination may very well supply a suitable clangor. When the incident is, later, recollected, the bell will perhaps ring out as though the glass had surprised the sound with the sight; and one may unwittingly slip into saying that the bell in the fetched image was ringing wildly. Through the pane of a bus window I once saw a drunkard, his arms flung about, his red face contorted, his great mouth opening and shutting. From his hurt and wrathful look, I had no doubt about his mood or the curses he was bellowing out, though not a tone, much less a word, made its way through the crystal wall between us. Even what we hear plainly in every-day life must be interpreted. It is of the nature of all things that each is a symbol. Sometimes we are tricked, and sometimes willingly.

This is the secret of the actor's art, and of the novelist's. If John Flemming has a vivid picture of Marjorie Daw from the letters his friend Delaney writes him, it is because Aldrich turned over to his creature Delaney his own power of illusion. We, too, see Marjorie—by means of the same magic which the author himself uses to make us see Delaney and Flemming. So Dickens, on his own account, produces Sairey Gamp, the inspired liar, and then delegates to her the production of the Mrs. Harris who, even by the standards of fiction, is utterly fictitious! Ambrose Bierce, in "The Damned Thing," conveys a powerful conviction of the existence of an invisible beast, at first by auditory imagery, combined with visual relevance:

. . . we heard, at a little distance to our right and partly in front, a noise as of some animal thrashing about in the bushes, which we could see were violently agitated.

but later, a patch of wild oats is strangely disturbed:

. . . It seemed as if stirred by a streak of wind, which not only bent it but pressed it down—crushed it so that it did not rise; and this movement was slowly prolonging itself directly toward us.

Plausible modulation, composition, of the form of what can be sensed, will thus produce overwhelming suggestion of what can not. Such modulation may employ the element of form in the fictional symbol on a much more extensive scale, involving the pattern of the entire story: imagery detailed in so many words as description in an early part may be made to flash into the mind's eye, afterward, by mere naming of place or person, so that the later experience may astound us as one of pure suggestion. Suggestion or no suggestion, *some* presence there must be. As Whitehead put the matter, in a discussion of symbolic reference with a different but applicable tenor: "A reflexion in a mirror is at once a truthful appearance and a deceptive appearance. The smile of a hypocrite is deceptive, and that of a philanthropist may be truthful. But both of them were smiling." Our conviction, when we read a story, that what we confidently assume to be the character's thoughts and emotions and personality are there to be experienced by us arises to a large degree from this swiftly natural symbolic transference of illusory phenomena of sense into evidence of sensorily imperceptible but totally credited animation, as of life in the world about us.

A superlative instance of the suggestion of which I have been speaking occurs in "The Fall of the House of Usher," where it not only contributes an enormous secret effectiveness to the story, but may be said, in a demonstrable sense, to *be* the story. Roderick and Madeline, the last of the line, appear to struggle feebly, if they struggle at all, against an unapparent antagonist, which is their extinction. So, with less exertion, because it can exert none, does the House, their ancestral home. In this tale, Poe's skill as an artist, remarkable as it is, is only secondary to the divination of his genius. The conflict by which the action moves is concealed with unbelievable cunning by making the single imagery of the victims—the perceptible bodies and building—house *both* forces of the struggle, their doom no less than their dwindled, unequal resistance. The problem of including, of presenting the sensorily unpresentable assailant is solved by making it appear to us through the ravished flesh of the brother and sister, and through the great fissure in the wall that runs from roof to foundation, within as without. For all its disturbing mystery, Poe's conception is no more supernatural than nature, no more unreal than reality. That the great romancer knew what he was about must be plain to any careful reader. There is hardly an image in the story that is not the sign of death-in-life: the defective building steeped in the sickening exhalation of the tarn, Roderick's morbidly sensitive face, Madeline's flushed pallor and the fact of her burial alive, the painting that represents light in a sealed vault, the view of the moon between the halves of the house as the fissure yawns, the collapse of the ancient stones and their vanishing into the tarn.

There are, in addition, such passages as the one in which Roderick ascribes to the inanimate stones the sentience of living things, or the one in which the unnamed narrator gives this first impression of the exterior:

. . . No portion of the masonry had fallen; and there appeared to be a wild inconsistency between its still perfect adaptation of parts and the crumbling condition of the individual stones. In this there was much that reminded me of the specious totality of old wood-work which has rotted for long years in some neglected vault, with no disturbance from the breath of the external air.

Poe had no patience with bald didacticism. Yet, knowing the tragic impermanence of human contrivance, and having witnessed those signs of the death-chamber by which the Invisible at last almost bursts through upon the world of sense, it is characteristic of him that he should have dared to transform the imageless into the vivid lacquered symbols of this masterpiece of fantasy. With the instinct of all great symbolists, he made his symbolism, in its divergence from delineative portraiture, draw a strange power, not from mere omission, which is failure, but from such disposition of actual presences that the enchanting salience of what seizes the sense is the hiding place of some other force, which can thus work as though with supernatural strength, and with a baffling mordancy like that of secret guilt. It is not surprising that such a writer should have applied his gift to the creation of mystery stories, in which the disordered pattern of the scene of crime is haunted by the significance of presences still to be identified as clues, and then reshaped into the form of discovery, of solution.

Not only in fantasy, romance, and symbolism is the absence of some image in mid-reading an influence on the story. In *Tristram Shandy* or in *Ulysses* such postponement is an engine of suspense, as the timely appearance is the piecing out of structure. The characteristic works of Henry James may equally be said to move by the principle of suspicious anticipation, which is satisfied piecemeal by encounters that reveal fresh incompleteness, and is ended only by some such scene as the one in which the truth about the golden bowl is *pictured,* or the one in which Strether's question as to the nature of Chad's relation with Madame de Vionnet is answered by his accidental *sight* of them boating in the country, and their realization that he has discovered them so. It would be absurd, as we have seen, to declare that the image is the story; but their relation, as we have also seen, is of such intimacy as to make us understand how the skillful ordering of images may not only heighten but at times provide mechanism for the battle of wits between writer and reader. In that sense, any climax or conclusion remains, while we are still in the body of the narrative, an image—if not quite omitted, then surely absent in its being deferred. Furthermore, any episode visualized and concluded as though it were complete, but reintroduced later for the elucidation of a meaning or even a quality not at first comprehended by some character (perhaps because of youthful inexperience) can deepen the drama of the fiction and expand its scope.

Proust is a master at this sort of recapture, of discovery and recognition all the more astounding because the discovery and recognition occur in the midst of what supposedly has already been discovered and recognized. One instance is his playing upon the matter of the composer Vinteuil's relation to his daughter, which is repeated and enlarged like a musical motif; but any reader of *The Remembrance of Things Past* can produce a dozen like this out of his casual recollection of the events. So adept was Proust at this enrichment of imaged memories by their juxtaposition and fusion that he employed the procedure for various purposes, at times in a single passage. There is such a passage, of some length, in *Within a Budding Grove,* which he devotes to an appreciation of the art of the painter Elstir, especially his coastal scenes. The encomium arises quite naturally: Elstir and the hero have met at Balbec, a seaside resort, and they meet again at the great man's studio there. In expressing certain conceptions of the painter's originality, his peculiar contribution, Proust makes the narrator compare the paintings with the local scene, and with similar settings elsewhere. We are at times scrutinizing nature, and at others, selected works on canvas—but always, of course, within the literary conveyance of the novel. This last, the discourse of Proust, is itself a blend —description, narrative, criticism, and psychological disquisition—so smooth and limpid as to direct attention away from itself to the illusion of scenery or of graphic art. Somehow we are made intimately acquainted with Balbec as a setting for new developments in the action, yet without any sense of formal description for that purpose. At the same time, since it is Elstir to whom his contemporaries owe a modernist view of the characteristics of the place, we learn a great deal about his mind and personality, again without obvious technical formality. Also, he is somewhat important because of his relations with more important characters—Swann, Odette, the Verdurins—with whom he is currently not on the same terms as in the past. The alterations are illuminating, of him and so of them, and are part of the vast scheme of shifting standards which is a principal study of the novel.

The pages, then, are so full and so various, that we have

little or no time to think of them as pages, as writing. The passage builds up an illusion of a place, of the life there, and of the people there for the summer whose lives are lived principally in other places. There is triumphantly suggested to the reader who is at all conscious of his reading a belief that the text is really a transcript from life as it is lived in the world, that this is not Realism, but a report of realities. The fact that the delineation of locale and people is concerned with ideas about society and the higher reaches of civilization and culture and progress, makes the illusion of the story at once a presence noted but not dominantly singled out for notice. The illusion of the story is therefore richer pictorially than the imagery of those fictions in which it comes up only in the course of the action; and though at first the action seems slowed by the discursive style, that proves in time to be an error of hasty judgment, for actually the plot is made to thicken and deepen and broaden with a scope and a solidity no action story has ever achieved. *The Remembrance of Things Past* is a vast net of episodes ultimately revealed in their interwoven relationships; each of them is at least once treated as though of time present to the time of the recital, but also with reference to another or others remembered or anticipated or only imagined.

In his different way, Joyce rings the changes on time in *Ulysses*. Something more will be said of this later; at the moment I wish only to note that both of these famous moderns have, as it were, reinforced the dimensions of space with the new temporal ones, constantly running out in all three directions the lines upon which may hang the illusion of existence as imaged. They have thus produced an effect of the complexity of that existence, including no little of its perplexity, an equal reality. The role of the image in accomplishing all this, needless to say, so far from diminishing, has multiplied. There are Elstirs of the novel, too; and their sharper vision of actuality has been shared by contemporaries who, with no intention of discarding or discrediting the older-fashioned, relatively static imagery of Flaubert or Stevenson or Willa Cather, are equally not inclined to live without the disclosures of the more dynamic novelty of the newer mode.

There is much more to the whole fiction, of course, than imagery. Yet it is difficult to understand how any story as art—that is, as creation of illusion of presence—could long dispense with the image and not dry up into second-rate brochure, or some odd species of unbelievable journalism. In instance after instance, drawn from every mood of the imagination, regardless of point of view or other technical device, we have re-marked the substantive contribution of the sensorily perceptible to the equally present but sensorily imperceptible elements of emotion, idea, form, character, language as dialogue, and conflict. In the large flow of the medium of the whole fiction, these relations are boundable only as currents in water. The image, and especially the visual image, is needed to contribute at least a delusory fixity—if of no more than the appearance of surface, then at any rate, that. Let the heroine lean her head against a tree trunk, and then from the perceived woman and tree, and from the surrounding earth and foliage and sky, there comes to us some substantiation of forces amid which her thought and her mood may be as vague or as clear as is wished. Anybody, doubtless, may think of *blue* and of *rustle* and of *hard* and of *sweet* without sensory experience of them, but one cannot really live so among the realities they name. As the struggle comes out in the thunder of cannon and the glimpse of uniforms through smoke; as a character chuckles or furrows his brow over the editorial he is reading in his imaginary newspaper; as feelings and ideas become apparent in the movements and facial expressions that suggest them, so the image arises as primitive and indispensable shape, whether of things material in the world, or of energies announcing change in themselves through the alteration of what appears for them. Perhaps the horse and the sonata as we sense them are products of the unsensible forces by process of which our image is partly made. Equally, the realities of formative power that lurk in the image are in time made manifest to us by it. The horse as seen and the sonata as heard, are, from an extremely important point of view, *the* horse and *the* sonata. The fact that art has often been defined in terms of form is of interest to students of fiction; and there is a sense in which the image, as the illusion of what is sensorily perceptible, is, itself, form.

Chapter 4

Pattern

THE TRADITIONAL CONTRAST of *fact* and *fiction* is of some interest etymologically. *Fact* is derived from *facere,* meaning "to make" or "to do"; *fiction,* from *fingere,* "shape," and therefore, "to invent." In origin, then, either is a thing that is or has been brought about; yet usage has given to the one the character of actuality as by divine or natural establishment, and to the other the character of human design or contrivance. Usage, of course, is an anarchy unto itself: there is an enormous class of facts established by human contrivance and nothing else in the universe—"It is a fact that today is Tuesday"—"It is or is not a fact that the rod is eighteen inches long." The fact that there are so many of this sort of facts is possibly one reason for our maintaining a distinction between *fact* and *truth*. A student of fiction can hardly be blamed for an occasional chuckle over the precaution. Returning to our original contrast, we may say of *fact* that it refers to some event, quality, or relation presumed, or perhaps better, regarded, as simply and actually existent; whereas *fiction* would be applied to what is known to have been created by human interposition, by and in and for the mind. Hence the imagination is felt to dominate in fictions more than in mechanical inventions, such as airplanes, which before they occur are fantastic, but which as soon as they become familiar enough in the world, are, of course, plainly recognizable as facts. For this reason we say that fact arises in the world outside; fiction in our consciousness. We regard *fact* as somehow simple being, but *fiction* rather of man's shaping. Our attitude toward fiction, as toward all art, recognizes in it therefore importantly, if not preeminently, the aspect of form.

One of the strong impressions we carry away from reading a story is that of pattern, whether in the sense of design preparatorily conceived and then executed by the author, or of a partly recognized and partly occult tendency which is achieved in the telling, or of something in the finished product which affects us as structure, outline, and the like. This formative or formed element is protean; it comes to us in many guises. Fiction itself, for instance, is said to be a form of literature; or its illusion or its action is one of its forms, of which sundry others might be the general mood, the point of view, the intellectual position or purpose, or the more elementary components, like certain settings, or characters, or the very paragraphs and sentences and larger unitary parts, each with its own form. The agreeable accommodativeness of the term-of-all-work is plain indication that custom is aware of a virtually omnipresent reality in fiction, that must therefore be recognized as a principal element of the whole fiction. In fact, they very loose absent-mindedness of custom here is what has made me cautious of using the word everywhere I pardonably might. Instead, I have spoken of kinds, moods, points of view, schools, lengths, and presences, and indeed have preferred any appropriate designation to the doubtless proper, but perhaps vague, and at any rate confounding omnipresent word, *form*. In particular, I have chosen the word *pattern*.

Now, by *pattern* I mean entity as assemblage. Something is itself, yet is also a relation which is manifestly associative, and on the other hand, obscurely exclusive. The parts are interdependently cooperative. Pattern therefore merges a continuity that is contained with an identity that is single and public. It is the paradoxical reality of communal singleness: there are the member entities; there is the relation of the whole of each member to its part in the union; above all—of course above all!—there is the comprehensive entity of which the parts are parts, of which the pattern is the pattern. Pattern is accordingly a complex of relationships among the parts, and between them and itself, and between itself and the unseizable whole which it patterns. Pattern is to reality what the flame is to the light. It is no more the whole reality than is the substance, to which the pattern gives form, the whole reality. How strange! that this thing which seems of the very essence of appearance should itself elude our apprehension, and manifest itself as the indubitable but only conjectured principle within the various other elements of which we are aware, such as phenomena, imagery, feelings, and thoughts. So far as fiction is concerned, for example, there is a convention by which, when we speak of the pattern of a story, we mean that story. That would be to identify fiction with the shaped creation. That would be art merely as form. A conception so limited and so artificial is a warning to us to be both modest and daring. Indeed, the very hopelessness of exhausting the varieties of fictional patterns stimulates us to ask, what, at any rate, are some of these patterns?

There are two types, which I call "horizontal" and "vertical" patterns to emphasize their contrast. The former is the site of the story, the domain of space and time which it covers. This includes the duration of the elapsed period of the grand occurrence, together with illusory environment, social as well as scenic, and therefore of course the agents. The writer cuts himself a piece of this world or of some other, of his own age or one past or future, which contains some occurrence of greater or less magnitude and complexity. I say he cuts this off, because, although the events will seem to be affected by the irrelevancies and interruptions of our life on earth, he knows that nothing of the sort is true. In a sense of "plot" curiously like the surveyor's use of the word, he has a terrain set out and dedicated to a certain fixed purpose. Because this area is isolated from the flux of worldly things, and because the illusion of happenings will be entirely *within* the terrain, I have called such illusion static. Presumably that is what Joyce meant by what he called the "stasis" of a work of art. It is somewhat like a map, somewhat like a stage-setting between performances, somewhat like an old battlefield preserved as an open-air museum. A great deal of work may go into the preparation of the static illusion. Fielding laid the ground-plan of *Tom Jones* with the utmost care. The researches of Balzac and Flaubert are part of the history of literature. Jane Austen worked with a calendar, Thomas Hardy with a map and almanacs, and Stevenson spoke proudly of the map he had prepared for *Treasure Island* before attempting to write that charming romance. In *Middlemarch* and in *Point Counter Point,* where related groups of persons are dealt with, each a little at a time, and time after time, there is design as of a curved line spiraling over spokes, and converging toward their hub, like a half-coiled spring.

Something of the same kind is to be found in the tales of Henry James. Around his central theme, centered in one character, he commonly disposed other characters, whom he himself compared to lamps, whose function it is to cast their light upon the principal. When this main character is also a lamp, as is Maggie Verver or Lambert Strether, the reflections are reciprocal. I am not now stressing these lightings up, but rather the basic arrangement, the premeditated scheme for them. Another of James' skills was the designed order of the encounter of his characters, not only as the ground-design of the action, but as a two-dimensional sketch to guarantee the inclusion of every necessary episode. He charted this pattern like a playwright, so that each scene to some extent would gratify the curiosity aroused by the preceding, yet carry tension forward to the next. Let me repeat that this is not the enactment of climax, but only the conjectural order of the climactic steps; putting them together so is somewhat like making a ladder on the ground, or on a carpenter's bench, flat. James' patience in planning, to those who have had an inkling of it, is a mark of his highly developed technique, and a trait of his nature as an artist. His best works are among the great compositions of fiction, with the best of Jane Austen and Flaubert and Turgenev.

Such writers must have their inspirations as others do, but

ultimately they leave nothing to chance. No matter what takes their reader by surprise, they have prepared it, with a nice proportion, a tactful timing, a true economy, a baffling ease. Their vitality is a grip upon the original, transient inspiration, a power to reshape airy illusion as though it were marble, into that harmony of part and whole which it is the measure of their genius to exact. So far as James is concerned, the adjustment of the contrapuntal elements of the static illusion—only one of his many skills—is in itself tolerably complex. I have called this the site, and the word suggests another of the same stem—situation. In James, as in his early admiration, Hawthorne, this is a feature of the work because it is an appetite of the man, but James' counterpoint is vastly richer. Among the situations he fuses to make the one grand, smooth effect of the story, the main ones are three: there is first of all the situation of the main character, his relationships among the people of this world, the network of strains within his character, and between it and the environment. In *The Spoils of Poynton,* this situation is the mainspring of the action, and in *The Golden Bowl,* it is the business of the action to unravel it as the knot of the intrigue. Related to this kind of situation among persons regarded as entering into or struggling out of entanglement, there is a group of instrumental patterns: the original equilibrium into which some disturbing force has come, the vague shape of the trespass and the vaguer shapes of its alarming potentialities of outcome, and the dormant or aroused attitudes of the characters closest involved, any of them probably—and the principal certainly—himself the theatre of conflicting insights and preferences. Secondly, after this cluster of situations, there is the grouping of subordinate characters about the central one, for the special advantage of each in casting their lamp-like glow upon him—for example, to bring out something in the consciousness of an inarticulate girl in *Washington Square,* or of a child in *What Maisie Knew.* Thirdly and last, there is the inventory of the sections of the narrative from introduction to conclusion, the chart of the procession in which each major event will have its place, that and no other, so as to permit the precise modulation of all these interwoven situations, the maintenance of their manifold persistent identity throughout rising complications to the climactic peak.

It must be plain that in my attempt to treat the horizontal illusion or static pattern as a thing apart, I have again and again been forced to refer to the vertical pattern of the dynamic illusion. In fiction, setting and action are experienced as one, except for purposes of abstraction. Analysis can distinguish the one from the other, but with progressively greater and greater difficulty; the process of abstraction here is simply a lifting of either aspect out of disregardful experience into focal; and whichever of the two patterns we raise into such prominence, we must raise the other at least into periphery. For reading, it would be about as sensible to experience illusion of setting and illusion of conflict separately as it would be to carry the face of a watch in one pocket and the works in another. Yet what is not rightly possible to do when one is reading fiction as it should be read is of course quite possible when one is examining its ingredient patterns; and the reader may proceed to abstract any pattern in this way quite safely, so long as he keeps in mind what it is he is doing, and is not deceived about the extent to which he can actually do it. Those of us who were required in youth to diagram on graph paper the jagged line of rising and falling action in *Julius Caesar* will recall a perception of this pattern as reality, but also a keen sense of skeletal silliness. Even in the kind of abstraction performed by fluoroscope, the kind, I mean, which leaves the analyzed organism whole and functioning, there is still, except for the most habituated, a distracting strangeness in the midst of recognizing the perfectly understandable relation of organic action within organic setting.

In what I said about James with respect to horizontal pattern, I spoke of an original equilibrium which is threatened by a trespass. Conflict is present in being promised. But the original equilibrium may itself be charged with conflict if it is a patterned deadlock of forces which the trespass will so upset that the earlier, suspended struggle is dwarfed by involvement in a never and more complex one. At the outset of *The Wings of the Dove,* Kate Croy and Merton Densher are lovers resolved not to give each other up, in spite of a family ultimatum against an improvident marriage. The opening situation of the novel is therefore the closed stalemate of an earlier action, reported as though from the past. The trespass comes in the form of Milly Theale, who is attracted to Densher; and since they are reported to have met before the opening of the story, the trespass, too, comes from the past. The first chapters are accordingly charged with a drama which the past has generated; and since no small element of our interest lies in picking up, as we read along, stray hints of what has gone before, the very treatment of the introduction has the force of complication. This effect of action thickening from the start is maintained throughout by progressive complication up to and even beyond the end; for, in the closing scene between Kate and Merton, and in the last words of their dialogue, there is still no assurance that the marriage they have so struggled and schemed for will ever occur, or, if it does, that it will be such as they have dreamed. From the point of view of Kate Croy, as the character who is most powerful in initiating developments in the action, the entire novel may be considered the working out of a conflict internal to her. Her resolve has constantly been two-fold: to have Densher and to have an income suitable to the life they should share. Circumstance, however, not only frustrates the fusion of the two aims but forces them into opposition; and this opposition persists at the ending and beyond, because it was present at the beginning and before.

James' resourceful tactic of modulation is closely connected with his provident strategy of situation. He has won the respect of many readers and critics because he can arouse and hold attention. In his own way—and what a way that is!—he was a born story-teller. For readers who do not wish to follow a story but merely to be carried along on it fast, his intentness on giving each step of the action its precisely qualified momentum may very well be maddening; but those with a tenacity to emulate his intentness are rewarded by an astounding density of absorption in a breathless quiet of tension they neither can nor wish to shake off. James keeps to the business at hand as few others know how; even his discursiveness is all for the event of the moment. Rarely does he fall into those large generalizations of psychological or philosophical comment that loose the sinews of action, as George Eliot and Proust and Mann frequently do. In his poorer work his spotlight is dim, yet it is ever trained on the event evolving from the one before and moving toward the one just ahead. His ideas are not given in explicit discourse; they are embodied in characters who are the presences of a movement restlessly continuous. Hawthorne symbolizes his convictions in persons and events that stress the symbolic; if his stories are not quite sermons, they are certainly ceremonies, and his originality itself is quaintly, personally ritualistic, suggesting the closeness of the beliefs so elaborately veiled. James, having drawn from life some allegory of worldliness and integrity, proceeds to redomesticate it within the Nature from which he has elicited it, and to return it there so nicely that there seems to be no allegory at all, but, as in daily experience, only the World, possibly the occasion for our formulating ideas upon it, but itself quite apparently innocent of them. So it is often not easy to decide what he means in any tale of his; his views and his message are *lived by* the story as his complexly busy deputy; his ideas, like his situations, are merged with his conflict, and consequently concealed by the devices which lodge it in us. In each of his masterpieces there is an unbrokenly mounting struggle with no instant of cessation or letdown. Some one, or some force in some one, is at every turn beset by an adverse, resourceful force. Not till the circuit closes in the last contact of the patterned parts can there possibly come the first deep breath of release. The bromidic adjective "gripping," which is generally applied to stories of physical action, and often with accuracy, is the only word for James' influence on readers who are ready for him. He exploited the obsessive power of curiosity, as Poe did that of fear, by feeding it the momentaneous variety of change in the object, of minute alteration enlarging possibility, of unpredictable consequence leading on to the exactly rounded outcome. No one was ever more determined than he to present the pattern of the moment of consciousness, of consciousness moment by moment. He did this by making each emerged moment live, and he did that by seeing to it that the animation of the conflict never mortally missed a breath.

So far I have dealt with the peculiar relation of illusion and conflict by suggesting rather than by exhibiting the juncture. I do not wish to leave the matter so vague; for since the line of merger may be plotted with much nearer accuracy than I have yet attempted, I cannot quit the subject without closing the gaps my sketchy hints leave open. For the purpose, I will resort to diagram; and since any diagram about the imagination could be no more than a figure of speech made of lines instead of words, I will not draw it and have it printed on the page, but will verbally describe it. The reader, knowing that he no more than fancies it, will have constant reason not to mistake it for truth, certainly not *the* truth; and I for my part shall be under greater pressure to make its suggestiveness as usefully precise as I can.

I will begin quite simply, by using metaphors familiar in the discussion of fiction. We are used to speaking of a story line, which leads, as we say, to a point. To signify this motion and termination, I picture a horizontal line, drawn from the left of a page, so that the point will be near the extreme right. I am aware that I am oversimplifying, but for the moment all that I wish to indicate is a progress to a destination, an end not in the sense of a breaking off, but of a completion, a satisfaction. Such a point, for example, would in a fable be the moral, or that tendency throughout the anecdote which is made explicit as the conclusion. In the fable of the Fox and the Goat, the moral, "Look before you leap," expresses not only the ending of the piece, but the direction of its movement. The two verbs, moreover, are a faint afterglow of the final image of the illusion: the escaped Fox jeering at his dupe in the pit. In our diagram, that image would be the next to the last point in the line. The fable is moralistic in organization as in function. Its little story is image-coated precept, but, characteristically, the precept is stated. The moral, in its aptness, is no accident, and so to call it a mere tag is more forceful than exact. It is, after all, the "point." I labor the issue here because in most fiction the point is not obvious; it is omitted from the text, and therefore from the private monologue. Even some fables have been written without the moral; and in the last two or three centuries the general practice in imaginative narrative has been along the line of Poe, not of Hawthorne. A great many readers (whether or not they really know their minds) say that they don't like preachy stories. On the other hand, it has become increasingly hard to get people to condemn as preachy any book expressing views identical with their own. The matter is somewhat confused, one must agree. But certainly most writers prefer a vivid and interesting illusion, perhaps with a message not too difficult to infer, but of course not expressed, and certainly not at the very end of the story. With all allowance, then, for certain great exceptions—Proust, for one—and for a catholicity of taste which is hospitable to the exceptional, the fact remains that contemporary authors conclude a piece in an image, the terminal one of the illusion, which thus becomes the ostensible point.

What this means is that the very last words of the text deliver one end, and imply another. The tension is all the tighter because the illusion is directly perceived, as by the senses, with the repression and back-pressure of some meaning or connotation intuitively felt. If my metaphor will not be taken too seriously, I will say that the image is stamped on our minds by a press that loses no force in remaining invisible. In fact, the impact may be so strong as to rouse us to look for the meaning (and find it), or may enable us to recognize it as some reviewer expresses it. Many readers, however, vigorously deny that there is any such feature, arguing with more reason than truth, that it is "just not there." Now, to refrain from spoiling innocent sport is one thing; to be silent on a matter of fact in serious discussion is another. The idea, or the feeling, or the pattern represented by concluding imagery *is* "there," as evil is present in a treacherous blow, or goodness in tending the sick. The constant sharpening of the symbolism in the course of a story, made possible by the extent of the narrative and the directive drive of the conception it substantiates, is what gives the ending its whittled penetration. Our "story line," as I said in introducing it, is an oversimplification. It pictures only the conceivable average direction of many lines steadily converging in their patterned conflict toward a rendezvous. When they arrive at it, it proves to be themselves in cross-section, and our point, being divisible, is hardly a mathematical one. It is as though a line of color vibration should cut across a line of tonal vibration at exactly one place, and, in addition, a line of the olfactory, and so on—to produce, perhaps, the illusion of a girl singing in a beer-hall.

With this revision of the notion of our point we must accordingly revise the entire diagram. The oversimplification I erect a right-angled triangle on our line, the hypotenuse gives way to complexity, yet we may proceed by degrees. First, slanting down to the apex-point over to the right. This, for the moment, will represent the illusion, the world of the story, the environment imagined as though perceptible by the senses. I picture this triangle drawn in solid lines, and for me it represents that continuity of the story in which movement of details, and alteration, and, therefore, presumable passage of time, will hold my attention to imagined occurrence and may stir in me an intimation of its suppressed significance. But since this last is, indeed, suppressed, I give to it another triangle, equal to the first an continuous with it, but *under* the line and drawn with separate dots (as though the first were reflected in water) to signify those elements of the story which are not manifest. What we now have is a large bisected triangle, of which, to render our experience of fiction, the upper half represents the illusion which we can plainly see, and the nether, the invisible meaning, which we can only gather as we read. For every point on our greater triangle we have either something given for something withheld, or something withheld for something given. Yet this only comparatively; because the separation of the two aspects is greatest at the broad base, where the story commences, with less and less to be learned at every remove from it, and least of all at the apex, where the point-image of the upper half and the point-meaning of the lower half are joined in the strategically placed presence of the former. But now all this talk about halves will no longer serve. The illusion is not single; neither is the significance. Each is many things: the one, imagery, movement, change; the other, not only intellectual, but emotional and aesthetic as well. The diagram in two dimensions must in turn give way to one in three, to provide room for many cross-sectional phases. Instead of a triangle with the axis horizontal, we need a cone in that position; and instead of a visible upper half and a hidden lower half, we now have a surface that faces us, and a hidden surface on the other side.

What we have now is an apparent triangle, which is really a cone in profile, with its base to the left and its apex to the right. Now it is possible to see why the "point" is so complex an affair: it is the rendezvous of every line from every point of the base. Of these, the one from the center to the apex is the general direction (our oversimplified, discarded horizontal line) and its further tip is the locus of their growing together. The cone might therefore be the emblem of the concrete whole fiction; the triangle, of the abstract. As for the unique whole fiction, that is a spiral motion starting about the base, but in the course of each revolution tending toward the apex, as though along grooves of just incompleted circles. Thus there is still a sense of the apparent coupled with a sense of the withheld, of locality with drive, of illusion indicative of imperceptible conflict. Viewed from our side, the spiraling about the cone and toward the tip might represent the progress of action fiction, as in Smollett, Scott, Cooper, Hugo. Viewed from the base, the centripetal tendency would appear single and alone; I have already spoken of this pattern in connection with *Middlemarch* and *Point Counter Point*. It is of course the design of a typical work by James, with the pattern of lamps surrounding a theme. It is the spider web of *Remembrance of Things Past*, with the narrator starting from and returning to the center, yet somehow always carrying it with him, too.

I now drop the diagram altogether. If it has been of value, that can scarcely have come from its resemblance to any corresponding reality, but rather from its suggestiveness of many patterns integrated into the one effect—the whole fiction— the pattern of all the patterning. What I have tried to suggest is, above all, that the conceptually abstractable patterns of illusion as imagery, and illusion as conflict, are inextricably united, are one, in the pattern of the illusion as the event. This is to the others what the heart-beat is to the systole and the diastole. We may analyze a story into its static and dynamic phases; if we could really separate them, we should kill it; and no living art is born of their mere adjacency or even synthesis.

In occasionally calling the entire matter of a story, even a novel, an occurrence, what I have had in mind is a comparatively large pattern of happening, with none larger than itself in the given work, and divisible into component steps. It is recognized as an entity, and so may be characterized by a phrase or a single word. This unitary quality may identify the occurrence for the author as he comes upon it, or it looms before him, in his imagination: the form taken by one life in autobiographical fiction like *David Copperfield,* by a length of genealogy in *The Way of All Flesh,* by a military or political campaign, or by any incident of private or social development which is an illuminating instance of some idea, principle, or contention. Although this sort of spontaneous shaping of chance into episode—the grain or the knot in the wood—might of course include case history, the category I refer to is not an ordinarily human one, but an aesthetic. From the top of the Empire State Building, Manhattan is reduced to a map, and the traffic of neighboring streets has the repetitive operation of mechanism. What is revealed is the natural contour of the island on the one hand, and on the other, the mechanical pattern imposed on it. All that we do when we peer down is to recognize an existing form, spatial or temporal, that is there to be recognized. Now, existence is replete with temporal forms, and we are endowed with the ability to pick them out of the flux of things as we pick wild berries out of a tangle. Any one of them is an occurrence of the sort I am talking about with reference to fiction, including any process by which an occurrence is determined or expressed. Therefore, in a Sherlock Holmes story, or a novel by Conrad or James, the pattern of *the* occurrence is a pattern of occurrences.

Our realization that time is of the essence of such form, in the identification, the expression, and the reading alike, is so casual as perhaps to be careless, to make us mistake the collaboration of time in action for a mere accompaniment. As well call the sap an accompaniment to the plant. The time of literary experience, in our recognizing the units of the text, and in speaking-hearing the units of the private monologue, is the fluidity of the action's flow. It is the actuality out of which arise the illusions of time in the fictional occurrence and of the time of the narration as planned by the writer to conform with the rhythms of reading. It is therefore one of the many ingredients the writer must feel and attend to in checking the text he is preparing, when he is his own first reader. I call this the actuality of time in the whole fiction because it is that interval in the duration of the reader's life. It is of course the time of contemporary events in the world from which the reader has withdrawn, in order to read. The reading time is part of that interval, and here is the basic ground for calling it the actual. Now, whatever the reading period is, there will be a coverage of so many pages and words, and therefore an average for each unit of the time spent. This varies with readers, and with readings by the same reader, depending on such psychological factors as the interest and the ease or difficulty of the text. The implication for the unique whole fiction is obvious. Yet there remains an average of some sort, not, I grant, fixed, but with a ratio between any part of the duration and the whole, and therefore of part to part.

To match this proportional index, there is a second. It is based on a length of text covered in a session of reading, with respect to the shorter length of any included section recognizable as a unit—an episode, a description, a stretch of dialogue, or the like. One had only to think of the degree of pleasure and so of patience with which he greets writing of this character or that, to see how important are the tempo and the change of pace with respect to "text-time" and to the reader's living time while he is experiencing the illusion of the story. One can see, moreover, that with both these aspects of time there is bound up a third: the succession of the events in whatever order the text presents them, whether this last is the same as the chronological order of events in the occurrence which the story presents, as in David Copperfield's autobiography, or some re-arrangement of simple chronology into complex applied pattern, as in Conrad's *Victory* or Edith Wharton's *Ethan Frome,* or the Homeric epic. Fourth, and final in this tabulation, there is the time of, or perhaps better *in,* the occurrence itself; that is, the credited years or moments of the horizontal pattern in which the characters live out their fictitious lives, perhaps in consultation with their fictitious clocks and calendars. For the sake of summary, then, we have first of all the elapsed time of the reading of a story; and second, the average time required for any division, such as a chapter or a page; and third, the relation of this to a passage of one kind or another, was we deem it slow or fast reading; and finally, the mimic time of the world of the characters, manifesting itself as their seasons, day and night, or what you will.

Should this pluralism of times appear to make fiction an unnatural thing, it is necessary only to recall the transcontinental passenger who has to lose or gain an hour between two successive moments of biological duration, so that he has to change the time of his watch, in order to be in step with his sidereal environment. There is also the transoceanic loss or gain of an entire day. Thus, all around the world, amid the variety of chronometries, each of us breathes the contemporary instant of the present, though again, for one it is the age of waiting for the unconscious beloved to open seeing eyes, and for another, that zero which is any moment of dreamless sleep. The doctor will not interrupt his taking of the patient's pulse at the instant when the train crosses the time line. A poker player in the club car grudges the time to do so; other passengers make a delightful ritual of it, since they have time on their hands. The relation of the time of the stars to that of a clock or an earache or a kiss is natural, and so is any relation within the complex of times in the whole fiction. With or without knowing it (in all probability, most commonly without) one kind of reader will prefer to maintain a time pattern of the simplest sort, and another of the most involved, while for a third a certain pleasure will come from change and variety imposed by different authors and techniques. For all alike, there will be a settling into and maintenance of the temporal pattern of the work in hand; and this is one of the subtle aesthetic practices of fiction as art; that is, as experience for the experiencing.

Somebody, let us say, is sitting in his chair with the rays of his lamp on his novel. His eyes move across the lines and down the page of the story; he fingers and turns the leaves; he breathes and shifts and perhaps sighs. Through the open window come the near or far sounds of the night, and also a breeze that plays with the curtain, and blows on the lamp, the chair, the book, all the things in the room, including the man. It is darkness in this hemisphere and day in the other; millions of creatures are slumbering, working, playing; airplanes are aloft, a cabinet meets, a drunken sailor in a foreign port strikes the blow that will start the next war, and sparrows and leaves and raindrops fall. None of this at the moment reaches to the focal awareness of the reader. Equally, nothing comes to him from the other darkness through which his blood courses, in which his last meal is being digested and his next appetite is being prepared, in which his interpretation of the print and the soundless voice speaking it are only two more operations of the cunning reticence of body in the abstract. That cunning, indeed, has drawn into itself the very print and monologue, stealth by stealth, and now is holding them off at the horizon of the momentaneous experience. Their timing and that of the man's pulse are now one, with perhaps some adjustment for a skimming, a rereading to recover the thread of thought, the delightful discovery of a misprint, or several futile stabs at pronouncing "chthonic" or determining its meaning from the context. So, as I say, the text is experienced peripherally, like the book in his hands and the slippers on his feet; and the private monologue has long since yielded place to another illusion at a further remove.

In this illusion events have already been related, and one is being related; but the relation, the retailing, ah! that is peripheral, too. For events have *occurred,* and one is *occurring* —or rather, what these people have done and said, are doing and saying, in this place, at this time, teems with what they are still to do and have done to them, to disclose and to learn. Not all of it yet, of course; time enough for that rest, too, in the characters' future, pages and pages ahead, later in the night or the week. Meanwhile, to regard what it is they are saying and doing, to respond to the present moment of *their* environment as one's own, is a possibility conditioned upon obliteration of a sweet confusion of the facts about oneself, by a disregard habituated beyond recollection of its training —a lifetime ago, when they took one's ability to watch a memory and ignore everything else, and turned it into the power to listen to, and later to read, a story. The skills they used for the purpose were many, including one that is an open secret universally—a bird's knowing how to fly without consciously knowing anything about flight, a violet's canniness in not growing up a gladiolus, the tight little way a pebble has of being a pebble—in a word, the time saving trick of any and all action, of its not needing to know what action it is or that it is action or that there is any such thing as action, even when it is action of knowing something, like teaching a youngster to read, or learning to read as a youngster. How silly it would be, then, to say of our man reading his story, that since, while he reads, he does not explicitly know about his maintenance of temporal and other pattern, the statement that such things are part of his experience is plainly false! Ah, the more inclusive truth would be simply this: that one may comprehend the whole fiction so far and so far, and then —it eludes us!

The pattern of the fusion of time and disregard is a pattern which no one may ever draw, but one which every teller of tales must know how to bring about, as the very tiniest baby fish knows how to swim. When my very animation is breathed into print and fancied audition of speech, and thence into the illusory occurrence of what I read, there goes with it, equally subject to occult transformance, the moment of my being, the time of man. Invisibly the very sense of the vanishing of the superimposed patterns of time works everywhere throughout the whole fiction, a pervasive necromancy, an unplumbed comfort. Now, it is highly improbable of any story that the elapsed time of reading is exactly equal to that of the composing and writing, or either of these equal to that of the occurrence narrated. Yet, in the imagining of a story, all three patterns are conjointly one, doubtless for the invaluable convenience of not having to ignore each separately; that is, of enjoying an illusion one pays no attention to whatsoever, the disregarded illusion of playing truant from time, of slipping out of the life of one's time to have the time of one's life.

A peculiarity of such legerdemain is that the merged, blurred times retain their patterns for analysis, and so, of course, have them to begin with. The time of reading, for example, is strictly chronological, in spite of interruptions, and in spite of skipping around in the book. One may compute it, as flying time is computed in air travel. The time of the printed text is also chronological, page after page. So, frequently, is the time of the occurrence. Events occur to imaginary people as they do to real ones, in sequence, with the one possible and only apparent exception that events may occur to various people, separated in space, at one and the same time. This possibility, as we saw a page or two back, in our vision of the world's time that included the reader's, is an actuality of every single moment. Tolstoy adapted it in *War and Peace*, Sterne in *Tristram Shandy*, Joyce in *Ulysses*, and Dos Passos in *Manhattan Transfer*; and in fact the device is as common, for incidental purposes, in fiction, as the phenomenon of four voices in two conversations in one operatic quartet. Nevertheless, keeping this exception in mind, one may maintain that the time pattern of the original imagined occurrence out of which a tale or a novel is made is chronological. So, too, may be the time pattern of the relation of these events, as we have already noted in connection with *Moll Flanders* and *David Copperfield*.

Then, all the major time sequences of the whole fiction

may be chronological. Many stories are written on this uniform scheme. It makes for swiftly simple progress, because, although the actual and imaginary periods of elapsed time are unequal, the index of the average rate of the reading time sets the general proportion, keeps all the sequences proportional, and so synchronizes them. The case is so marked in Scott and Cooper and similar writers as to bore some readers, whom it does not sufficiently occupy, whose disregard it does not exercise with nearly enough complexity. On one plane of cultural complexity, some people prefer the more difficult detective story; on another, the mazes of Meredith, James, or Kafka; and the same reader may go from either plane to the other. Yet the simpler synchronized form I am considering at the moment may be made vastly entertaining, and has produced great fictional art. Lively characterization, humor, pathos, symbolism of social or other issues of interest, vicarious experience, or, most characteristic of all, stirring events of rapidly mounting climax, have made excellent entertainment in the hands of Smollett, Stendhal, Mérimée, Dickens, Trollope, Mark Twain, Loti, Arnold Bennett, Colette, Norman Douglas, Richard Hughes, and Isak Dinesen. Furthermore, the chronological ordering is prevalent rather than invariable. A thread of intrigue will require the advance to halt briefly for the retailing of events out of the fancied past; or the first appearance of a new character in the course of the action calls for a pause to introduce a sketch of his past life. Such whorls of retrogression vary the straight line of movement from present to furture just enough to contribute an offsetting of monotony. They will be found sprinkled throughout the comparatively uniform propulsions of Cervantes, Prevost, Mrs. Radcliffe, Jane Austen, and Samuel Butler. Even Defoe, who is as consistently unilinear in this regard as any one in the history of fiction, is nevertheless, because of his great power of improvisation, sometimes induced to halt and go back in time when the value of the material appeals to his shrewd showmanship. The entire episode in which Moll Flanders discovers her mother in Virginia is a present haunted equally by the past and by the horrible threat of the future. The fact that the situation is exceptional for Defoe simply shows that even a most consistent chronicler will occasionally step out of line. What I speak of as chronological singleness is not the same as the annalistic directness of the Anglo-Saxon Chronicle. There are, strictly speaking, irregularities, yet they do not alter the fact of a prevalent, dominant, characteristic, direction.

One such variant, for example, which complicates the singleness only to the extent of doubling it, is to be found in the so-called frame story. We run across the device in de Maupassant's tales: a group of characters engage in discussion of some question; one of them, to demonstrate his view, launches into an illustration from life—the story proper; at the end of the piece, the disputants ruminate on this anecdote. In Bierce's "An Occurrence at Owl Creek Bridge," the central section takes place in the consciousness of a man about to be hanged; this is framed by an opening and a closing section presenting him in his environment. Sometimes the frame alternates, in the text, with the actual story, as in *Lord Jim* or *Ethan Frome*. Sometimes it is only a preface, without any balancing conclusion, as in *The Turn of the Screw*. Although the frame story need not by any means be a simple chronology set between two pieces of another simple chronology, that arrangement is a well-known favorite. With some exceptions, it is the pattern of certain famous collections of narratives, of which *The Arabian Nights, The Decameron,* and *The Canterbury Tales* are perhaps the best known. There can be no question that the more usual pattern of the frame story modifies the time pattern in two places. The compass direction may seem consistent, as in descending a gorge and climbing up the other side; but the temporal environment does change. I have included it with the pattern of uniformly straightforward chronology only because the comparative simplicity of the alteration tends to support the conception of the whole fiction by suggesting a transition between one pattern of time in which the complexity is successfully disguised, and other patterns in which, degree upon degree, it is brought to light and even emphasized.

So that the comparison may be easier for me to introduce, I will temporarily detour from a consideration of fiction in prose to one of fiction in verse, for the advantage of shorter examples. These will be three: the old ballads of "Robin Hood's Death and Burial" and "The Twa Corbies," and Browning's "My Last Duchess"—all three of them old favorites. In the first, Robin is at once said to be so ill that he can barely make his way to Kirkly to have his cousin bleed him. She treacherously opens the vein, and locks him into his room to bleed to death. He is unable to escape, but he feebly blows three blasts on his horn, and thus summons Little John. Forbidding revenge upon a woman, the outlaw asks the boon of shooting one last arrow, so that he may be buried in whatever place it falls; and his request is honored. From the opening event of his falling ill to the final one of his burial, the occurrence is given in the succession of time. The order is once inverted, in Robin's declaration that he has never hurt a woman, nor "men in women's company." But the general, negative character of the inversion, and its brevity, make it seem more a profession of principle than a record of past events. Otherwise, the way in which the events presumably occurred is their climactic pattern, and so the recital presents them. The action covers a period of a few days; the piece is in nineteen stanzas, sixteen of four lines, three of six, a total of eighty-two; so the reading time is a matter of minutes. The pattern of the great fighter's end is followed strictly, with severe exclusion of quite pertinent matter: not a word, for instance, is offered about the cousin's motive. The little story is therefore a model of the single modulation of all the time patterns of a fiction, as though they were unequal circles arranged about a common center so that any angle from that point would include proportional segments of all.

The arrangement of "The Twa Corbies" is different. The two crows are given fabular powers of conversation. One of them, in the fourth line, asks

> *"Where sall we gang and dine to-day?"*

and in the sixteen remaining lines the other makes a grim suggestion, which includes the story of a knight recently slain and left unburied in the woods.

> *". . . And naebody kens that he lies there*
> *But his hawk, his hound, and lady fair.*

> *"His hound is to the hunting gane,*
> *His hawk to fetch the wild-fowl hame,*
> *His lady's ta'en another mate . . ."*

Since neither the murder nor the motive is stated, they are not given, in chronological or in any order; and the order in which they are hinted is that of chronology backward, reversed. In a certain spot lies the body of "a new slain knight." There is only one person, his "lady fair," who "kens that he lies there." In spite of the recency of the whole frightful business, she has already "ta'en another mate." In addition to this inversion of the past, there is prophetic inclusion of the future, for the crows—

"So we may mak our dinner sweet"

with additional hideous details of that repast; and also for human contemporaries—

"Mony a ane for him makes mane,
But nane sall ken where he is gane"

and for the universe of stolid nature—

"O'er his white banes, when they are bare,
The wind sall blaw for evermair."

This brief masterpiece of sardonic horror anticipated by many centuries certain naturalistic conceptions, such as we are accustomed to think of in connection with Hardy or with more recent writers of the hard boiled school, and it did so with a mastery of indirect relation worthy of Browning or Meredith or James. The piece opens with a frame supplied by the unknown minstrel

"As I was walking all alane,
I heard twa corbies making a mane"

and reports the birds' statements, of course, as events in the chronology of their talk. But the events of the occurrence, as we have seen, are not only out of their time order in the relation, but some of them we ourselves have to determine. The mechanism of mystery fiction is exploited to heighten a dawning horror, and the prophetic touches crown the whole with bitter reflection. The time pattern thus contributes its complexity to the experience, imaginatively, emotionally, and intellectually. The bones of the narrative have been picked clean. When I consider the length of the ballad—the twenty very short lines—I wonder whether it ever had a reader whose mind did not hover and hover over it, unable to struggle out of its small, dense, terrible enmeshment. I feel that I must repeat just one of my observations, to broaden its meaning. The temporal pattern of the structure of "The Twa Corbies" may very well have been the inspiration of a split second, but it neither was nor is an accident in the sense of being irrelevant to the action, the mood, the meaning. The re-patterning of the various times in accordance with the time pattern of the telling, or the relation pattern, is the life and the soul of creation. It gives the ballad its unique quality: we are forced to piece out for ourselves, against obstacles of significant omission, most of the elements of the experience, and finally the experience itself. Whether or not the reward is worth the effort, is a question each reader must answer for himself. Certainly it is the only question worth attending to.

The lifelikeness of Browning's Duke is directly related to the complexity of the time structure of his monologue. He is no simple detail of a man, brilliantly suggesting what we must imagine in order to have the rest of him in our mind's eye, nor is he even an impression of the clash of two or three contradictions. Rather, he is a full, living man, likely to surprise and upset our estimate of him at every fresh fact he offers about himself. By comparison the Duchess seems rather an aspect of a person, an impression caught by an artist on canvas, a gift for life and joy misunderstood by that Italian renaissance Soames Forsyte, her noble spouse. Her qualities, and the events cited to exemplify them, are in fact his patterning, the object his enraged possessiveness has assembled. In this respect she is a detail of him, a means of making him betray his morbid strength, his cunning vulpine dullness, his brute's polish, his patronage of artists, and his glibness in collector's art-appreciation. We learn of these traits through what he tells us of her and of his jealousy of her vestige in the portrait, and also of his relations with Fra Pandolf, the painter whose real name he will not tell, of the sculptor Klaus of Innsbruck who cast a bronze Neptune for him, of the new marriage he is dickering for, of the Count who may be his father-in-law, of the guests and the servitors to whom he alludes. We learn all these things in the course of the few minutes he spends talking to the Count's negotiator, giving him information, referring to things that cannot be divulged to an inferior, and letting him know that he has noted the impertinent admiration which the portrayed passion of the Duchess' beauty wrung from that inferior at first sight—probing and scorning and terrifying him, and putting him firmly in his place. What we read, then, is this monologue of his with its references, a single speech whose sentences, phrases, words, together with certain gestures and other movements, are the events proper of the scene. The elapsed time of reading and of the recital of the text are therefore about equal. The words, as I say, follow each other in chronological sequence. They are the only class of events here of which this is true. Even the thoughts, the meanings presented by the words, are occasionally interrupted by parentheses. The events for visualization in present time, that is, the time of the scene of which we are spectators, are once or twice inverted in the recital pattern of the monologue: only after the Duke has begun to speak do we learn about his drawing the curtain from the portrait just before the beginning; and the visitor's involuntary, admiring glance precedes by several seconds our learning of it in the host's cool rebuke.

Otherwise, the past events supplied about the Duchess, Fra Pandolf, and Klaus of Innsbruck, and the past and future events relating to the Count, his daughter, and their messenger, have no order except that of the appositeness with which the Duke mentions them, dropping each into its fitting place of reference in the course of his half-prepared delivery. Yet there is enough spontaneity in the free, allusive flow of his speech, in the brief outbreak of temper, in the groping for words as he sputters over the dead woman's resistance to his will, of the nonchalant remark about the Neptune, to give the whole episode the quality of instant life. More deeply, the fact that past and future events are referred to in no order except that of the Duke's needing them, and their coming to him for the exemplification of his thought, gives them a unliterary, an unpatterned casualness, which in turn builds them up into the illusion of a man—not a part of one—speaking, thinking, remembering, anticipating, and beneath all, feeling, feeling powerfully. It is his being so many-sided that permits us to ponder over him, and find him still more-sided, as we do each other. In his complexity he may be viewed as a representative of his city and century, and from a yet wider angle as a representative of human nature in a stage of barbarism verging on civilization. He is the human concretion of so many traits, his individuality is so indivisibly his complexity, that he may at any point provide symbolism for our speculation. By contrast, Robin Hood comes to us as the living symbol of a certain force in a bygone society, the hero and rallying center of a vast class of people, and is only secondarily and by an assumption we need not examine accepted by us as a certain man, as *that* man. In "The Twa Corbies" we have a situation and a mood aroused in us. But in "My Last Duchess" we have one man presented in detail of a quantity to suggest a great deal more, so that it is he who seems to include his era and place, his rank and thus society, a number of dramatic situations, and a kaleidoscope of human moods and traits.

Each of the three poems gives its own pleasure in its own way, and each exhibits an organization of time-patterns strikingly interrelated with the effect. It would be interesting to compare them on grounds of aesthetic excellence, or to try to determine how much of their structure is referable to conscious purpose, and how much to creative instinct; but what more immediately concerns us is the fact that the patterns are what they are, and are useful for modulating the fictional medium in a variety of ways for a variety of ends.

Every event of a story accordingly has all three aspects of time all the time, though ostensibly only one at a time. The static illusion, comprising all the possibilities of the piece as the author conceives it, is the source of the triple reality of the event; while the dynamic illusion, with its stress on spontaneous uniqueness, gives the event its momentary uniqueness as we experience it. This inherent twinship of concealed and evident reality is what is modulated into the action or plot, in which the event as the part and the continuity as the remainder are constantly adjusted and readjusted to each other by the invisible hands of time and attention. *What* is adjusted and readjusted is conflict, by which, as I have said, I mean a number of a variety of conflicts, or forms of conflict, so composed in their relative prominences as to make up the pattern of "a" conflict. For example, although in the Robin Hood ballad the writer-reader conflict operates as the momentary holding of attention, together with the withholding of outcome, this phase of the complex conflict is not nearly so important for that piece as it is for the other two, where it is far more nearly the characterizing feature of the conflict, and fairly dominates. Consequently, the conflict *in* the illusory occurrence of the death of Robin Hood is a far more prominent feature of the ballad than of the other, or of Browning's dramatic monologue. To put this idea from a different point of view, what we have been considering is a variety of structural patterns based on the simple chronology of the imaginary events, either retailed pretty generally in that order, or else refashioned into some other order dictated by a need or a purpose which is part of the pattern of the recital. In fiction the *characteristic* material is the events, the provision of conflict. Time is not their mere accompaniment, but their essence; and in the author's modulation of them into this or that design of action or plot, time is one of the collaborators for the production of form. It is so, in being itself a form, to be perceived everywhere in its discernible patterns, for, like anything else, it is born of the universal creativity.

I turn now to another assortment of structural patterns, each identifiable by its *treatment* of the events of the illusory occurrence in some one part of the recital pattern. Regardless of its place in a sequence, for example, an event may be stated briefly or at great length. The amount and quality of elaboration in a given instance is determined by the precise need of the conflict in establishing the form of the entire story as a satisfaction of that particular experience. Since any part so formed is one of the sequence of parts of a narrative, I will speak of it as a *structural unit*. So far as I can tell, there are in narration proper (as distinct from incidental description, exposition, and argument or persuasion) just four of these structural units. These, in their pure states, or modified, or mixed, I believe to constitute narration in the most narrowly accurate use of the word, and therefore the narrative element *per se* of the whole fiction. Once more, as in the case of the word *form* itself, I need a more particular terminology than that of general usage. We commonly speak of any part of a story, indifferently, as a "part," a "scene," an "episode," a "section," a "unit," a "division," and the like, applying any one of these designations without particular identification of the thing so designated. This indifference seems to me entirely too loose. In naming the basic structural units, I have taken over the words used for two of them that are quite familiar, namely, the *scene* and the *anecdote;* but for the others I have been compelled to coin names—the *chronology unit,* and the *time composite.*

The *scene* may be variously defined, depending on how it is regarded. From the point of view of the entire story as the imaginary occurrence, it is one subordinate extent of the action, conveying a turn of the conflict, so important as to require division into its component events, although with no apparent break in their continuity in time, and placed in one self-contained environment or setting. In any sense of the word *environment* that includes people, the scene would have one group of characters throughout, or certainly the important ones for the conflict; that is, the coming and going of a waiter might not break up the scene into small scenes if he is simply an animated property of the stage setting, but if he plays a role in the conflict, his coming or going would mark a new scene. Clearly, then, the scene is a structural unit dominated by the classic unities of action, time, and place, if by *unity* we mean the illusion of persistence and sameness in each, and therefore in the three together. This persistence or continuity is at any rate the ideal for each "unity" in the combination, whatever may be the exception, seeming or real.

I have offered one apparent violation of the unity of place in the instance of the waiter. Another would be the progressive change of scene glimpsed through the window of a moving train, or effected by people walking or riding. However, such movement of setting, throughout a scene, is a *persistent* change, the *same* change continuing, admitted as a quality of locale to begin with, and therefore unchanged in character—unless it works some fresh development in the conflict. Whether or not such perambulatory scenes, as in motion pictures, violate unity of place, is a matter of point of view; ideally, setting is static, or is commonly considered or treated so. On the other hand, the relation of unity of action and unity of time appears rigid. Exceptions here are much more dubious, much more questionable as merely apparent. An inconsiderable gap may not seriously violate the flow of the action, but it breaches the continuity of the unique event beyond any doubt at all. So far as I am concerned, this observation is simply further proof of the inseverable intertwining, if not indeed the identity, of energy and time, not as logical abstractions, but as the actuality from which we abstract them. I do not say that space is out of that identity, but only that we seem always to think of it as though it were apart; and thus in our arts we take greater license with space than with time. According to this quirk of ours, what any painter does is natural, but what Joshua did is a miracle.

Next, I should like to define the fictional point of view as it relates to the scene. If the story is candidly written from the point of view of the author, that is, with the "I," then his omniscience is the coign from which we survey the scene as the meeting place of the unique environments of all the characters involved, the public environment, combined, perhaps, with the same social field, as the author tells us that it appears to any character who has thoughts about it. Point of view in the technical sense, then, is an operation by which the scene, as a unit in the illusory occurrence as the author imagines it, is connected with the business of his relating it. The scene in the occurrence is not only identifiable as a certain pattern in the continuity of a presence in consciousness, but in addition has been appraised as a scene for its inclusion, and for the manner and extent of its elaborated treatment. Here point of view, as a principle of selection and modulation, is joined with the author's sense of the value of the scene in its bearing on the conclusion of the story, and so on its rounded form, its identity. The author may err in instinct or calculation, so that we may be subjected to a scene that is a bore or an irrelevance, or, on the other hand, we may feel that we have been cheated of interesting or clarifying details. For the conclusion of the story is the outcome of the conflict; so that the decision whether or not to make a certain event into a scene, and if so, of what pattern to let it take on, is determined both by the ending of the conflict and by the point of view. Since the conflict and the point of view are patterns, the structural unit —in this case the scene—is ostensibly a subordinate identity in the actual continuity, the merging (by part for whole) of the illusion as imagery, the illusion as conflict, and the illusion as point of view or pattern proper.

What I say here of the scene of course holds true for any structural unit; so that the final determination to conceive and treat a unit as a scene is due to the great importance of the particular event in the scale of action or climax, an importance calling for the utmost illusion of uniqueness so far as that story is concerned by division of the major event into so many minor events that the transit from one to another of them appears to be immediate, smooth, and without break in the stream of time. The continuity mimics the passage of time in life and thus matches the time of the activity of reading. In the synchronization, the events seem contemporary to our focal attention, and we disregard the fact that the action is related as of the past, in the past tense. The time of a successful scene is always the present, during our experience of it; and since the fine division into component events makes possible an increased imagining of sensory detail, the scene is quite likely to become an intensely vivid presence. The instant, contemporary maintenance of setting, characters, and action as a single yet constantly changing and continuous environment is what I mean by the uniqueness of the scene. No other structural unit has the same potentiality. Ideally, the scene is a present occurrence, so immediate that we disregard the fact that we are experiencing it, and the actualities of the text, monologue, pattern and authorship generally, and so persuasive that we have complete faith in the unpredictability of the immediate outcome. The possibility that the author may know how the scene will come out, or may not know, is quite taken care of by the illusion that there is no author, that what is happening is just itself. There are people, I hear, who have never read with such absorption, but like the imageless thinkers, they can hardly be thought to constitute the rule, or anything but an exception to it, and therefore no model, much less the ideal.

In "The Twa Corbies," someone who calls himself "I" introduces the rural scene of the talking birds. The first-personal point of view of the private monologue is then turned over to the crow who asks the question about dinner, and again to the other crow, who reveals the fact of the knight's murder. The crows are crows, and they speak; but they do nothing else, so that the scene does not hold attention for itself. It is a vehicle for the past event, and we can concentrate on the tragedy, and are left free to solve its mystery. In "My Last Duchess," the scene grows up around the Duke's monologue, from the opening statement that the portrait is painted on the wall, to the closing one about the sculptured Neptune. The guest is seated, and then rises; the two men stroll toward some door, in order to descend and "join the company below." Both as setting and as movement, then, the little scene offers some competition to the events recalled or anticipated by the speaker. One of these, the painting of the portrait by Fra Pandolf, of course in the same room, is rendered by the Duke's sarcastic mimicry of what he intimates must have been the artist's praise of his sitter, compliments in which her coloring plays so bold a part as to give the past a most unghostly solidness. One's imagining of the furniture and the costume of the period (regardless of accuracy) heightens the illusion; and there is the uninterrupted flow, smooth or staccato, of cultivated speech. As the fictional narrator, the ostensible first person, the nobleman dominates and disposes throughout. Even when the traits he boasts of, such as hereditary pride and noble will, are betrayed as petty insensitivity or something equally unflattering, it is he who does the betraying. His unbridled egoism is the cause of his self-betrayal. A similar transparency of characterization has been achieved by writers of prose fiction in the use of the delegated first person, to render the speaker both as he sees himself and as he does not—by Miss Edgeworth in *Castle Rackrent,* Thackeray in *Barry Lyndon,* Faulkner in *The Sound and the Fury,* and Lardner in "Haircut" and a number of other short stories. Returning to Browning's Duke—whatever we learn of him and the others, because or in spite of his intention, comes from his words, and therefore from the fictitious first person. The scene is comprised by the point of view, a relation that enables the structure to emerge steadily out of the agent as the "character," and as steadily to reinforce our sense of the Duke's character as his individuality. For we must not too readily accept the notion that the scene as a unit of structure necessarily includes the agents; of course it often does, but it may be included in any one of them, as a presence in his consciousness, as it is again and again and again in *Remembrance of Things Past.* Is not any fictional scene contained in the consciousness of the author? and does it not become so, again, in that of the reader? Well, characters can do anything readers or writers can—in illusion.

I have called the scene a structural unit, because it may be one unit of many in a structure, and because it may be *the* structure of a fiction, as in "My Last Duchess." It may also, as in Dickens, be a comic or pathetic or otherwise interesting event perhaps not structurally necessary for the entire story, though no reader would ever wish it omitted—the trial in *Pickwick,* the wooing of Mrs. Nickleby in her garden by the madman next door. When a novel is loosely organized, when it is a string of occurrences with more story than plat, more incident than causal relation, like the old picaresque tales, rather than a single great occurrence comprising lesser ones as its vital organs, then the scene, like any unit, is likely to carry an independent burden that makes its structure necessary indeed. The loose arrangement of a typical piece by Smollett or by Scott offers fine opportunity for a variety of exciting struggles. Each is the occurrence of its portion of the book; each will be a scene or succession of scenes, or among a variety of structural units will have its big scene in which strength is pitted against strength, skill against skill. The actions of the characters are made into the action of the re-cital. Like the action, the time and the place are experienced as presented to the attention scenically, however ancient the age or remote the locale. Like the ballads of Robin Hood and Chevy Chase, such fiction feeds its readers' need of vicarious strenuousness, the immediacy and the uniqueness of the scene giving it the power to stand by itself as one of a string of mighty emprizes. In this use of the scene as setting, fiction is at one with the theatre, as both are with the older epic, and the tales of folklore out of which epic was compounded. The big moment, the event so important and so fascinating that it must be told in all detail and sequence, is *the* moment for experience; it is, above all, created fictional experience at its most intense, the imagination's way of life, oblivious of everything including itself, except as the thing imagined. The scene that truly interests us is reality and romance together.

The other familiar structural unit, of equal or greater antiquity, is the *anecdote.* In the Greek, the word originally meant "not given out," and so was once used of unpublished stories. At present the general meaning carries over this connotation of a privacy of some sort into the separation of some incident from its context of events, so that it may be related partly for its own interest, but still more because it is a property of the larger thing, an example of a personal trait, or of the working of a principle, or the reasonableness of a thesis of which it is understood to be a metonomic fragment, or symbol. This reference to something other than itself, which shares with it our interest in the experience, somewhat lessens the illusion of the uniqueness by comparison with the scene. Again, the fact that the anecdote is an illustration or a pendant accounts for another characteristic, its comparative brevity. Structurally, the principal feature of the anecdote is its sticking to whatever it conveys. All well organized fiction does this, but the anecdote does it in every part, from beginning to end. Each event seems an arrow-post directed toward the end, from which there is a similar indication, backward on the others. The point of an anecdote need not be intellectual; it may be a feeling, and so there is an entire category of little humorous stories, or jokes, which promise from the start the laugh that is to cap the end. It has been said of O. Henry that his stories are expanded anecdotes; although this definition will not strictly fit such of his works as "A Municipal Report," it remains true of his yarns that even in their expansion they are notably brief; and many of them run along in a jocular patter to which the humorous twist of the ending is a kind of highest moment. Certain magazines feature what are called "short short stories" or "short shorts," and the markedly anecdotal flavor of these provides one more instance of the impossibility of fixing forms within the whole fiction.

As a matter of fact, so far as the anecdote is concerned, it is unlike the scene in being more dominantly a functional than a structural form. It has structure, but the structure is very simple and flexible. In not being confined, as the scene is, to rendering events in strict sequence, it is also free of any need to conform to the demands of the three unities. As a result, it is equally at liberty to include dialogue or not. True, there are scenes in which no one speaks, such as the one in "The Black Cat" where the madman kills his wife; but the fact that the scene in a story, like one on the stage, most commonly involves speech, makes dialogue a necessity of practice, if not of the form in the abstract. The anecdote has nothing like this tightness of formal organization. In time pattern it has to follow only a single simple principle to be recognizably itself: every part of the recital must plainly point ahead to the fact that the conclusion will make the whole what it is; not only that there will be a conclusion, and that it will be important, but that there is practically no other importance. So long as this is to hold true, the recital must be brief. Fables, parables, and apologues are therefore among the chief categories of the anecdote. So may myths be; but if, like fairy tales, they are written or read exclusively as fantasy, then the elaboration of detail and consequent expansion of content and length will diminish their obvious anecdotal quality. With such stories shortness is only a secondary mark of identification. On the other hand, an anecdote may be cast in scenic form, as many fables are, or may in slightly expanded form contain one or more scenes, as in the case of the parable of the prodigal son.

For purposes of fiction in the narrower sense in which we commonly apply the term to a novel or a short story, the anecdote is a minor structural unit. As such, its main uses are for illustration and conciseness. It is brevity saturated with significance and glistening in the light of meaning. If O. Henry is a master of the expanded anecdote, de Maupassant is a master of the instrumental one, a technical development quite in accord with what I believe to be his characteristic symbolism. He availed himself of the anecdote's incisiveness and economy to reduce the substance of a long novel to the length of a very short one, as in *Pierre et Jean,* or even to the length of a quite short story, as in "The Necklace." The latter is an astounding piece of engineering: it contains only five scenes, none of them with a surplus detail, four of them having to do with the necklace in some important event of its use, and the other, which comes first in the recital order, with expensive finery generally; the structural units that make up the rest of the story are anecdotes, succinct comments, and similar thrifty adequacies. This in a piece seemingly too short and simple to have any structure at all, apart from the surprise ending!

But de Maupassant is neither alone in the practice, nor did he initiate it. In the sort of novel that is descended in part from the periodical essay, there is a natural tendency to follow the tradition of Sir Roger de Coverley. Fielding refused to call his fictions novels, because, he said, any scribbler with pen and paper could write a novel; it required a higher order of talents and education to emulate Mr. Spectator. The introductory essays to the eighteen books of *Tom Jones* were intended as structural elements of the history of that youth's life. As to the purely narrative parts, the author said that he would not give equal space to every event. Where nothing of importance had occurred over a period of years, he would skip that part, but would devote many pages to one event, if it were sufficiently "marvelous." Hence the great scenes for which his career in the theatre had trained him so admirably; and by a different application of the same principle, the anecdotes, like the ones about Sophia's muff and Western's chastisement, which in their lesser way not only enrich the essay-history but speed its movement. Irving, Dickens, and Thackeray were superb anecdotists of the discursive sort. More recently Katherine Mansfield, Hemingway, Dos Passos and Willa Cather have shown like skill. When one character wishes to exemplify his view of another, or to tell what is typical about some place, or activity, or aspect of life, the author may drop into anecdote as naturally as the imagined person would. The nature of the form, as arms-length rather than close-up examination, and the opportunity it provides for detached observation make the anecdote invaluable.

In discussing the scene, I spoke of its constituent events as divisions and subdivisions of a larger one. The larger would, so to speak, be the lesser what the topic of rhetoric is to the paragraph; by itself, it could summarize and therefore indicate a scene of the grand fictional occurrence, but not present it as it would appear in the recital. The pattern of time is obvious: the extensive section of the author's illusion is merely summarized in stating the topic event. I gave an example from "My Last Duchess" in the Duke's sarcasms about Fra Pandolf's flattery of the Duchess while she sat for her portrait. An even briefer instance is

> *"The bough of cherries some officious fool*
> *Broke in the orchard for her . . ."*

This would have possibilities of enlargement—for another story; but Browning wanted only one of a series of illustrations for the Duke to retail as evidence for a thesis. To repeat, a single statement may suggest the scene it does not present in detail, may summarize it in a sentence or a clause. A series of these summaries, each bearing on the same aspect of an action more comprehensive than any of them, and presented in chronological order but with time gaps for omission of irrelevancies, is a structural unit which, for lack of a better name, I have long been used to call a *chronology unit*. Metaphorically, the chronology unit would not, like the scene, be as solid as a wall about a garden; but, like a picket fence, in spite of the apertures, it would recognizably mark an enclosure. More precisely, the chronology unit is synoptic, though not in the technical sense of a mere skeletal outline.

It is not an abstraction from, but a presentation of, fictional occurrence, and although it is composed of summaries, it is itself no mere summary. I make use of Browning's monologue again: when the Duke says

> ". . . and if she let
> Herself be lessoned so, nor plainly set
> Her wits to yours, forsooth, and made excuse—"

he is summarizing a number of marital scenes by expository characterization, not listing them in detail. In what I call the chronology unit, on the contrary, each event in the series is summarized explicitly, so that the structural unit is of course permeated with summary; but the sequence grows into synopsis, and that, finally, is its pattern.

One can easily see its use and advantage. It is an excellent device for introducing a character by accounting for him, or letting him account for himself, up to the time of his entrance into the story, or during the time of his absence from it. It sews him in, as it were, with a large, quick stitch. Similarly, it can be used to present a state of affairs of long standing in the neighborhood, a household, an economic class; and thus may serve to introduce the conflict. It is most commonly retrospective, but can be anticipatory or otherwise imaginative; Liam O'Flaherty adapts it to an episode of planning for the future by a newly married couple in "Milking Time," from *Spring Sowing*. In the mingling of patterns which makes the fictional medium a matrix of novelties, the chronology unit may take on an anecdotal cast; but the anecdote can be merely *one* temporal unit illustrating some larger entity, whereas the chronology unit cannot present fewer than several events, and normally comprises many. As my name for it indicates, it has not only a definite functional form, like the anecdote, but, unlike it, a definite structural form. This, though simpler than the scenic pattern, is no less individual. In fact, the very simplicity makes it far easier to define, if not to recognize. More, though the anecdote may blend with either of the other two somewhat, the scene and the chronology unit are structurally exclusive of each other. The one, in mimicking uninterrupted flow of time, *presents* the illusion of uniqueness; the other only *indicates* uniqueness, because although each summarized event refers to some continuity in illusion, at every new step even this indirection is broken by manifest abridgment of the temporal flux. This effect is doubled when the constituent events are imagined as separated spatially, as by geographical distribution. When we say of a story that one part of it is very dramatic, whereas another is told in rapid narration, we may very well be contrasting a scene and a chronology unit.

In fact, I should have preferred to say "narrative unit," to heighten a contrast of fiction and the theatre; but where would that leave the scene and the anecdote? They, too, are narrative units, and I should be only increasing a confusion which I am eager to avoid. However, now that I have made as clear as I can what I am designating, I am glad of the chance to pay a tribute to the chronology unit as the structural pattern of a kind and a numerous class of fictions. I cannot remember reading one single story which is a chronology unit throughout, but I have read many of which it is the prevailing, the dominant scheme. There is an Oriental toy, consisting of a little tab-like disc of paper which, when dropped into a tumbler of water, grows into a flowering plant, pot and all. The chronology of the author's projection of the static illusion, as it drinks in the author's experience of the dynamic, may undergo a sea-change. Certain events swell into full-blown scenes; others merely bud in summary; others exfoliate as bits of background; finally, there is the characteristic configuration of stem and twigs, the basic organic form. Defoe, in his persistent simulation of biography and autobiography, is a typical chronicler, or narrator. He loves to cover the longer and the shorter periods of his subject's progress through life in a flow of events, rather circumstantial than fast, just as he loves to tabulate the profits and the prices and the values of commodities and services. In his chronicling retrospection he does indeed dwell from time to time on what, in other hands, would be a scene; but this he rarely presents in the illusion of immediacy. Rather, he talks about it, or Moll or Robinson or Roxana does, in the remote reminiscence of middle or old age, conscious of the great interval that has elapsed, and peering across it with better memory for outline of fact than vision of events. Thus the scene, in his books, always seems to be explained or characterized or editorialized—anything but presently vital before our observation. The details are often all there, in neat inventory; they are evidence that once there was such a scene, but they are not the scene itself. What Colonel Jacque published to the world was not his log; but the log haunts the autobiography. The only exception, the *Journal of the Plague Year,* is indeed scenic with the most graphic hideousness.

Smollett had much more notably the illustrator's pen. In his earlier books, and in his very last one, there is no steady flow, as in Defoe's stories, but a racing current of incident upon incident, rushing along as fast as a person can read or imagine. I cannot name his superior for speed of events coupled with vividness of the objects of the illusion. He attempted a rendition more consistently scenic in *Sir Launcelot Greaves,* and an elaborately discursive essay recital in *Peregrine Pickle;* but the former is doubtless the poorest novel he ever did, and the latter, in spite of its having some of the most uproariously funny scenes in English or any literature, is at times almost unreadable for the endless, mugging periods and a good deal of unfunny pedantic humor. It is most successful in those episodes of physical hustle and violence that are in the tradition of *Roderick Random.* Again, in *Humphrey Clinker,* where Smollett showed that he had learned to twinkle as well as roar, it is nevertheless the parts involving practical jokes and horseplay, the parts about Lismahago, and the bit about Matthew's bathing in the sea, that are the true Toby. Such things in Smollett are handled in the chronicling manner; the general chronology unit swells some one event into an anecdote here, and there a scene, or a series of scenes, or a great section alternately scenic and chronologic, with some of the scenes worked out only so far as he needs them, and some of the chronology units with time breaks of comparatively brief interval. The events are not only narrated, but painted, with swift sure strokes—was there ever a novelist more sure of himself than Smollett? In Scott the canvas is grander and so is the soul; but for sheer propulsive sweep of events running one into the other, the proper comparison for Smollett is with Byron, the Byron of *The Prisoner of Chillon, Mazeppa, The Island.* There is much of the same unresting narrative movement in *Moby Dick,* but with intervals of slow action in the imagined occurrence; and also in Hudson's *Green Mansions,* but with frequent substitutions of the pictorial for the breezelike passage of events. Mann has the power, but prefers to use it rarely, indeed seems to resist it, to subdue its speed to a kind of throbbing pressure. Yet his constant recourse to the chronology unit in *Buddenbrooks* is one of the chief engines in packing the illusion of swift genealogical succession between the covers of one book. His generations come and go in the lyric rush of time; while Butler, who relies more on the anecdote to alternate with the scene, produces more the effect of time's mocking patience, a victory discounted in advance and so without triumph. In Proust, one is surprised, like the narrator, to realize periodically that a decade is gone. In Joyce, the time span covered is rather short; it is only the associative mind that moves quickly, with the appearance of getting nowhere, like an insect raging in an inverted wine glass. Of the last three writers, it is only Mann who gives the impression of comparatively rapid movement; yet in his restrained use of the chronology unit, he seems austere beside Byron or Smollet.

I have kept the fourth of my structural units to the end here, because in pattern it imitates the others. Like the anecdote, it is less notable for structural than for functional form, because, like the anecdote, it is markedly representative, and therefore passes on some of the attention it might claim for its own identity to whatever it characterizes. Now, a characteristic of anybody or anything may be a common or frequent one, or it may be one evinced very rarely. The anecdote can represent the familiar trait or the unusual one, because it delivers a single occasion, with the understanding that it is selected to present an aspect of the larger thing it represents. An anecdote of Lincoln's benevolence in a certain connection can be told in such a way as to show that he was consistently benevolent, whereas an anecdote of his loss of temper can make it clear that this was a rare lapse from usual practice. But the structural unit I am now introducing is confined to representing what's consistent, and may not be a single, selected instance of what is typical. It must first abstract from the often repeated occasions those events which never fail to occur, and those only, and must then artificially put them together into a pattern which, since it has no trace of spontaneous accident or irrelevance, can hardly be mistaken for one certain happening, even as an example of a whole species of such happenings. The anecdote renders the characteristic, the typical, by way of unique occurrence. But the structural unit I have in mind presents only what is typical about *all* the occurrences, as though they were superimposed till the chance elements in each fell away, leaving the single configuration, the invariable elements of many events. The pattern we get is not a form of what actually exists in Nature's time, but a conceptual norm, announcing itself as such. This product, by analogy with the composite photograph made by printing a number of different portraits on one sheet of paper, I call the *time composite*.

A time composite, then, indicates the unity in time of strikingly similar events, by eliminating their differences. If Nature, in producing events of a certain kind *seriatim* were to allow only their likeness to appear, then each could without change of a detail represent the species. The time composite

99

therefore operates so as to imply that if the events behaved that way naturally, it would itself be their one and only pattern. As a structural unit, therefore, it sets events in the framework of time, but deprives them of the uniqueness which time confers on them. The scene presents a unique occurrence as a unique experience. The anecdote presents something which remains constant—a quality in things or in personality—manifesting itself on a unique occasion. The chronology unity presents a series of events, each expressed by a summary of its uniqueness; for the events are generally dissimilar, except for a common tendency or direction. The time composite gives the illusion of plural identity, of one and the same event occurring again and again. In it, uniqueness is nothing but the sign of Nature's blind, awkward, fumbling at repetition. We recognize the good intention, and with eyes and hands steadier than hers, we remove the blemishes of contingency, and edit her barbaric yawp as our unnaturally regular composition. The time composite takes hold of a pattern which Nature suggested but never finished, and finishes it for her. The other structural units implement time without necessarily saying so; the time composite frankly and explicitly squeezes time out of the picture.

The frankness may take the form of the author's telling us that he is presenting a common occurrence as a typical or habitual one. The typicality may also be half hidden, half disclosed, by adroitly tucking in an adverb—"always," "every evening," "once a week," "unfailingly on the dot of noon"; or an adjective—"the same," "invariable," "unchanged." He will characteristically use verbs implying custom or habit, as in "we *used* to sip it slowly, to make it last," and also the auxiliary with the same meaning: "They *would* promenade for an hour after dinner." As expression of habit, custom, convention, this structural unit is admirably suited to conveying the idea of routine, monotony, stagnation, conservatism, narrowness, contentment, mechanism, poverty of resource, budgeted strength, fixation. It can therefore present a monotonous situation interestingly and can indicate the rack of prolonged boredom in a short characterization, so that in reading we recognize the tedious not only without affliction but, in fact, with absorption. As such, it is frequently encountered in de Maupassant's works, where it is used to strike the characteristic note of a person, a district, a class, an eccentricity, a long-lived emotion, an *idée fixe*. De Maupassant exploits not only its succinctness and economy, but its protean need to unite with, to disguise itself as, one of the other structural units. In the tale of the two Parisian friends who resume their every-Sunday fishing expedition despite the fact that the Prussian invaders have advanced close to their haunt on the river, he uses a time composite organized as a chronology unit to introduce their itinerary, their comment on the scenery, varied according to the season but the same year after year, their anglers' passion, their warm friendship, their average-ness. By this simple device, unfailing in his hands, he seems to launch his action, although he is only introducing his setting and characters. The disguise of descriptive and expository matter as narrative, by narrative means, is a marvel of deception. Many of his introductions are compounded of the same thrifty action. In "The Necklace," the wish-fullfillments of Mathilde Loisel take the form of an imaginary scene of what she conceives to be luxury, a revery to which, we are told, she is addicted. Another time composite disguised as a scene renders the monotony of dinner at the Loisels'; and the husband's invariable remark of delight over the unfailing appearance of soup complicates this mixture with an anecdotal twist.

The fact that the time composite must take on one of the other forms makes it useful simply for varying them. For example, Katherine Mansfield tells the story of Miss Brill in a form prevalently scenic. But since the scene is that of her Sunday off, there are periodic reminders that the events are a matter of weekly routine. The day is therefore set against the background of its normal activities, and the treatment makes possible a sense of permanence and security—so cruelly to be shattered. The background breaks through, very close to the end, at a time, ironically, when its solace for the lonely old maid is gone: "On her way home, she usually bought a slice of honey-cake at the baker's. It was her Sunday treat. Sometimes there was an almond in her slice," and so on— except that now she hurries past the shop. Poe, as one might expect, avails himself of such technical adaptations of structural units one into the other. The alcoholic degeneration of the hero of "The Black Cat" merges the chronology unit with the time composite; the blinding of the first cat and the murder of the wife are told in brief passages each of which is certainly a scene and certainly an anecdote. The changed, eccentric behavior of Legrand at a certain stage of "The Gold-Bug" is conveyed to the reader in a scene in which the friend converses with the servant; but what is conveyed is structurally composite. Kipling uses these fusions to establish social background: the opening of "The Phantom Rickshaw" provides an especially rich example. In such fashion, as I have said, the static quality of exposition and description may be relieved, by organization as action; or either of these forms of discourse may begin in its proper style, and then turn into an anecdote or a chronology unit intended to carry on the same function.

The mingling of structural forms is one of the chief sources of novelty in story recital. From a certain point of view, the author is doing two things all the time: he is maintaining one and the same conflict throughout, and he is doing everything in his power to keep this persistence from degenerating into monotony. He may even wish to conceal the fact that there is any conflict, as in a certain adroit kind of "slice of life" narration. Then the ringing of the changes on the structural forms may be used to direct the reader's attention away from any possible recognition of form, so that he simply follows the imagined occurrence. The author's authority, his disposition, his inspiration unaware, or his conscious analytical choice, will determine these arrangements; and the order of sequence and recurrence, together with incidental descriptive or other discourse, will grow into the pattern of the specific story. In addition to the interlinkings within the strictly narrative pattern there are numerous potential junctures of that pattern with other elements of the fictional medium. The scene, for example, can lend actuality to allegory; the anecdote can economize the time of realistic recital; the time composite can tinge symbolism with a drop of naturalistic mechanism. For originality of treatment, as of all else, the fountain-head is the creative spirit; and that, in the worldly concrete, is the author's uniqueness. Whether by exquisite tact or by technological design—or now one and now the other—his originality is the mark of himself. It is therefore he who makes it impossible for us to exhaust the patterns of fictional pattern, who makes impossible the final utter comprehension of the whole fiction, since so much of it is lost to him, and to his own eyes. Yet something of the patterns and of his originality in them persists; and at rare intervals in the history of the art there will arise some writer in whom some modulation is stamped with what the world calls absolute originality, though the derivation of component elements in it can be traced— some Cervantes, some Sterne, some Poe.

Most recently, as I have said several times, it was Joyce who gave us a time pattern of this outstanding sort of originality, the sort that appears to come to us without precedent. In *Portrait of the Artist as a Young Man,* and much more in

Ulysses, he transformed Dujardin's "interior monologue" into "stream of consciousness." I am a little sorry that it is called so, because *stream,* though accurate in suggesting forward movement in the fictional occurrence, does nothing to describe the far more characteristic complexity of the structural unit which Joyce plotted for the single major event. We saw in connection with the scene how one event of some scope and duration can be divided and subdivided into its constituent events, and how any one of these can be an allusion to the past or a remark about the future. Furthermore, a scene including several people can exist in the mind of an imagined person remembering or anticipating or only fancying it. In any case, the constituent event has always hitherto been treated as though it were a whole integer, like 1, 2, 3, in a simple progression. Joyce's method, to continue the arithmetical figure, is rather like considering each such constituent event as a cluster of small fractions. It then may be regarded as a "major" event; so that the moment of consciousness may be treated with closer approximation to its instantaneous variety of content— a jostle of bits of experience from the environment, the body, the consciousness, in the form of phenomena perceived as physically external to the character, together with others as his sensations, and others as responses of imagery, feeling, reasoning, and verbalization out of the past as memory or habit, in the present as pleasure, pain, recognition, delusion, error, and out of the future as anticipation, hope, dread, reverie, fancy, rehearsal. Each of these bits (to vary my figure of speech) represents some stream of occurrence by being the part of it that is focussed on. The representation of all these regions at once makes the moment of consciousness an illusory spatio-temporal form on more levels than one. It resembles a traffic center with approaches not only from several compass points but also at street, underground, and elevated levels. To any one seeing it for the first time, it might very well portend hopeless confusion or disaster. To the policeman administering its operation, or the motorist accustomed to it, it might be simplicity itself. To the motion-picture camera it would be orderly flow; to any one rectangle of the film, a moment in the ceaseless confluence and effluence. Hence my dissatisfaction with *stream* of consciousness: there are really many streams, and the event is a cross-section of traffic which seems pattern-less, not because there is no pattern, but because there are so many patterns that one must be practiced in order to grasp the entire pattern. I wish some one had thought of saying "traffic of consciousness," a phrase which not only suggests continuity, but also indicates the complexity of each moment taken in cross-section, in a way which modern psychology has taught us to understand. Be that as it may, one can see that Joyce's structural unit is an invention approximating the form of instant experience more closely than any other. By means of it, every element in the fictional medium is present in the occurrence, giving to the staid old technicality known as "complication" a startling freshness.

As the microscope revealed dramatic struggle in a drop of water or blood where no one would have suspected it, so the fine adjustment of the structural unit of stream of consciousness enabled Joyce to create absorbing fiction out of materials formerly rejected or not even regarded, since the minuteness of the elapsed time of occurrence would seem to involve only themes trivial to the point of worthlessness. To his admirers, at any rate, Joyce has given up-to-the-minute proof of one of the oldest saws of criticism: any subject is good, that is, workable, so soon as some one comes along who actually works it. The happenings of a single day in the lives of not especially remarkable people, doing only the things they are likely to be doing any day, may be made into a novel of great length and interest, if some way can be devised for exposing and exploiting the universality of conflict in some minute and hitherto unnoticed area. It is not that the old ways are not good, but that the new one is good, too. Conflict, on the grandest and the tiniest scale alike, is the indispensable subject. The rest lies in what the author has in his power and expression to give; that is, in himself. If one Irishman can write an entertaining account of controversy between big-endians and little-endians, another can reveal the drama in a spiritless avoidance of violence and tragedy—the dodges, for example, an ordinary man might resort to in keeping himself occupied away from home until his wife's lover can safely have his assignation with her, and leave. It would be necessary, I repeat, to find the means for uncovering the fine tracery of conflicts in the boredom, the passive resistance, the resentful heartsickness dulled by long custom. With every clearance of struggle, there would be appearance and narration. Time itself, the empty container of motion, would disgorge thematic material. Each moment—every single falling drop of the torment—would yield to scrutiny its triple destiny of past and present and future. At every heavy-footed, overladen step the massed burden would grow to such volume that the very length of a *Ulysses* would show the vanity of trying to do more than approximate an exhaustion of the matter to be told.

104

Any chance idea that may come to an author is capable of being elaborated in full. When winter has picked out the skeleton of a leaf, how marvelously ramified we find the tracery of that single simplicity! The author's valuation of what comes to him, his instinctive or careful choice of the number of the themes to develop, together with his resources and ability for developing them—these are what determine the form of a fiction in its bulk and extent. Whether it be a novel, a novelette, a short story, a short short story, an anecdote, all the themes are potentially there. The differences lies in the number *developed*. What at first appears to be a very great number of pages and words, as in *Ulysses*, will prove to have done economically what a more slovenly artist would have taken several times as much space to do. Flaubert in *Madame Bovary* will seem to have achieved an incalculably richer lifelikeness than de Maupassant in "The Necklace," or the pupil will appear to have surpassed the master in the husbanding of means, depending on one's standard or on one's view at the moment of comparison.

If *Portrait of the Artist as a Young Man* seems in its slightness little more than a novelette, that is because Joyce chose to present, but not to develop, the multitude of its themes with the nice, selective succinctness he had already achieved in some of the tales in *Dubliners*. There are a great many characters in the *Portrait*. Young Stephen had a great many relations with them. In the stages of his growth and with the changes of his views, these relations ramify; and he himself is a tangle of beliefs and doubts and disillusions. We can see from a reading of *Stephen Hero*, the posthumously published earlier version of the same work, that Joyce first gave a great deal of development to some of the secondary themes. But in the novel which he gave to the world each of the subordinate story lines he chose to retain is delivered in a single finely shaped outline suggesting more than it says, but stating its principal value clearly, with an accuracy as of the goldsmith's art in an old Japanese sword-guard. Before that, in "A Little Cloud," one of the last pieces in *Dubliners* to be written, there are more characters briefly referred to than one would suspect from casual reading, and many more aspects of their personalities are touched in with tiny strokes than one would have patience to count. Here, as in every superior short story, one can see how the projection of a single effect rests not on the omission, but on the admission and suppression of others; on an appraisal of just how much treatment to bestow according to auxiliary value; and on such repression as will not only give the main theme the necessary prominence, but force from the depressed ones that back-pressure to which the short story as a form owes so much of its packed tightness. The ratio of the number of themes developed, as against the number of themes presented, is what makes the basic difference between the short story as a pattern and the novelette, or between either of them and the novel. Apart from this, mere length, even in a fable, is wordiness.

At the beginning of this chapter I said that no one could exhaust the possibilities of form in the whole fiction, and a few pages back I repeated the statement and offered some particulars to support it. Certainly I do not believe that I have arrived at any such goal. As a matter of fact, I have deliberately concentrated on those patterns I think to be most characteristic of the whole fiction as an art distinguishable from others. Accordingly, I have drawn my topics in the main from the imaginative elements of the illusion as image and the illusion as conflict. If these are not the narrative phase of fiction, we most often speak about them as if they were. Since I am attempting, even in these analytical and abstractive chapters, to maintain a presentation of the whole fiction in dealing with each element of the medium at a time, I must make use of accretive review. On the other hand, I cannot enlarge here on the modulation of pattern with respect to the elements that remain to be dealt with in chapters of their own—feeling, thought, language—without subtracting heavily from the content of what I mean to say there. I shall therefore postpone some of the discussion of form, to include it in other chapters where it can operate partly as review. There is, however, one such consideration which, though it belongs in the next chapter after this, belongs here a little, too. I have left it over from the discussion of the momentary event in stream of consciousness so that it may serve me as conclusion and transition.

The region proper of the stream of consciousness is, of course, the consciousness itself, which registers any presence in the regions of the world or the body. Also, there are presences within consciousness, such as memory images, which I term *contained externality*. Thus the consciousness not only observes and records events happening in the world around it; it is itself the field of action whose events take place. In Joyce especially the doings of consciousness are right before us, as, in an action story, the movements of worldly things and bodies are. The agent's focus of attention, revolving with incredible speed, is trained upon a presence of one region and then of a second and then of the third with continuous shift of direction and adjustment of range. The rapidity with which each of these concerns of focus appears makes the group *seem* to be a union of contemporary ingredients, otherwise possibly without relation, yet with at least temporal pattern. Each of the parts, regardless of its origin, is thus an object of attention; we receive them as the character does, and from his particular point of view. The text itself does not tell us in so many words how this is achieved; it simply guides our focal attention in a way that mimics that of the character, and we accept the illusion without realizing it. The procedure is guaranteed, in the text, by the following device: each part of the pattern, as a concern of focus, is expressed in the fewest possible words, the first capitalized, the last followed by a full stop; every such presentative sentence, made brief and even mutilated for speed, names or symbolizes only what is occurring to focus but names it plainly, so that the text omits such traditional designations of operation by consciousness as "he sighed to himself," "which he did not examine at the moment," and so on. In this way, the linguistic aspect of stream of consciousness, so far from being a hoax or a perversity or a snobbery, is part of the function of the thing, and is one of the distinctions of its difference from Dujardin's interior monologue, which is couched in the sentence of traditional grammar, with subject, predicate, and modifiers, all properly composed in syntax. Joyce's adaptation is a departure, a new step, in the faithful imitation of a certain kind of confused but alert thinking, by compelling the reader to imitate in reading the same sort of complex and strained awareness he himself often practices in perceiving the realities of everyday life.

On first thought, one might assume that the focal attending, since it is so influential an action of stream of consciousness, is the only one. Yet, as we have seen, disregard is also at work. In it presumably lie all the presences of the character's thoughts, including the past operations of consciousness, such as memory and habit, and including all external presences so perceived. Now, all of these, as mental action, contribute obscurely to the character's awareness of any presence in any region at any moment of his experience, and determine not only the quality of his response, but also some collaborative influence in the *selection* of objects *for* focus. One person, as we say, will notice certain things; another, others. What applies to stimuli from the world and the body applies with at least equal force to stimuli from presences in the mind.

What one remembers visually, for example, in response to, in association with, some object, is what one has in order to remember it, what one has to remember *with*. Not only focal attention, then, but consciousness in the large, is the action of our structural unit. Indeed, the moment of the stream of consciousness is very hard to conceive of as static in any way, since it is consciousness in the act, in the unique act of privishing, which is to say, of living.

Out of the flux of these tiny units, Joyce produces an illusion of one of the famous cities of the world, its expanse, its transecting thoroughfares, its traffic, its public and private places, and its manifold activities. He produces a large number of its citizens as individuals, each remarkably an identity for later recollection. Many of these we get to know in a variety of detailed information that would make any one of them eligible, in rounded reality, to be the central personage of a novel of his own. Three—Stephen Dedalus and Leopold and Molly Bloom—go far beyond even that standard. There is included in each of these three, by the time the book ends, a minutely detailed autobiography such as makes up the whole of *Moll Flanders;* an education of the hero at least equal to that in *Tom Jones* or *The Ordeal of Richard Feverel;* a presentation of nuances of passion and mental attitude as full as any in Stendhal or Chekhov or Proust; a physical portrayal worthy of Balzac; an impression of the mind of the moment as vivid as the one in *Tristram Shandy,* but in construction masterly beyond anything that Sterne attempted. Now, as I take it, it is this complex pattern of a person's impulses, history, background, acquired tendency and idiosyncrasy, habits, and dependable and unpredictable reactions that we refer to when we speak of his personality, of his unique character. So, together with its service to illusion and conflict as forms in the pattern of the whole fiction, the structural unit of the stream of consciousness creates the illusion of the person unmistakably as himself. I shall have more to say, and very soon, about patterns of character. I trust that what I have said here has conveyed something of my views on character in fiction as one of the forms of its form.

Chapter 5

Character

FOR FICTION, the word *character* has two chief denotations. The proper, as the generic one, is synonymous with *agent,* a doer of the action. He may be any imagined person who appears or is only referred to in the illusory occurrence, like a passerby who does not so much as distract the attention of two principal characters while they are conversing; he may be of any degree of importance from that insignificance up to the value of the principal, who not only does things necessary for the plausibility of the illusion, but in addition plays a dominant role in the advancement of the conflict. I say that this is the widest acceptance of the term, because its application is as suitable to the god Mercury, the rooster Chantecleer, Bunyan's Mercy, Aesop's pot that called the kettle black, Swift's Lilliputian Queen, and Carroll's Queen of Hearts, as it is to Simon Legree, Madeline Usher, Sherlock Holmes, Becky Sharp, Jude Fawley, or the Duc de Charlus. It is this acceptance of the term as indicating a participant which enables us to speak metaphorically of death in "The Fall of the House of Usher" as an antagonist, although he is not specifically one of the agents, as he is in "The Masque of the Red Death."

The other chief denotation emphasizes rather the nature of the agent in personality or personification, depending on whether the agent is a human being or something else, like an animal, a thing, a force, an abstract idea. Here "nature" would include not only the genus or some species of that, together with the necessary details of appearance and constitution and behavior which give the class identity, but also the distribution of those qualities in the specific pattern which gives the individual *his* character, which is and is presumed to be his character and his alone. The two meanings, of participant and of temperament, are of course intimately related; so much so that it is quite common in critical discussion of a certain character in a book to make comment on his character as though he were one of us in our world.

It may or may not be pertinent that the word itself is derived from a Greek verb meaning "to cut deep," and therefore to engrave or mark, especially for recognition. There is nothing of that left in the critical term as we now understand it; so that it is a curious accident that our usage combines the ideas of action and identity. Something of the same sort inheres in certain other uses of *character,* as in the expression "algebraic characters," or "the general character of the process is synthesis." This phase of symbolic reference, of naming at a remove, or by the substitution of sign for thing, is quite characteristic of *character.* In the first place, there is the symbolism, plainest in allegory (as the most forthright mood of didacticism by indirection) whereby the character has a meaning which is a component of the meaning of the story. Hawthorne's ambitious guest is "explained" in being so "characterized"; his gray champion is the recollected self-reliance of an older generation steeling the resistance of a new one against oppression; Ethan Brand "stands for" the unpardonable sin of cutting oneself off from humanity. The Fox is guile and the Goat gullibility; Persephone's coming and going are Spring and Winter; Sancho Panza is common sense, practical and limited; Effie is need and Silas Marner is duty; the Buddenbrooks rise and fall according to the power or weakness in their men; the Forsytes are the British cognates of Babbitt.

In the second place, there is the technical symbolism of imaginative literature, which need not detain us beyond the mention of a few examples: Ivanhoe as hero, Madame Beck as female villain, and all the conventional categories of foil, fictitious narrator, comic interest, and the like. In the third place, there is the extremely subtle symbolism between any one character, so considered, and the medium of the whole fiction. Whenever he is in focus, for example at a time when he is physically active or thinking, he—perhaps momentarily, but if so, then for the moment exclusively—is the story. He is then the convergence of the lines of the action, so that many of them fail to appear to us as such, since in their operation through him alone they seem to be nothing but him— Quixote charging the windmill, Eliza fleeing over the ice, Eustacia Vye denouncing fate, Hans Castorp daydreaming in his room at the sanatorium. This power to represent the entire fiction, for a while, by being it, is made possible by the fact that the character, in the sense of agent or deputy, embodies such qualities that their pattern qualifies him to sustain and administer the task. I have exhibited him in isolation here for the advantage of simplicity in introducing my conception; yet as a matter of fact any character represents the story any time he is mentioned; when he is one of several or many, the representation is lessened because it is shared, but

110

it is as truly representational in concert as in holding the stage alone.

Now, symbolism of this sort rests on a peculiar and delicate relation with another I am about to present as my fourth and last. What is technically known as "a" character in critical terminology is, in the experienced illusion, an inhabitant of a fictional world, whether presumably ours or some other. He is a dweller in it. He is a manifestation of it. So, in great part, is his character; in being a denizen of our planet, for example, he is no Martian. By the same token, his world is a manifestation of him as an artificer in a Bronze Age, or an engineer in a Machine Age, or as any one living in a world of which his contemporaries have made some such "age," whether he has participated in that or has not the remotest awareness that it exists. A certain savage race may not have changed its customs in any important respect for eons; yet a member of it in a story told of pre-historic times would be one sort of man, and in a story with a background of civilization to-day, quite another. What is true of each of us in this general way as a symbol of his great world, is much more solidly true of our symbolizing the nation, the city or province, or the immediate neighborhood in which we are citizens or strangers. So, as one of the population of a world of illusion, the character is a locus of communal energies; and since there are far too many sorts of these energies for them all to be equally manifest in any one personality, he is the assemblage of such and such ones and their manifestness as that pattern half disguised in his individuality. The illusion, the occurrence, of a story is like a tapestry woven so cunningly that one might gaze and gaze and never dream or warp and woof, but see only a place and people and happenings. Yet each of the tapestry people is a figure, and the threads of his being are tied in with the two weaving dominances of right- and left and up-and-down. To conclude this statement of the complex symbolism of character in fiction, I will repeat what I have said about other things in other places: character is one of the necessary elements, of fiction, identifiable as such in the medium; or else, from another point of view, character is one of the elements which in their intricate fusion give rise to the whole fiction.

Equally, the element of character may be the dominant feature of the whole. We know by now that, openly or secretly, a fiction really operates by the principle of illusory conflict. Yet there is a familiar scheme by which stories of plot, like detective stories, are distinguished from stories of atmosphere, like

Poe's tales of terror; and another of these classifications has the name of stories of character, like Lardner's "Haircut," Ruth Suckow's "Old Maid with Cat," Flaubert's "Un Coeur Simple," and Chekhov's "The Darling." In fact, from one point of view, perhaps narrow but nevertheless valid in what it embraces, what the world has come to think of as fiction in the past two centuries is imaginative prose literature devoted to a presentation of something about human life as the author believes it to be lived. If the world does not hold this attitude toward fiction in general, it certainly does toward what we designate by the word *novel,* marking that off from the less frequently produced romance by Scott or Hugo or Stevenson, or the fantasy of Poe, Verne, and Kafka. The novel proper is chiefly concerned with an examination into the nature of life and the nature of man. Thus, when we say "novelist," we are thinking most often of writers like Balzac, Hardy, and Tolstoy. Of course biography, history, and the social studies share this concern with man but in them the phenomena investigated are the hard, determined, specific facts, which are never omitted no matter what else may be, so that they are the objective of the study and nothing further. But these facts are precisely what need not appear in the novel; when they are expressed at all, they must be absorbed into the fiction, must flow in the illusion, seemingly quite incidentally. To produce this effect is an art of great difficulty in itself, sometimes beyond the power of even so celebrated a story-teller as Bulwer-Lytton in *The Last Days of Pompeii,* where the text is acrawl with footnotes, or in that part of Dreiser's *The Financier* where the matter on the panic of '73 is an undigested wad of paper containing the notes of a research digest. Let me repeat: conformity to fact in fiction is never more than a negative, or perhaps better a subordinate, virtue; that is, it should never break in upon romance as scholarship, or upon realism as obvious report of reality. Its unobtrusiveness is its highest instrumentation; there is nothing better that it can do than to heighten the illusion that it is the illusion which is real. The fidelity of life which is really the novelist's triumph is life-likeness with or without fact—an unfailing truth to human response as conception and emotion. This would never be data; it would be form as plausible conformity to the way things are.

When I drew Bulwer into the discussion, it was partly to show that what I have in mind when I speak of character as the prime ostensibility of numerous fictions is no matter of realism or naturalism only. Either or both together as different aspects of one inclusive mood of course must be recognized as virtually synonymous with the word *novel* in recent times, certainly for the vast majority of readers with a taste for literary art. Seriously or comically, the novel has been the popular medium of imaginative literary speculation upon character. This has been so in English, for example, since the days of Richardson and Fielding. Furthermore, in its prevailing realism the novel has tended to convey its psychological conceptions through the illusion of individual personalities—Isabel Archer, Theobald Pontifex—with a dense concreteness suggestive of the social dimension in the person's experience, and with no little reference, at any period, to contemporary trends in philosophical or psychological thought. The person thus implies the race and the local contemporary *mores,* as a solitary star shines for universal system.

If we turn from realism to romance, or to symbolism, or even to fantasy, we see, after a little reflection, that modern fiction of those moods has made character its concern, too. It has adopted a different species of imagery from that of portraiture, a shift of center from the probed or merely exhibited identity of the one man to the grand latency of all humankind. The element of character is made less obvious by dissolving it in a suffusion of high meaning or high feeling or high fooling. We are not entirely gulled. In the fancies of Barrie and Wilder, in *Green Mansions* and *South Wind,* and *A High Wind in Jamaica,* we know by impact if not by plainness that we are in touch with human nature as truly as we ever were in *Rasselas,* in *Candide,* in "The Pit and the Pendulum," in "Dr. Jekyll and Mr. Hyde." We know that *The Trial* and *Finnegans Wake* bring in the same matter strangely, as a puzzle; but we know that it is there, trick or no trick, as we know it to be in the flutterings of the White Rabbit, and the tears of the Walrus. In *Anna Karenina* each character possesses completeness in being one entire person. In Wilde's "The Happy Prince," or Bangs' *The Houseboat on the Styx,* or Ade's *Fables in Slang,* or the Capeks' *R U R,* this wholeness of personality pervades the entire story.

Smollett, in his *History and Adventures of an Atom,* under the pretence of recording the fortunes of this particle of matter in the body of a Japanese, satirized contemporary public life in England. The symbolic device, honored by antiquity and popular in the eighteenth century, lay simply in having something represent a fractional factor of society and circulate through the whole of it. It maintained a certain objectively critical point of view, taking the form of a golden ass or a golden guinea or a lap-dog, or any thing or creature that might pass readily from owner to owner and so turn up in a selected variety of situations at a number of social levels. The entire person in the book would then be society; the ostensible characters would be its organs, not only the guinea or the lap-dog but the "people" themselves. There is therefore a family resemblance between this sort of thing and Goldsmith's Chinese visitor to England in *The Citizen of the World,* and to the entire *dramatis personae* of *Rasselas* and *Gulliver.* But for my purposes here, Smollett's atom offers the best comparison, since it allows me easy verbal transition from the body of the fancied Japanese to the British body politic, which the fictional text referentially embodies. The relation of each component agent to the greater organism is reminiscent of the "transparent man" exhibited at world's fairs, whose organs in their various colors light up in his glass self one at a time, so that the circuit of the complete show is a mute illumination of our anatomy. This is allegorical method, even when the large character which lends its meaning to the illusion is some body of natural or theological law, or the body of principles associated with the name of Locke, Leibnitz, Darwin, Marx, Schopenhauer, Freud, or whom you will, and manifested or attacked in the imaginative presentations of Sterne, Voltaire, Meredith, Butler, Dos Passos, May Sinclair, and Malraux. It is the method of all symbolic narration, declarative or significantly allusive, in which Man and Nature are writ large, and of the romantic narration too, as the expression of universal feeling, or perhaps better, of emotion as a kind of universe.

The procedure, to repeat for emphasis, is to give each phase of some grand entity an identity of its own, perhaps in the non-human image of an atom or a blue-bird, or even in the human semblance of Christian the pilgrim, Gulliver, Don Juan, Ethan Brand, Roderick Usher, Zuleika Dobson, Rima, or Babbitt—and to employ the sensory illusion and the conflict of fiction in establishing and maintaining the relations among the abstractions thus symbolized, and between them and the character in the large which they jointly and totally imply. To tell the truth, this is the method of realism, too. But in realism the design is hidden, is relegated so profoundly into the background of awareness by the importance of single characters who are complex and rounded whole people, that the character of Man is apprehensible only in its inclusion in the make-up of each of the agents, or in their reciprocally responsive conduct, or at times in a something as real, as thin, as hard to put a finger on, as the imagined air they breathe. There is, of course, a certain kind of realism in the treatment of character-in-the-large, so that I can understand why a critic should speak of Cabell as a Realist, even in *Jurgen*. Yet I am certain that most readers, with Flaubert or George Eliot or Tolstoy in mind, would, in spite of recognizing an intellectually realistic turn in *Jurgen* and *Figures of Earth* as works of a mixed mood, nevertheless feel, as I do, that in the mixture the dominance is one of romantic symbolism of the ironic kind. The fact that the categories are frequently debatable in this way is one more evidence of the role of the artist manipulating the elements of the medium for the creation of novelty in the whole fiction.

The power to project or to entertain imaginary character, either as an individual or the personified aspect of personality, comes from our belief that each of us has "a" character. The personages of the illusion are unceasingly accompanied by two real people, the writer and the reader. This relation is patent when an author reads aloud to a friend, or when he discusses his writing with some one who is familiar with it. In such exchanges the author may very well have a kind of detachment, an outgrowth of his having read his own product by, and therefore to, himself during composition and revision, so that the encounter is somewhat like a discussion between or among readers. True, there are novelists who demand, in Miss Edgeworth's words, "large draughts of praise"; but there are others capable of objectivity, just as there are readers who cannot brook the slightest departure from their own or the fashionable opinion. Otherwise, new and unaccustomed art would have its verdict much faster than it usually does, neither suffering from the opposition of mass inferiority with reference to the strange, nor requiring the fanaticism of partisanship. For it is part of the unique whole fiction that the creative spirit shall envisage, or certainly shall behave as though envisaging, an audience, a public. This may pardonably be conceived as including at least a portion of posterity, even if the matter is quizzically denied, as in Lamb's cool statement that for his part he was writing for antiquity. From the point of view of the reader, too, the author, and Lamb in particular exemplification, is a personal presence determinably, whether or not the determination is ever made. Those of us who reread Jane Austen and Peacock do so because the company is a very special delight not obtainable elsewhere. The tales are now twice-told; the novelty seems all in the style, inimitable beyond the power of custom to stale. Yet even at first reading the recognition of an author as this and no one but this author is possibly an impression of great strength.

It is not only a possible but an unavoidable impression when the author speaks frankly in the first person as Fielding does; or hovers about each character with open disapproval or caress, as Meredith does; or periodically raises from scrutiny of the action the still wrinkled brow of analysis, as George Eliot does; or calls himself "Christopher Isherwood," as Christopher Isherwood does. Also, why else the unremitting carriage of manner in Zola, Wilde, Daudet, Kipling, Beerbohm, Sherwood Anderson, Cabell, James Stephens, Hemingway, Faulkner, and Pearl Buck, and by whole movements like the Celtic school? Even when the writer makes no feature of himself or goes so far as to retire behind the illusion and stands there hidden, "paring his nails" in the arrogance of his self-concealment, it has always been possible for the trained sensitive reader to penetrate by curious study to the creative individuality, to determine at least some major attitude, the recurrently identifying tone, the expressional temperature. I do not say that every reader goes so far as this. I am fully aware of the fact that to many readers the propensity is presumptuous, or even queer. Hence I am not saying that the focal awareness of public by writer, or writer by reader, is a necessity in fiction. What I do say is that the actuality of the relation—focal, peripheral, or disregarded—is the source of the power by which character and characters and characterization become alive in the persons of the imaginary agents, and impress themselves upon our attention. Furthermore it is this living relationship that enables us to evoke, in fancy, personalities we have never met, and, not only that, but to lend to an isolated trait, or an abstracted aspect of universal existence appearing to us in the guise of complete identity as though of a person, the response which in everyday life we are certain we yield only to man, woman, or child.

The sort of fictional character that is an agent, though not a person like one of ourselves, may be encountered in several varieties, but these are fundamentally all alike. A non-human character differs from this man or that woman not only by negative exclusion, but by some positive criterion of kind, or one of only partial identity. Some of these who are not as we, are God's creatures in their own right, superhuman like the Angel with whom Jacob wrestled, or any of the numerous tribe of demons. Others are subhuman—Moby Dick, Poe's

Ourang-Outang in "The Murders of the Rue Morgue," the snake Conan Doyle's "The Speckled Band," and the animals of Albert Payson Terhune and James Oliver Curwood. These represent the lower creation presumably as its genera really are. So, after a fashion, do Buck and the other beasts of *The Call of the Wild,* although in presenting their nature —their courage, loyalty, intelligence, and so on—the primitivist in London seems to have gone the limit in humanizing them. I dare say that from the point of view of an enthusiast about animals such characterization may seem only a tribute to reality; but the tribute has the singing quality of idealization, if not of outright romance. To me, London's Buck, as a conception, represents a stage intermediate between Poe's ape and the talking beasts of Kipling's *Jungle Tales.* Their character includes our power of speech, rendered in the words of our speech, so that the romance is frank, although it manages to stop short, somehow, of the fabular. That one matter of idiom, however, makes a difference of kind; animal and human behavior are mingled; and though the basic concept is different from that of Aesop, or of Swift in respect to the Houyhnhnms, the basic procedure is the same. When a horse serves or injures a man as a horse would in life, that is one thing; when he discourses on the merits of cleanliness, that is a horse of a different story.

The same analysis applies to any other variety of agent that is not simply a human being. Ideas, for example, are imageless. Time is not for the senses, nor justice, nor evil. Yet what is sensorily imperceptible has exerted upon us some one effect of its own, and this is movingly like some one effect exerted on us by a thing sensorily perceived. So the duration of time is a mountain, continuousness a river. Justice is the light of the sun. Evil is the lightning. Now, time or the hill endures; their duration is what they have in common: and from the interlinking of metaphors, the visible "becomes" the idea, and the idea "is seen." In much the same way, a colorless microörganism is stained into appearance; one has only to find the right dye. Once the physical reality has been metamorphosed into the idea, the symbolism may progress until time is the magic mountain, or the antiquity of the universe is Father Time. Now we are in the picture because the picture is in part something about us. As we lend our nature to the appearance of beasts, so we lend our appearance to the nature of things. The beast or the man, being a creature, stands before the view of consciousness with something still of the concrete uniqueness; and the sequential acts and words

117

of the Fox in the fable, or of the Red Death at the masque, have temporal identity which can be modulated into conflict within the structural unit of the scene. We have entered, I say, into our mythology and our fairy lore and our demonology and our fables and allegories. Vulcan and Circe are we, and Grendel and Siegfried, elves, angels, imps, and trolls, dryads, gremlins, the Lilliputians, the furies, and the muses. They may not be the likeness of our special Creation; but each, in spite of the most individualizing difference from the others, is the image of our creativeness.

What we have done with the qualities and the forces of our world, we have paralleled in the classification of our kind. I mean that to the personified beast or idea we have added the conceptualized type. Now the type is itself an idea, in being a composite. It is an artificial pattern, no less real because of this artificiality than a chair or a ship, and similarly of certain invariable characteristics. Its utility may or may not be its truth, but is certainly its value. We have every right to speak of a typical oak, a typical dachshund, a typical monsoon, a typical diphtheria. We may go so far, for emphasis, or for clarity in indicating that we have a conception in mind, as to speak of the typical Frenchman or Chinese, although of course no one has ever met him. It is only when, in ignorance or willfullness, we attempt to clamp the type about some unique individual, that the truth and the reality vanish, leaving nothing but the narrow, the suspect utility of superstition or prejudice. Whatever the determination of the type, some degree of fashioning has entered into it; any shrewd skeptic can prove the manipulation by pointing out the fingerprints of our disregarded mental handling. The type is a construct. It is not only an idea, but our idea of that idea. For all its applicability to the average, in spite of the fact that in practice the generalization so often seems valid, it is of course secretly responsive to guidance by our unexamined attitudes, which is to say to our ideas operating as feeling, drive, will, and private advantage. To regard the typical coolie as a reality of natural or Divine creation certainly "works"; but how, in each instance, and for whom? In classifying mankind for good or evil our consciousness is interwoven with our objectivity, so that the resultant character of any human type is inextricably part of our self. What a pity that our rationalism, that sees so clearly whatever is before its nose, is so seldom as acute in hearing the breath (or the sniffle) which issues from inside it.

Nonetheless, the type is enormously economical in enabling

us to respond at a stroke to great numbers of individuals of any one sort, by attending only to their essential and invariable qualities, and brushing away the accidents of the individual representatives. This device is invaluable for symbolism of a certain kind as the sole method of characterization throughout. Even in realism the type is useful, as for example when what is needed at a given moment is someone for the main character to deal with simply in the course of his business as a person moving about in the fictional world: a gamin, a sales girl, an irritating fellow passenger. So much of our life is lived symbolically anyhow, that we do not find it strange that a character in a book should also live that way—drive according to traffic lights, ask a direction of a policeman, smile at a baby going by in its carriage. Many of our relations with people are habit patterns of this sort, which make it unnecessary for us to deal with them as individual personalities. I am deeply convinced that most people deal with most other people in this snap-judgment way most of their lives. At any rate we do not naturally give unimportant strangers more than an elementary, a primitive response. Types are like branches, any branches, which our simian hands seize, and on which we swing through the dense social woods.

Human types in fiction may be classified as social, ethical, aesthetic, and psychological. The first two I will lump together because they are often so combined in the "characters," as they used to be called, of Theophrastus, Hall, Overbury, Fuller, La Bruyère, Marivaux, Addison, Steele, and other essayists. "Character writing," in this special sense, which no longer carries the old fashioned name, is a kind of literary composition in which there is treated a single type of person, in terms of his profession or moral qualities—the soldier, the schoolmaster, the squire, the poetaster, the good child, the bad child, the honest man, the cheat. The profession, trade, or public office is personified in what appears to be one man, like the fisherman in Aelfric's *Colloquies,* with the effect of simplifying a segment of society into one figure, as for a frieze. The reference is not directly to an abstraction, but to its embodiment in human practice—not, let us say, to medicine, but to the doctor. Fielding's Thwackum is the theologian pedagogue. Rousseau's Emile is offered, if not as the child of nature, then as the natural child. Thomas Day's Sanford and Merton, and the numerous brood of Miss Edgeworth are other instances of large sections of the puerile race summarized into individuals, but veiled so thinly in individuality as to fool no one, not even an alert youngster. Very good fiction, indeed, may be written with no other sort of characterization; Aphra Behn's *Oroonoko* may be read with interest to this very day, two and a half centuries after its appearance, and *Rasselas* and *Candide* are even more famous specimens. The type characterization lends itself to the plain-spoken didacticism of philosophic, tendentious, or satiric attitude. The idea may become the ideal, or the anti-ideal, and all three sorts of treatment may be given freshness and novelty by talented hands: *The Sir Roger de Coverley Papers, Nightmare Abbey, Uncle Tom's Cabin, The Isle of Penguins, Green Mansions, South Wind, Antic Hay, Painted Veils, The Blind Bow-boy, Main Street, The Good Earth, God's Little Acre,* and, with few exceptions, the people of *The Grapes of Wrath.* In fact, social or ethical types have persisted as some of our most famous literary conventions of character: the Child of Nature, the Child of Art, or as we would say to-day, of Civilization. The Noble Savage, Innocence in Distress, The Man of Feeling, the Nympholept, the Titan, the Noble Peasant, the Noble Artisan, and a host of others conceived by the moralist, the economist and the political doctrinaire.

Thus types originated by humanitarian optimism or criticism become standardized and join the array of aesthetic or technical patterns available for quantity production—the brave knight or cowboy or simple bucolic, the sweet young thing, the fallen woman, the temptress, the self-made man, the tired business man, the neglected wife, the victim of circumstance, the creature of environment, and the recent troop from the vocabulary of Sigmund Freud. Writers of ability, but with no power to originate characterizations, or to portray the rounded individual, have made familiar types interesting by the charm of other talents: compare Scott's heroes and heroines, or the *dramatis personae* of Longfellow's or Tennyson's narrative poetry with either Chaucer or Browning. True, Chaucer used types; but if his Squire and his Prioress are of that category, his Pardoner and his Wife of Bath most certainly are not; as for *Troilus and Criseyde,* the individualities who people its action make up a contribution to modern characterization beyond the power of criticism to appraise. After Poe and Doyle, the detective was the mechanical puppet Grub Street, but Chesterton and Carolyn Wells and W. H. Wright and Dashiell Hammett produced new forms. What Steinbeck did with the natural man of the eighteenth century ideologues in his *Tortilla Flat* goes beyond resuscitation it is nothing short of re-creation.

The sort of types I have called psychological are not of

course to be rigidly compartmented from the professional, the ethical, or the aesthetic. Nevertheless, the very nature of the type as personification of abstraction justifies a separate classification for each sort. From the point of view of humanity in the large, as in psychology, each of our traits is a component of our personality. Any such trait, abstracted and personified, then becomes a type. Some in the category, like holiness and valor, have ethical and professional reference, so that Mr. Worldly-Wiseman may play a role in the same drama with Christian and Apollyon.

Yet there need be no reference outside the frame of man's traits. The domain may be restricted to that of human nature, so that in a certain light, Poe will read like the anatomy of terror, and Katherine Mansfield like the anatomy of heartbreak. This restriction is very noticeable in some subspecies of fiction. Once upon a time a certain sort of psychological typification bore the name of *humour*. Ben Jonson officially introduced it into English drama around the beginning of the seventeenth century, and around the end of that century Shadwell enthusiastically revived it. I suppose that Smollett was its most consistent practitioner during the following century; also, Fielding wrote an excellent essay on the subject for his *Covent-Garden Journal*. The humour characterization, as every schoolboy is taught, derives from the medieval notion of four bodily fluids. An excess of any one of them would produce an unbalanced clinical type physiologically, with psychological stigmata—the sanguine man, the melancholy, the choleric, the phlegmatic. From this origin, humour came to mean any temperamental propensity amounting to eccentricity or ruling passion. In Jonson's *Every Man in His Humour* Captain Bobadil is the boastful soldier, and so on. According to Fielding, humours might be tragic as well as comic, and he gave Macbeth's ambition as an example. His own Blifil is a humorous characterization in this sense. The humour personality may therefore be a matter of degree, with one extreme a very thinly personified type, and the other a real man, but of an unbalanced, and distorted nature. Any reader of Smollett knows his fertility in the production of the later sort of creatures, partly because that was the way he doubtless conceived the average character, and also because the humourous character offers little or no obstacle to a narrative of onrushing incident. In its single and invariable quality, it is quick for the author to present and the reader to recognize, and incapable of producing surprises or other complications once we have placed it. To call Scott a humourist in the same degree would be an exaggeration; yet the stock figures of his romances show how much he learned from the tradition. Today the word *humour,* as I have here used it, has gone out; the practice, which of course still survives, seems to have become mainly the inheritance of Hollywood, the comic strips, and the soap operas, in their purveyance to the junior high school aesthetic.

There was a time, however, during the doctrinaire decades of the French Revolution, when the English radicals made use of the humour for their social criticisms. Mrs. Inchbald, Holcroft, and Bage seized upon its convenience for political moralizing and satire. Godwin, who like them would now be completely unread were it not for *Caleb Williams,* appears to have introduced a development of some importance—a conflict of humours in the one man, somewhat prophetic of what we mean by our word *ambivalence.* His Faulkner is a man of honour in both the moral and the aristocratic meanings; the rational goodness in him quarrels with irrational pride of rank, and this conflict drives him to crime and tragedy. Again, Godwin's Fleetwood is a person of so exquisite a sensibility as to go from the peak of joy to the pit of despair in an instant; he cannot strike a balance with the world, and ruins his life and the lives of all those close to him. Godwin's extreme devotion to reason, or rather, in the spelling of his time, Reason, impelled him to construct types in which irrationality of some sort played havoc with individual development. His personifications of some human trait looked upon as two-sided, with advantages and disadvantages, made character the locus as well as the source of conflict; and his philosopher's treatment of human nature by means of clear-cut abstractions makes his agents seem at times oddly like syllogisms, or geometrical demonstrations, or exposed clockwork turned into people by a latter-day Pygmalion. It was by no accident that his daughter wrote *Frankenstein.* His doubling of the simplicity of the humour deserves study as an elementary modulation of over-simplification into complexity, a step in the direction of viewing character as not only complex but bewildering, and so a kind of first step toward the stream of consciousness of our century.

The humour characterization is closely related to that other exploitation of a single trait—the caricature. Sometimes the two coincide, as in Micawber, when the characterizing bent is made the subject of ludicrous exaggeration. Smollett employed the humour and the caricature side by side, for example in Matthew Bramble and his sister Tabitha. Yet of course the two forms may be absolutely distinct. The humour is literary; the caricature, originally a form of pictorial art, retains much of that aspect in fiction by playing up the appeal to the senses. Again, the humour need not have in it a shred of the comic. Finally, the caricature may exploit a physical feature or a mere mannerism not at all suggesting a dominant personality trait. For that reason, caricature can get its effect by emphasizing individual or even unique differences and subordinating all else, so that what is produced is a single, whole personality—not a strict likeness, but a sort of lampooning portrait impossible not to identify precisely. Hence caricatures may be drawn not only of types of fictitious individuals, like the judge in Bardwell vs. Pickwick, but of actual celebrated persons, like those who sat for Max Beerbohm. In fact, the question of whether a certain graphic composition in caricature or simply comic painting, that is, comic romance or comic realism, may arise in a borderline instance. What would then be called for would be an exact special judgment of how much the amusing force of the picture is a rendering of reality in the subject, as against how much of it is a rendering of the artist's impression or intention; and such a nicety of discrimination between the realism and the symbolism of the piece might very well be impossible, not to make, but to get readers to agree with. When people of a geographical locality denounce some books for caricaturing or otherwise falsifying the life there—*Carmen*, or *Kim*, or *In the Tennessee Mountains*, or *Tobacco Road*—a stranger finds it hard to know which side to take, especially if he suspects an issue between fact and poetic truth. Nor is the problem at all simplified in the whole fiction. This potentiality of the caricature for experience: namely, that it may unite the typical, the individual, and even the unique—makes it a transitional pattern of characterization, and I have accordingly dealt with it last in this scheme of types.

Before I turn from the type, however, I wish to add some remarks about it generally. One of the problems of characterization in fictional art is to establish credibility with or without regard to verisimilitude. Now, this involves a related problem: to wit, that in the illusory occurrence each event must be experienced as unique, no matter who is doing or saying whatever is being done or said. In the solution to this problem, so far as types are concerned, the image is of course, incalculably influential; and the more vivid it is, the more subtle the persuasion of individual identity. This is obvious in caricature—the hideous teeth of Mr. Carker, or the sigh of Jo the fat boy. Whatever one sees in the one case or hears in the other, *and whatever accompanies this perception,* is what one imagines for himself, and is accordingly, *that* identity. One may, in what is called everyday life, doubt the evidence of one's senses, but not the presence before one's imagination. That, I take it, is the secret of the tyranny of nightmare.

In addition, once the type has been imagined with some such occult uniqueness, the art of narration can further fortify that uniqueness by means of the minute particularity and linked continuity of the scene as a structural unit. This contribution may be quite independent of expressed imagery, as one can see by carefully comparing a scene in Hawthorne where there is little or no delineation of the parties to it, with the often elaborate and circumstantial delineation of some scene in Swift. Also, the more powerful the undercurrent of conflict in the sequence of events, the more ready we are to believe in them; so that with vividness and close-knit action operating together upon us, the type will have quite as much verisimilitude as one needs for the fictional experience of it. There is a further force contributing to this plausibility, and although I have already given it discussion, I must repeat it here. We live much, if not most, of our lives symbolically. Many things are typed in our responses to them, often without analysis or focal recognition by the mind. Our initial behavior toward an employer or other supervisor, toward someone in overalls or a business suit or an ermine wrap, toward a freckled face or one rouged with a certain notification, will be not only behavior toward a symbol, but symbolic behavior. If we do not all react with the same typicality in each case, each of us is likely to have his typical reaction, and that is likely to be a recation, or a modification of a reaction, of his community, or of a point of view he shares with people like himself. In a village, the stranger is suspect; in the heart of a metropolis, the wariness takes on the technique of typing. Perhaps that is why O. Henry's New York is believable to us as a great concourse of types.

Now, what this really means is that millions of people have been classified by custom and habit. The capitalist, the laborer, the sales-girl, and the showgirl are types functionally, as are the grouch, the yokel, the rowdy. Each encounter with a type is actually an encounter with an individual exemplification of it; and the behavior called out in us, even in dealing with a category, is therefore at least partly individual. What we do ourselves, we are inclined to credit in the action of others, even of those who are inhabitants of a world of illusion. The novelist can safely develop one personage in individuality, as Defoe does, or a few, as Richardson does, and let the others range down in scale to mere suggestions of people. So a painter may apply a varying scale of detail and complexity in picturing figures in the foreground, middle, and rear of a canvas. In a story by George Eliot, there will be a Romola or a Marner who improves, and a Godfrey or a Tito who degenerates, while the others of their world perhaps age, perhaps die, but do not otherwise change, and so are not especially enriched in their personalities. Elizabeth Bennett responds to changing influence from her environment with momentaneously suitable adjustment, but Lady de Bourgh is a personified reflex or arrogance. In *Tom Jones,* there is the humanly variable hero, and there are a number of other *people;* by comparison, Bridget Allworthy, Western, and Lord Fellamour are humorous in the obsolete technical sense; Allworthy is an ideal, Blifil an anti-ideal; Partridge and Molly are comic "characters"; Thwackum is a talking Idea, and Square would be no more were it not for the chance disclosure of his dealings with Molly, in a posture most unabstract.

This last example is an indication of the ease with which a type pattern may be complicated toward individuality by an inconsistency. Indeed, the maintenance of type characterization depends on sticking to whatever is the pattern of the qualities of the composite. What is selected from reality is not something as it is, but its essential something; hence the abstraction. Yet reality, or life, is still the source. Nor need the pattern be presented as a bare outline; fertility in producing congruent detail may mark the creative ingenuity of the superior allegorist like Dante or the great symbolist like de Maupassant. The richness is a wealth of detail of this or that idea, or of people-of-such-sort. If it were not for the consistency, controlling all the elaboration of minutiae, where would the allegory or the symbolism be? There might very well be significance, as in any flower in any crannied wall, but how fix the signification? No. Inconsistency is reserved for realism of individuals, where, appearing often in the guise or surely with the force of apparent irrelevance, it erases some area of what would else be the sterotype pattern, unbalancing our habitual reaction, confusing our conceptions into quick humility, forcing us to recompose more complexly the form of the character we are experiencing, and leaving, in the place where there was simply somebody, the

125

less easily definable but much more powerful presence of one person and nobody else.

I have been speaking of the typical, as it is declared and focal in the type. It may, *per contra,* be instrumental, that is, ingredient or basic or skeletal to more rounded characterization. Aristotle declared (and Fielding cited him in approval) that every character should be conceived in his typicality, with the addition of whatever made him differ from others of the same type. Here is a scheme which, in line with Aristotle's advice about combining the familiar and the unfamiliar, plays off inconsistency against consistency in the treatment of individuality. We have the consistency of a class, inconsistent with other classes, and this consistency the character shares up to the margin of his differences. With or without reference to its originator, the pattern has a harmony which I suppose may be called *classic.* At any rate, that is what I will call it. Fielding adapted the pattern for use in fiction. He was outspoken in his contempt for the lack of art in novels, to the degree that he called his own works "histories." In announcing his use of the Aristotelian formula for characterization, he offered as illustration his treatment of the several innkeepers in *Tom Jones:* all had the qualities of the trade, but each in his own way. Whether or not he was the first to employ the method in the English novel, he was certainly not the last; what I am calling the classic model has become the traditional, with a numerous issue of very great works indeed. I suspect that much of whatever in this regard strikes us as unorthodox or at least different in Sterne, Dickens, the Brontës, and Joyce is their departure, in one way or another, from this norm.

That the tradition still survives, that it will persist side by side with other practices, who can doubt? It has every advantage of ease and clarity, both in its organization, and from our familiarity with it. True, it can, like any formula, degenerate into mere contraption, so that the character is not created, but only fabricated, as in Godwin and Bulwer-Lytton, and, on a very low plane, in the derivative fugitive pieces of any time, including our own. Yet in the hands of the sincere and gifted artist it has produced and still produces superbly expressed figures; at random, I think of Balzac, Flaubert, Galdos, Trollope, Conrad, Galsworthy, May Sinclair, Thomas Mann, Aldous Huxley, and Willa Cather. To cite Fielding again, lesser spirits follow originators, but these originators follow only "Nature." Originality is first a production by consciousness, out of itself, or a presence; but secondly it is single-souled attention to the presence, in order to convey it. This latter process does not require reproduction down to the last detail, though such may be the triumphant illusion. In approaching an imaginary person for rendering, there may be selection, so that the strong impression the character makes on his creator will pervade the presentation, and emerge from it at the end. The analysis and recomposition of imagined personality for characterization is a habit rooted in our daily procedure antecedent to any appearance in art; and though the classic way, as I here call it for discrimination, may be neither the only nor the best way, it is one very good one with a splendid record of achievement. To fiction as art it offers a very fine form by which to achieve the proportion and balance of the single person's nature and behavior. If it has so long ceased to be new that it can now be expressed with neat efficiency, it is by no means easy to manipulate with the effect of life; and its effectiveness has certainly not exhausted the resources of talent to produce novelty by means of it.

A quite different method for rendering imaginary people in their individuality has already been partly considered in connection with caricature. I pointed out that caricature, in emphasizing one feature or mannerism or aspect of a person, need not falsify the rest except in this disproportion, so that the result may be a peculiar portraiture, perhaps lopsided but not thereby necessarily inappropriate. Analysis may enter into the operation, but again, it need not. The seizure of the salient thing to be exaggerated may be all in the lightning intuition of the moment, and thereafter the author may simply follow through. This impressionistic hunch that the obvious anomaly is a clue to what is characteristic, and that all that is required is enough heightening to make manifest what is already vaguely felt about the man, is a method of characterization combining the classic faithfulness to type with a romantic love of strangeness and individuality. The impulse to caricature is irresistible in most children, who are quick and helpless in response to whatever arouses shyness, affection, fear, resentment, or just a fit of the giggles. Their drawings of people come out pretty consistently as caricature, whether so intended or not. Inexpert drawing is not the only cause; sometimes the little artist sets down with fidelity not what he has seen with feeling, but what his feeling has seen.

The imagination, in fact, proceeds in all of us according to this reorganization on the basis of strong impression, as the natural historian reconstructs some prehistoric monster on the basis of a single vestigial bone. The analogy is intended to be suggestive, and certainly not exact; for fancy is free of any compunction about contingency, or for that matter, about anything that may chain it to purposes not its own. It exploits the very feelings that the scientist weeds out of his process. This statement holds true not only of art, but of the most ordinary matters of everyday life. We are in accord, from infancy, with many assumptions we have never examined or even really once looked at. This is simply another phase of our living symbolically as part of nature. Thus a reputed wit will get a laugh when he does not want or look for it. Those to whom an Irishman is funny in the nature of things will laugh at his accidental hurt. The stale commonplace of the witness stand, that only the exceptional witness has ever *seen* what he says he has seen, and the inability of many people to describe accurately lost articles which they have had by them for years, will sufficiently attest the extent to which we perceive physical objects by function rather than by appearance. Accordingly, our strong impression of a person may be fitted out with a pattern suitable to it, whether the rest of the man corresponds to the conceived composition in much or little detail, or not at all. When I hear a deep, resonant voice over the radio, I may instinctively give it a big powerful frame to issue from; a languishing soprano may raise the vision of a willowy blonde. The process of affixing a suitable "person" to a shred of information we carry to such a point, that if in a dinging-car I overhear something about a crack boxer, and later something about a divinity student, I may never suspect that both references are to the same young man.

The gift by which imagination realizes its own impression on the basis of a fraction of the reality of one human character was dowered to a superlative degree on Charles Dickens. *Some* reality he generally started with; that, doubtless, is the ground for our belief that his creatures *somehow* walk our earth. To say this is a little like saying that the most gorgeously improbable clown has a whole real man inside him. But when we read Dickens, the real man inside the clown is inside us. Now, the power to incite illusion of this order, unfailingly, instantly, and in hundreds of attempts, shows how personal a thing genius is. About Dickens one may as well begin by saying what one would have to end by saying: his characterizations are of the kind that would be produced by any man exactly like Dickens. Each one is a signed piece. Maybe he did not mark every person he met by the single trait or twist shared by no one else in the world; but it seems safe to say that of those he met who were so distinguishable, he missed very, very few. That was *his* humour! Browning had the gift of knowing in advance which one speech of a conceivable play would give the gist of it, so that in his dramatic monologues he never needed to write, he could simply omit, all the others. Dickens' gift was a divining rod for the single aspect of individuality in a man, a woman, a child, which, when he touched it, magically lit up and flooded the entire strange spirit with illumination. In his addiction to conventional types for his heroes, heroines, and villains, he sometimes went beyond Scott, and sometimes as far as Bulwer. In this he was quite in line with the Crummles repertory; yet the Crummleses themselves are not stock figures. Many of his characters, furthermore, are humours, and some of these of the very finest—Pecksniff, Scrooge, Quilp, Bill Sikes. But Sairey Gamp and Tony Weller are no humours, nor are Mr. and Mrs. Mantalini, nor Cap'n Cuttle, nor Cousin Feenix. These are comic delineation in the grand tradition of Hogarth. To find their equals in unforgettableness, one must go to the very top of English comic writing, to Sterne, Jane Austen, Mark Twain, and to Chaucer and Shakespeare. It would in fact be pardonable to say that *they* must be compared with *him,* since in the sheer number and mass of his outpouring nobody in English literature ever excelled him.

Thomas Wolfe, who neither wrote nor created like Dickens, nevertheless shared one quality of greatness with him—he often felt toward people as Dickens did. As for Dickens himself, it is curious to note that his love of the theatre and the theatrical exerted on him two effects distinct and indeed opposed. On the one hand he drew freely on the stage for any conventions of situation and language that he needed for use in his novels. On the other hand, he appeared to take a mischievous delight in flouting the conventional by turning out, as I say, hundreds of examples of the utmost in psychological idiosyncrasy. He turned out so many of them, so fast, that he had time to note each, as it were, only by a single symbol, in a kind of shorthand characterization. (In his youth he had been one of the ablest stenographic reporters of his day.) One can understand why Chesterton had special reasons for his enthusiasm for Dickens: no other writer of fiction has ever proceeded on a more unquestioning faith in the uniqueness of the soul. It is this basic spiritual inconsistency of the members within the race that gives to his every figure of ludicrous or cruel distortion an identity not to be confused with that of any other of the master's creatures, or of literary or other art, or of this world. The confidence seems almost arrogant—to snatch from personality after personality one characteristic and one alone, never doubting that this one is the tell-tale inconsistency setting the individual apart from the million, so that nothing need be said of all the massive remainder of the man, since that would of course be only our shared humanity.

Perhaps the very intentness of my desire to identify each of the sorts of characterization I have dealt with so far has betrayed me into the blunder of making them seem reciprocally exclusive. If I have been guilty of giving such an impression, I must make amends for my awkwardness; there is nothing in the whole fiction, as I understand it, that would long tolerate such a compartmentation. In all really good characterization, whatever the sort, the particular sort is simply the manifest and therefore the most conspicious; all of the other kinds are included, but with a removal of attention amounting to deceptive, false absence, or relegation into disregard. The talking beast of fable, for example, relegates humanity to a condition of remote control. The personified idea, such as Jupiter for lightning or Pluto for death, comes to us like an image which is being addressed by a sleeper whom we overhear in a wakeful state in *this* world; for the animism of the mind need not be considered the whole of its infancy, but only its infant somnambulism. Equally, albeit differently, the type relegates out of focus all the individuals from which it is distilled, yet without, as we have seen, squeezing out of itself every last remnant of the uniqueness of each of them. Thus Hawthorne's conception of the suicidal evil of cutting oneself off from one's fellow men, appearing deceptively in the person and clothing of a single man who wears the name of Ethan Brand, is nevertheless not masked in this individual beyond our power to suspect the presence of a human characteristic quite as much as a human being.

And just as a character in an allegory turns out to be a symbol within the ethical or psychological frame of reference of a single trait of mankind writ large, so any general trait may be referred to the frame of reference of one person. The device for effecting the transfer may be Fielding's adaptation of the classical analysis and recomposition. It may be Dickens' divining rod of intuition which taps the spring of quintessential identity. But whatever the approach, there is a procedure in creative characterization in which the presence evoked is the illusion of one whole man, of him and no other. The individual is then no mere personification, like Ethan Brand. No; the individual is an individual who *remains* an individual, like Tony Weller or the Artful Dodger. In our criticism of Dickens we are prone to overlook this realistic turn of his inventiveness, and to speak of his work as imaginative in the sense of fantastic, and with an implication of the unreal. This would be to imply that all of his characters are of a category different in kind from living people, instead of being, as they are, different only in degree.

There are eccentrics in this world. There are minds whom ignorance has stunted, or feeble wit left childish in bodies biologically adult. In the same fashion, there are trees which are *naturally* twisted because they grow out of the side of a steep hill, or which are in configuration distracted and wild from sustaining the storms of the ocean-side. The unpardonable sin of Ethan Brand takes on a different light when, instead of being self-cultivated in privacy, it is visited upon some hapless innocent in the very heart of society. The realists who were Dickens' contemporaries, in failing to include Dickens characters among their portrayals, were as restricted, let us say, in the one lack as he was in the more extensive limitation; if he seems to have lived in a world of eccentrics, their worlds, by omitting or playing down what is eccentric in every one of us, are as truly falsification of a universe in which Nature has again and again played the freakish fantasist beyond the strangeness of any fiction. Our criticism, in failing to acknowledge the realistic raciness in Dickens' comic romance—as it does in that of Rabelais, Swift, Sterne, and Thomas Wolfe—falsifies what it expresses more than he intended. In representing certain people in a certain way he did not fictionize them in the sense of "putting in things of his own" that were not "there." Rather, he created them out of a power to see and feel them as we can not, or as we can do only in his writing.

In much the same way, by calling it "poetry," we have patronizingly kicked upstairs the Brontës' power to reveal the reality of life denied and to reveal it in the terrible terms of the denial. Had they written in the faintness of wish-fulfillment, they might very well have enjoyed a sentimental vogue. Their lives were passion starved of passion. Their minds and hearts and bodies were wracked by an absence, and their novels are the anguish of that. Now, what may be expressed *of* the living organism negatively may be expressed *in* it positively. A baby without milk is not a bundle of vital statistics among which one is regrettably not included. Rather he is the heartrending little skin-and-bones of malnutrition. There is a physiology of hunger as well as of alimentation, of lovelessness as well as of love. The Brontës did not characteristically express the wistful vision of what they were denied, but created out of the workings of denial in their souls and their flesh. The presences of pain and longing and unachievement mingled their frantic cruelty with the beautiful image of desire; and so *Jane Eyre* and *Wuthering Heights* and *Vilette* are the worlds of people whose incontestable identities have been sculptured by want. These people are whole individuals formed, not by growth, but by ingrowth. Yet wholes they are, and each, at the first encounter, bursts upon us with the burning privacy of a furnace door flung open. They may be abnormal, but they are not fractional, and they are certainly not false. They are evidence that romance may grow out of some stony cliffside of reality crooked and fierce, that all of the roots of a life may writhe within one margin of living. Unless realism may deal only with averageness—an averageness dictated moreover by our trust in its existence, and therefore betraying wish-fulfillment—then Charlotte and Emily Brontë were the instruments of real emotion speaking its own sort of truth. In speaking of Dickens, I called his intuition a divining rod; theirs was an eruption, and their characters are flung up into our atmosphere out of a convulsive and irrepressible rage in the heart of nature. Other revealers of mankind record occurrences on the crust which we take to be the whole of our earth, but they too are rather the furies of what that dull rind would withhold and hide.

So much for the system of intuition in characterizing the whole individual, and also for that classic analysis productive of, and then resting upon, clear pattern. There is a third conception, more modern than they in the history of human thought, though not in the history of modern fiction. This is a process of characterization based on the presumption of consciousness as a *tabula rasa,* or blank page, upon which the sense impressions from the world inscribe, in chance combinations of association, the form of the unique personality. Hence the name of Sensational or Associational Psychology, apparently applicable to any of a long line of expounders from the time of Bacon down into our own, with of course special modifications according to the particular views of this or that writer or school. To put the thing crassly, we are determined in our character by our environment; but since the environment can and does change, we can and do change along with it; and to the degree that we may change our environment, we may contribute toward change of ourselves. There is, of course, the opposite view summed up in the epigrammatic cynicism *"Plus ça change, plus c'est la même chose."* In fiction, the associational principle has provided not only intellectualist programmes for publicizing by imaginative forms, as in the work of Silone or Malraux, but also technical innovations of characterization, with or without programme, radical or otherwise—Sterne, Godwin, Stendhal, Browning, James, Chekhov, May Sinclair, Joyce, Gertrude Stein, Dorothy Richardson, Gide, Dos Passos, and Kafka.

All vital art is to some extent critical of predecessors, even within emulation and affection. Certainly I have not meant to suggest that continuators of what I call the classic scheme do not deviate from or disapprove of this or that procedure; the novelists of the Fielding tradition, such as Jane Austen, George Eliot, Thackeray, Trollope, Hardy, and so on, seem to me to display a power of self-criticism as among draughtsmen vying to see which can draw the most nearly perfect circle; that is, each is trying to do the same thing better than any of the others. But the novelists who by virtue of the techniques they use are the critics of this entire group appear to deny (to continue the figure) that circularity is the true form, or that any flat or solid regularity is the true form. Rather they seem bent on showing that character is actually a cluster of intersecting masses rendered indefinable by the ceaseless mutations of chance association and individual disfigurement. True, in the midst of this confusion there are accretions of temperament formed by association too early to be readily dispossessed by later invaders, or perhaps stronger in their concreteness than any environmental attack encountered by the individual. These would correspond to the principal trait or traits of the analytical or the intuitional scheme; but they are conceived as developments by circumstance, and their permanence is at the mercy of the chance that shaped and so can unshape them. They are like submarine creatures not only overrun and tumbled and battered by their fluid surroundings, but affected to their inmost by chemical changes in the medium in which they live.

If Sterne is a spirit whose sincerest laughter with some pain is fraught, he is equally one who can assume no conviction untinged by self-ridicule. His adroit instability makes him a master of association, since the double approach of adopting an idea and satirizing it obviates effectively any settling into definiteness of design. Uncle Toby is a faddist of the art of war. Also, he cannot hurt a fly. It would be hard to say on which of these two accounts Sterne has the more endeared him to us. For although Toby Shandy is an adult male who, having fought in battle, was so sorely wounded in his body as to bear the hurt to his grave, he is also not quite grown up in his mind. In much the same thrilled happiness with which Blake's child put questions to the lamb, Uncle Toby ignores the barriers of speech in addressing those other creatures of God, his human brothers and sisters. Among these is Walter Shandy, his blood brother, in whom a certain learnedness is a shackle upon reason. The deep, powerful convictions he has drawn from erudite authority dissolve and run together the moment he attempts to express them. He is a character in whom the fixed principle of crystallization is this: it will not jell. Providence has given his good wife to him not as mate, but as a counterweight. In her vague massiveness there is barely the gleam that suffices for perambulating protoplasm. She therefore accomplishes her offices in her world with the effectiveness we rightly ascribe to intelligence, but without one shred of intention or awareness on her part. Her conduct is human by effect, but without cause; if one were to think long about her in this light, it would cramp his brain, and so her being the wife of Walter Shandy makes theirs a marriage of the most exquisite suitability. It is the same way with all their relatives, friends, servants, and neighbors. Those of them who have definiteness of outlook have achieved it on the basis of assumptions plainly absurd, contradictory, and misunderstood; and those with a gift for seeing through the folly of every reasoning, including their own, take their stand on an incertitude as solid and as stubborn as the rock. As a result, when the consciousness of any of them is invaded by perception of some act or word from another, he responds with the unfailing performance of mechanism, but of mechanism so loose in the parts that the automatic operation emerges in every instance with the triumphant uniqueness of unpredictability.

By such fortuitous process, the character of a rural and stick-in-the-mud society is perpetually agitated by bewildering chance; and above this scene of churned lethargy there hovers the mischievous Associator himself, watchful and ready to dart down into any area that shows signs of stability, and chatter it away. Although the fictional world expressed in *Tristram Shandy* is doubtless one in which events occur in chronological order, it is not so expressed. The recital sets all sequence aside. A chance remark of the dialogue acquaints us with some happening of the past; and this, it appears, must be scrupulously recalled and recounted (no matter what it interrupts, or at what point); but in the midst of the telling, the author cannot repress the need to inform us of some related matter which only he knows will occur at some time which must be regarded as future; and that incident in turn cannot be unrolled without the renewed involvement of the present (or at any rate, *some* present); for the Associator is himself as subject to the notorious fickleness of the Associationism as the fictional community is, and as all experience and Nature are, of which the tale is the included mirror. Therefore all the conflict and the tension and the action of the story are put at the service of character. No novel in any language leaves the reader with more intense vividness of a locality and its inhabitants than does this somersaulting impudence. By setting order at naught, Sterne creates form. The book is the conversation piece of all conversation pieces. It is not only about a certain family—it is that family. Operating upon inconsistency as upon a tenet of faith, it is the portrait of a cluster of individuals somehow alike in the teeth of the fact that each is like nobody else among them or anywhere, each an individual as impossible to fail to recognize or identify as the book itself. In *Tristram Shandy* the chance of the mind's associations is a device for ultimate establishment of the static illusion. Instead of conflict manifested within or against an imaged illusion, the illusion emerges from the conflicts (not the least of which is the game between writer and readers) as the fruit appears on the vine.

It stands to reason that the scheme of characterization used in a book which is virtually *sui generis* might not produce the same effect in other fictions attempting that scheme. What I mean is that an author who, knowingly or not, uses associationism not only may turn out stories in which the conflict is set in the environmental illusion in the usual way, but that that is almost always exactly what he does. If, for example, instead of exhibiting associationism in momentaneous operation, he chooses to proceed by giving its process in the large, he may on the surface write in a manner hard to distinguish from the traditional one enunciated by Fielding. Yet he would not represent alteration in the characters as mere aging, or passage through stages of maturity constitutionally typical.

His hero or heroine may be a person considerably refashioned by shift of circumstance, if not constantly, then at least from time to time, and if not in every respect, then certainly in some eminently characteristic one. The character would be always recognizable, but sadly deprived from one point of view, or enlarged or improved from another.

Moll Flanders is an example; the narrative of her changing history was prophetic of our more recent doctrines of conditioning and determinism; and this fascinating anticipation of attitudes of our own time probably contributes no little to Defoe's modernity and to his continuing vogue after two centuries. The gist of the matter may be put in Moll's remark that when she was poor and desperate she of course found virtue impossible, but that with each return of fortune's favor she at once set herself up again as a good woman. Otherwise, as she became confident and habituated in crime, she was transformed into the pickpocket or the prostitute almost as completely as though she had never been anything else; and her character, up to the time of any moment of her life might accordingly be defined as "the person who had had those experiences in that order." The same may be said of Roxana and of Colonel Jacque and of Captain Singleton. Each change of Moll's character or of theirs would be roughly equivalent to a change in circumstance, and the sum of the inconsistencies would approximate the unique person. Defoe's fictions read much more like stories than *Tristram Shandy* does, because they are plain narration, not disquisition that bit by bit builds up into picture. Here Sterne and Proust are very much alike, while by comparison Defoe and Stendhal are of an older fashion.

As for the matter of character, there are several features of Defoe's art that combine to set him apart from anyone else. In the first place, he develops only one personality to a book. This statement is so little an exaggeration, that I will let it stand as I have put it. In the second place, his chronology is that of autobiography, or reminiscence, by a person of advanced years, who sees everything with the eyes of that age. Our sense of change must make headway against the fictional narrator's sense of persistent identity, so that for a knowledge of the passing of time we must rely heavily on the various circumstances chronicled. Finally, there is almost no analysis: presentation of subjective states is exceptional and brief, in the manner of bare summary or of homily, with almost no presentative detail. The character as agent proves on examination to embody a close interweaving of social relations—the successive actions of society on Moll and her responses as reactions. Each social relation is thus rendered as an event, and the event serves in the place of the trait, since Moll is always by nature the production of her experience at any given date. This, I think, is the surest, as it is the subtlest, of the ways in which Defoe uses associationism; and in this usage the social and political reporter, and the author of the satires and *The Essay on Projects,* is at one with the novelist. It is curious to note how much in this one respect Defoe shares with Chekhov, and how a little addition of the more personal characterization by traits gives the Russian so much difference of color in his naturalism. In "The Darling," for example, a woman is characterized as changing all her interests and mannerisms, even her way of speaking, according to the trade or profession of each of a series of men with whom she becomes identified. The changed circumstance initiates her reconstitution, while the details of the reconstitution are properly the character, and the total of these alterations, as her addiction or bent, constitutes her outstanding characteristic.

Genealogical novels supply an interesting variant of the associational treatment, especially to the extent to which genealogy as inheritance is turned into genealogy as environment. A line of descent with prominent family characteristics places each member in a situation of adaptation, rebellion, or compromise. In *The Way of All Flesh* the genealogy is a current on which the individual floats or against which he fights back; in *Buddenbrooks* it is a house, domestic and commercial together, where he lives or from which he is removed, according as he belongs there or not; and in *The Forsyte Saga* it is a supervisory community, in which he minds the family business or is forced to tell it not to mind his. The temporal plan of Butler's story presents each generation prominently as a generation, with parents and children subordinated, so that the effect of chronology seems almost stark. In *The Forsyte Saga,* the generations live together in graded contemporaneity, with Soames as the center of a conversation piece. Mann combines the two treatments, so that there is always a family picture with a leading figure, but not always the same one, because in the chronological succession death or other change is periodically rearranging the pattern. There is social philosophy in all three, but in Butler it is explicitly satiric, and the ideas of his attack dominate the action and the characterization much more than in the two other writers.

He is manifestly the intellectual; they are more obviously novelists. In view of the fact that all three study the phenomenon of the family as environment, they therefore apply associationism in some way to the conception of character. They ridicule or criticize or deplore the typical characteristic of material acquisitiveness, and it is amusing to note that the sort of character they deprecate is very much like that of Defoe the man, with his merchant's habit of affixing a price tag to everything in this world or the next. There is, evidently, a genealogical aspect to the world of writers of fiction, as well as to the fictional worlds they create; and the descendants of commercialism are not altogether respectful of the founding fathers. On the other hand, Defoe has a more nearly kindred spirit to-day in H. G. Wells, who found himself cast upon an island which, if not deserted, was to him plainly a wilderness; for its rehabilitation he wrote a long series of essays on projects, exhorting all the Fridays to alter the environment and to make it a better material and social influence on the character of their children and their children's children.

The interest in time as a social phenomenon with great meaning for the individual is implicit in *Moll Flanders*. It is more nearly explicit in *Castle Rackrent,* in *Henry Esmond* and *The Virginians,* in *Les Rougon-Macquart,* in the Barchester novels, in *Men of Good Will.* Toward the end of the eighteenth century, under the stimulation of Rousseau, the interest took on a crusading vigor in fictions calling for educational reform according to various ideological programs: *The Fool of Quality, Sanford and Merton, Nature and Art, Hermsprong, Belinda.* There were reactions and continuations in Bulwer, Disraeli, Meredith, and Henry James; but in all instances, the two generations of the teacher and the taught were of course juxtaposed for contrast and thesis. It is not surprising that the force of this interest should later evolve into the genealogical novel we have been considering. Nor is it surprising that the interest should also persist as simply one factor of the content—not the dominant one, but one discoverably at work in the illusion.

For *Remembrance of Things Past* or *Ulysses* there can be worked out, not one genealogy, but many; and although genealogy is prominent in the former and buried in the latter, it will be found to be treated in both as a matter of great importance; that is, as the extent to which the character of any agent is descended from antecedent environments, so that

138

the generations survive in him. To those who may doubt that Joyce had any such intention, I will say only that he is far more specific than Proust in fixing the dates of parental biography and provenience. Since Bloom is impelled to repress the memory of his father's suicide, and also to seek a spiritual son to replace poor little Rudy, and since Stephen is looking for a father in place of the begetter from whom he is estranged, Joyce's precision in the matter of chronology must be considered as a conscious handling of an important theme. Besides, there is the *Portrait of the Artist as a Young Man,* which deals with the education of the hero in skepticism and disillusion about his environment and its traditions; and there is *Finnegans Wake,* an attempt, so we are told, to adapt to fictional purposes the Viconian theory that our human history is cyclic and repetitive, that the generations are a few successive epochal types which set the patterns of human character within each of them and therefore affect the individual in his. The forces producing the recurring variations are conceived to be universal, like the laws of science. From this point of view, the local environment, which inscribes itself on the individual *tabula rasa* through the man's senses, is in turn a *tabula rasa* in space-time impressed by the stimuli of the universe, that environment of environments.

Our century is one in which most writers of fiction have the college degree. In getting it, they have commonly taken courses in psychology, and know something of such names as Locke, Hume, Mill, Charcot, Wundt, James, Freud, Dewey, Watson, and Koffka. The undergraduate interest has often been prolonged into professional life, as a field of reading or as an interest of intellectual sociability shared by other men and women, whether college trained or not. Beyond comparison, the most celebrated psychologist of our time has been Freud. He has influenced not only followers, but adapters, opponents, critics, students, casual readers, and the many who know him and his terminology by hearsay alone. The words with which he and his followers have increased the speech of the world—*complex, fixation, libido, inferiority*—are to be met constantly in conversation, in journalism, and in sophomore compositions. Their meanings will be found exemplified in the drama of Eugene O'Neill and on the canvases of Dali. For good or ill, the impact of Freud's ideas has been notable in the publications of learned societies, in press and pulpit, and even in the home-brew primitivism of the flapper, the nudist, and the jitterbug. The effects, so far as fiction is concerned, are to be marked in the works of D. H. Lawrence,

Grazia Deledda, Wasserman, Gide, Mann, Sigrid Undset, Faulkner, W. L. George, Dorothy Richardson, Sherwood Anderson, Aldous Huxley, and Erskine Caldwell. In the fiction of a single writer, May Sinclair, the treatment of the relations of parents and children, of man and wife, of lovers, of unmarried parents, rests on a conception of human character so thoroughly Freudian as to amount to a marked deviation from the ideas of English fiction from *Pamela* to the end of the nineteenth century. Miss Sinclair's interest in the Brontës was the inevitable outcome of their unwitting anticipation of the ideas on which she has based her art, in *Three Sisters, Mary Olivier, The Divine Fire, Mr. Waddington of Wyck,* and *The Life and Death of Harriet Frean.* It is the culmination of a tradition in English fiction vital out of all proportion to the handful of oddly assorted writers who have represented it—Sterne, Bage, Mary Wollstonecraft, Mary Hays, Meredith, Hardy, Samuel Butler—a frank expression of the fact that men and women are with equal force capable of bodily passion. To this view nobody has for a long time offered serious dissent; the point in connection with the English writers I am talking about here is that the truth must not be omitted from a discussion of human character intended to be regarded as full; that is, not alone with reference to sin or sex, but with reference to what is organically essential in men and women. To read *The Three Sisters* immediately after reading *Jane Eyre* or *Wuthering Heights* is to see by the sun what has been groped for by moonlight. Considerable as the critical estimate of Miss Sinclair's contribution has been in some quarters, I feel sure that she will some day be recognized as one of the major reputations of the first half of our century, as the publicized mediocrities of our period fall away into oblivion and leave room for the genuine creators to stand out plain.

Perhaps I have been mistaken in thinking that so extended a statement is needed for the schemes of characterization as I conceive and have dealt with them. I will therefore confine myself to a single conclusion for all of them, whether they are symbols, abstractions, types, humours, or caricatures, or whether, as real whole people they are schematized on rational analysis, intuition, associationism, or Freudianism. My single conclusion is that *characterization is always based on some comprehensive attitude about the general nature of human beings.*

Having set forth a variety of the author's possible approaches toward characterization, I now turn to a consideration of the character himself. I will deal with him as he appears in the imagined occurrence, where he is the illusion of a living person, presumably in every respect. I will therefore conceive him in a kind of schedule or inventory of his aspects, and will detail as many of these as I can. He is a living organism. As such he is at all times conjointly a body, a consciousness, and an environment. The body may change because of growth, emaciation, amputation; the consciousness, because of sleep, swooning, or a mental ailment, like amnesia; the environment, because of seasonal or natural alteration, or simple removal. Since the environment is most obviously separate, we customarily distinguish it from the self, and contrast the two; but no one has ever produced evidence of a living self without some environment, which must therefore be considered indispensable, together with body and consciousness, to the reality of individuality. To sum up, a character of the sort we have in mind is an illusion of a person or self, because he is the illusion of a body, of a consciousness, and of a world, all together and in one. It is in this complexity of his that he differs from any type or idea or symbol fictionally disguised as an agent for fable or allegory; for from his assumed complexity there arise his uniqueness, his potentiality for conflict, and all his other services to the whole fiction. The statements I here make about him need not of course be rendered expressly in the novel or tale of which he is a part, any more than they are verbally expressed by Nature about us; but in any sense that he is assumed in imagination to be an entire man, they are inferentially applicable to him. The same is true of the rest of my discussion of him, in the inventory I am trying to make suggestively as full as possible.

His body is a presence in our consciousness marked by properties of appearance—color and light and shade. These present his mass, proportions, race, and posture, and the texture of features, such as hair, eyes, skin, wrinkles, scars, blemishes. He is rarely encountered naked, but he may be: Crusoe staggering onto the beach after swimming from the wreck; Hypatia stripped by the mob; Matthew Bramble "rescued" from the sea by the misguided Humphrey Clinker. Commonly, he is dressed; and his clothing expresses his historical period, his locale, his stage of civilization, his rank, class, fortune, contour, taste, idiosyncrasy, and personality. In fact, every part of his surface can be a clue to something about him that is not directly given, such as his health or his strength or some organic condition that is not itself apparent to the senses of an observer, like toothache or blindness. On the other hand, the mention of any perceptible internal condition of the sort will be symbolic of the appearance that goes with it, and will help to create the image. One way or the other, he must be absolutely credible on bodily physical terms, so that if in the story he is to undergo an operation or be soaked in the rain or be able to hear or smell acutely, the event shall be accepted without hesitancy as a simple fact.

There are writers who feature the perceptibility, in detailed, delineative portraiture akin to the painter's art—Flaubert, Conrad, Willa Cather; others indicate it as they go along with the story—Smollett or Hemingway; and others produce the effect of it almost entirely by suggestion based on impression of trade or personal disposition or any imperceptible matter—Fielding, Hawthorne, James Cain. Minute delineation is not necessarily realism, as we can see from the examples of Scott and Poe. Nor do all realists use it; and it is therefore one way of distinguishing the art of one realist from that of another—of George Eliot who relies on it very little, from Proust, who is fond of it and a very great master of it. The character's physical aspect, regardless of how it is projected into our experience, and whether we pay much attention to it or not, is nevertheless essential imagery in the illusion of a story, and its symbolic quality can give the action vividness and subtlety at a stroke. Besides, appearances are capable of intensifying our understanding of the personality of the character, and may be its most brilliant emblem, regardless of the mood in which the fiction is experienced: Don Quixote, Roderick Usher, Sherlock Holmes, Beatrix Esmond, Pere Goriot, Mr. Pickwick, Frankenstein's monster, Little Eva, Tarzan, Long John Silver, Tartarin of Tarascon, the Duchess of Guermantes, Thomas Buddenbrook, or any of the three musketeers.

For economy, I have relied on the visual appeal, but I have been implying one of sensory variety. The voice may be guttural or nasal, the hair fragrant, the brow cool, the hand bony. The character's own liveliness of sense impression may characterize him: Hardy's peasant may see the sunset with the eyes of a painter; Dickens' people are enthusiastic eaters and drinkers. Characterization that exploits the senses has been made most effective by authors as different otherwise as Balzac, Stevenson, and Mann. The curious lack of imagery in some long sections of Gissing's works makes his conversationalists seem to vanish in the midst of speech; Voltaire's or Butler's frugality of picture throws the ideas into high relief; Fanny Burney and Loti and W. H. Hudson create the reality of their agents largely by lavish detail, making the person part of the scene as some composers make the solo voice an instrument in the orchestration.

Above all, for fiction, the bodily character is important in changes of motion—expressions, actions, speech—by which the imagined man directly participates in the confluent action. Dumas, Scott, and Conrad come to mind at once in this connection. James, on the other hand, seems to vary his practice here, or to be uneven in it. At his best he knows how to escape the ghostliness of psychological analysis by relieving it with the relative materiality of voices distinguished in dialogue; so that *The Ambassadors* seems solidity itself by comparison with *The Golden Bowl,* and either of them by comparison with *The Outcry.* It must be obvious that the character's power to perform public actions which are observed by others (including the reader) is a main prerequisite for his agency in a fiction. The impatience of many readers over description is not hard to understand or sympathize with. Yet the extreme of too much notice of the picturesque in a tale is to me far less objectionable than the opposite. Any tendency of ours in reading to pass too quickly from evidence to habitual reaction, to thrust the evidence aside, as it were, in the very act of responding to it, reduces us to living symbolically with reference to characters as we do among ourselves when we are least observant. This making over of people into mere reflections of our own conduct is a reduction not only of the artist in this observer but of what is human in those observed; and there is in it the same degradation as in perpetual self-feeding at crowded lunch counters, hatted, and with the umbrella gripped between the knees. It is escapism into the midst of business by the mere vibration of busyness; and with reference to characterization in fiction, it is an escapism in which much didactic as well as light literature has been written and read. Never to attend to anything but the physical world would be a fixation from which thought and art—certainly, literary art—deliver us. But to refuse ever to regard the panorama made possible for us by the senses, in the moment when it is staring us in the face, could be nothing more or less than jail by choice. Not only are the interest and the beauty of our surroundings lost to us, but in failing to exercise a nicety of observation we are atrophied in the glory of living. If character in fiction is nothing but a means for exercising already habituated response, then we cannot grow by it, and a work of art becomes a trapeze in the monkey-house.

The consciousness of the character may, like his bodily appearance, be expressed in great fullness, to a slight degree, or may merely be assumed for the action. In a single work, the three procedures may be employed in alternation. We have seen how, and to what extent, in certain works of Sterne, James, Joyce, and Proust, the consciousness is the region of the illusion and the arena of conflict. Spatially and temporally, a certain amount of the action "takes place" there. By means of the limited third-personal point of view combined with dialogue, or of the frankly first-personal omniscience of an author as much at home inside his character's head as outside it, or by the fictitious first person of interior monologue, or by the combination of several or all of these in stream of consciousness, not only are the body and the world included by reflection, but the consciousness itself is represented in manifold departmentalization—feelings, sensations, images, ideas, memories, perceptions, anticipations, and racial, social, or personal impulses.

The recent fictions dealing with consciousness as the area of conflict owe no small debt to those who dealt with the consciousness of the character by the method of *indication*. This method is a great tradition, and a living one. It is the one the great reading public are used to (whether they know that or not) and to many of those, the *technical* shallowness of its penetration into the character's consciousness is condemnable as "too deep" or "dry." (People who find *Middlemarch* a labor of Hercules, or *Tristram Shandy* crazy, are not likely to find recreation in Dorothy Richardson or Joyce, or indeed ever to have heard of them. The indicated consciousness is therefore the furthest north of many accomplished and brilliantly equipped readers, whose notions of diversion or mental exercise do not nevertheless include polar exploration or deep-sea diving. To them *The Egoist, The Ring and the Book*, and *The Golden Bowl* are tough enough going. So when they read the reviewers on *Finnegans Wake*, they thank God for a tidy hearth and Somerset Maugham. When they speak only for themselves, individually or as a group, they are certainly not wrong; and even when they claim the right to speak for everyone, and so for me, they are still right—as far as they go. For I, too, have not only read, but reread and prized, the authors they prize. What is more, there are passages in Meredith and James and Browning which I find myself taking very slowly indeed.)

When the character has met with some problem or hurt, or some pleasure or narrow escape from danger, and has need of reflection or privacy, the action of the story may go, as it were, indoors into him. Such a retreat may be rare in a book, or it may occur frequently enough to vie in prominence with the outdoor action, the extra-individual, which is set in the fictional environment. In "The Killers," for example, Hemingway so rigorously excludes explicitness on the subjective states of the characters that the unaccustomed omission has the power of a vacuum into which our creative sympathy is sucked, to replace the abhorred blank with imaginative reality. The consciousness of the agent has therefore not been taken for granted here by reader or writer, for its omission has been made obvious, significant, and therefore symbolic. In *Moll Flanders* the entire fiction is one unbroken declaration by the heroine. What (after the fashion of a traveler at the customs barrier) she declares, is, as I have pointed out, her world, by which I mean as much of the world and its circumstances as have happened to her up to that moment; but even Defoe feels periodically the obligation, when things go exceptionally well or ill with Moll, to give her a moment in which to summarize the repercussion of events as effect *in* her. This summary she generally renders with the brevity of duty, in some few sentences of prudential or pietistic exposition, or, less often, of her subjective state as she conceives and formulates it—that is, labels it. Since the label names some mood or condition of mind which the reader recognizes and grants to be applicable to the facts, he credits her consciousness with the reality, for he wants her above all to get on with her story.

When a response in consciousness is such as to register in some change of the character's bodily appearance, provided that the character is the sort of person so to betray himself, we are compelled or enabled to divine his state. The method of indication is one of the devices of the stage as well as of fiction, and has the advantage of resemblance to a typical life situation when one studies the expressions and actions of another in order to probe for something. This treatment in literature is often combined with rendition of speech, the two devices either substantiating or belying each other. A sudden pallor and an outcry of pain, a jolly remark in a lifeless tone, will suggest an inner something that fits into the context of recital or else must be explained by what follows. Sometimes an omission of what may reasonably be expected in a certain sort of situation will not only provide drama by raising questions, but will heighten the questioning with hints of psychological conflict. When a chatterer halts in the middle of a word, when a greeting always answered in the past is met with silence, the determination of the character's frame of mind is a turn of the action, an occasion of suspense. James, as we have seen, is a master of this species of psychological missing clue. It is his gentleman's reserve in operation, the mechanism of his indication by indirection. Any sleuthing character of his, starting with what is strikingly absent, and impelled to find out why, both consults other characters whose knowledge of the aloof one may cast some light on the mystery, and also beards the mystery personally. By the fencing tactic of dialogue, the reluctance or secretiveness is ultimately forced into the open as declaration or disclosure or very strong presumption needing little more analysis of the evidence so gained, in a series of encounters each courteously proper.

The fact that characterization is inseparably related to the author's ideas, together with the fact that the essay as a mode of discourse is interwoven with presentation of illusion, often enables the author to help our understanding of mood and motive in the character at some fresh development by means of helpful explanation. If this way of doing things sometimes leaves something in the character unexplained, it is then a strong hint about something in the author. Really capable novelists, however, do not often fail to illuminate what they are trying to point out, although we may dislike the kind of light offered, or the angle from which it comes. A sincere intention to be just may proceed confidently from principles others might hold faulty or debatable, and yet show how the reality looks according to those principles. Thus, Pamela's confusion of prudence with virtue made it possible for Fielding and other contemporaries to catch Richardson in the act of confusing a success story with a maiden's prayer, and whatever mistakes he made thereafter, he never repeated that one. Possibly Shamela is too rowdy a demi-rep to sit on the witness stand. Omitting her nevertheless leaves Pamela and Joseph Andrews confronted, twin portraits in the fictional gallery, each with the creator's exegesis and pedigree. Pamela's character is conveyed in the first person by her letters: Joseph's by sections of narrative interlarded with bits of disquisition by the author. Richardson's misjudgment stands in the record for us to profit by; but so does Pamela. For though she is falsely explained as to virtue, she is still true to life in her naive and, in a way, innocent cunning. The object-lessons of fictional art are not always so clear cut.

The importance of detachment in realism and naturalism, where the character is imagined as a whole person with feelings and ideas inside him, is an importance verging on definition. To the extent that he is plausibly an individual, his behavior is, or is potentially, of a certain degree of independence. He is, let us say, self-propelled and directed; or if governed from without, has his own way of acquiescing or resisting. His independence, then, is that of a person in a community, with respect to the other persons in it. When the impact of this independence is strong enough (and it always is in the sophisticated writer's power to evoke illusion), we overlook a fact we have known all along: that in being the product of an author's imagination, any character is dependent on *that* creative conception. In what is called realism the participation or the relevance of the author's views is far less in evidence than in allegory, where they are characteristically prominent or even explicit, or in symbolism, where there is at least a powerful suggestion that ideas are somewhere about and that one is supposed to look for and find them. The impartiality of the realist is therefore one of the fictions of fiction, which the author creates, but also, so far as he is sincere, credits. That in his scrutiny of phenomena he may be detached to a degree beyond the power of most men there can be no doubt, but I deny that his impartiality includes absolute freedom from reliance on ideas. The most one may say in this connection (it is really a very great deal) is that, granted his principles, he applies them steadily and honorably. The notion that in naturalism the novelist is writing with freedom from allegiance to ideas is one of the most uproariously funny glumnesses of our age. What is nearer the actuality is that he is writing or trying to write about humanity as though from a point of view which is extra-human, or non-human, as seductive a fiction as mortal ever succumbed to. Insofar as any naturalist is for one moment ass enough to credit himself thus supernaturally, what a pretty picture he makes in bed alongside his arch-enemy, the authoritarian! On the day when a story is for the first time composed by a slot machine, I will credit the author's contention that it did nothing to interfere with the characters. Until then, I will continue to be grateful to the naturalist for a point of view so marked and distinct as to reveal reality in a new aspect, providing a consequent advantage of contrast and comparison with the old.

In line with the issue of scientific objectivity, naturalism gave wide currency to the conception of the character as an organism, every phase of which must be observed and treated. The eighteenth century founders of the English novel referred frankly to the body, and regarded it, according to their lights, as sin, forbidden fruit, or great fun. One of the important tendencies after the death of Smollett in 1771 was a reaction against this frankness, much of which had been as coarse as it was frank. The lady novelists were very active in the movement to clean up—Fanny Burney, Elizabeth Inchbald, Mrs. Radcliffe, Maria Edgeworth—and Godwin and Holcroft oddly enough represent the same aversion. On the other hand, Mary Wollstonecraft attempted the subject of the married woman's right to "live her own life"; Beckford's *Vathek* has an idyllic episode of physical love; and Bage's *The Fair Persian* delightedly mocks at the notion that a ruined woman cannot marry and live happily ever after. I admit that these exceptions are few and obscure. I am simply interested in noting that the seeds of revolt against Victorianism were planted, as those of Victorianism were, many years before Victoria was born. Of course, the current ran the Victorian way. Jane Austen is certainly silent on the physical aspect of sex, but her heroine is never afraid to confess to herself or her confidante that she loves a man; and should the heroine's friend or sister trip off on the path of dalliance, or should she know some one referred to as a natural child, the heroine seems pretty clear in mind as to what that means. Which is to say that Jane Austen's heroine, like herself, is no doll, but a woman in being a lady. Thackeray's record is a little more open and a little less admirable. What he said about fashions of candor in comparing Fielding's treatment of Tom Jones and his own of Arthur Pendennis may of course be extended to cover the case of Becky Sharp. He cannot be accused of unfairness to her; he was really most indulgent; at times her fairness fairly leers. With the Brontës, woman's passionate love of man is neither defended nor acclaimed: it is. In Meredith there is greater intellectual awareness of social issues, and a fine gallantry in the attack; but there is also a kind of female-worship urged upon the male which leaves the novelist a Victorian inside out. In Hardy the real revolution is struck: the bodily aspect of sex and so of life, and the revolting anti-naturalness of convention, both expressed in a plain honesty of statement, set man and woman on the one plane of organic constitution, but with no neglect of the higher possibilities attainable by human organisms as people with brains and hearts and souls. With some mopping up operations by Gissing and Butler, the battle against tabu was won. To call it a victory for truth is to say that we know what the truth is. But that it was a victory for candor, no serious thinker will deny. The high water mark of the movement, so far as I am concerned, is the career of May Sinclair; but telling contributions have come from Shaw, Wells, Galsworthy, Bennett, Dreiser, W. L. George, D. H. Lawrence, George Moore, Cabell, Sherwood Anderson, Aldous Huxley, Dorothy Richardson, and Joyce.

The slow change in the representation of the character of woman brought with it a corresponding change in the representation of the man. Even Rochester is no Ivanhoe; and by the time we get to Jude Fawley the hero is no longer an ideal. Furthermore, as man the lover was altered in portrayal to fit the newer picture of his mate, so the two were in time reviewed as parents and as "the older generation," an appraisal and a criticism set forth by Meredith, Butler, Shaw, May Sinclair, Galsworthy, and many others. Conceptions of the family, of parental authority and filial submission, have undergone an earthquake. Alteration there, and in education and social life generally, is still in progress, under pressure of world war and revolution and an advance in communications which dwarfs both. Blunt candor speaks everything. There is some indication that it has even caught up with that darling of the doctrinaires, The Child. To me there is more than a note of counter-revolution in the appraisals of childhood implied by Richard Hughes in his *A High Wind in Jamaica*.

The changing conception of feminine character has been influential in ushering in all these changes: but, in turn, there has been a growing tendency to represent the individual character as more and more complex. In a sense, the novel since the middle of the eighteenth century has, with few notable exceptions, moved massively towards the treatment of consciousness. One might almost define realism in its psychological phase as a mounting tendency to present the complexity of consciousness. Surely, if one combines that theme with the newer feminine characterization and the urgent aim at objectivity, one has all the principal forces of realistic tendency from *Clarissa* through *Anna Karenina* to *Remembrance of Things Past*. At the same time, one can see why critics should hesitate to call Defoe a novelist, or should not hesitate to call Dickens a romancer. The anatomy of feeling in Richardson, the union of character and action in Miss Austen's *Emma*, the painstaking discrimination of motives in George Eliot, the careful plotting of the steps of human reasoning in "The Murders of the Rue Morgue" and in *The Ambassadors*, the descent into the volcanic action of emotion in *Wuthering Heights*, these are but a few of the fine sectionings by which fiction has split and multiplied the simple notion of any man as one pattern or one mystery. If this is true of any specific character, like Studs Lonigan, Marian Forrester, Hans Castorp, or Eugene Gant, it is even truer of the single character conceived in the abstract. Out of its richness and variety the particular individual comes to us not only as himself, but as the representative of mankind evolved into civilization.

Many of us, fascinated and troubled by our own complexity and intent upon our own growth, have looked to the novel for such personal presentations. We enjoy them, and the imaginative experience of their individualities is part of our adult self-education about the race to which we belong. The many-faceted unity of each of these "people," like that of our own identity in being evident and perplexing, does not, of course, yield up the last secret of what man is. Some mystery always remains. Indeed, one increment of the increasing knowledge that wide reading brings is a kind of wisdom in accepting the fact of the vestigial ignorance, coupled with an incorrigible interest to learn a little more about what that ignorance really is. What the method of the full treatment of consciousness has already evidently added to the lore of exploration seems to promise more.

Yet, without that treatment, the method of dealing with consciousness by indication has also effected and is effecting a steady expansion of acquaintance with the subject. Not only did this broadening scope lead to and attain the device of stream of consciousness, but it has already adapted and absorbed into itself, for example in *Dark Laughter* and *For Whom the Bell Tolls,* whatever of the newer procedure could deepen and amplify its own. In Anne Radcliffe's *The Romance of the Forest* the continuity of action went indoors into consciousness, to take the form of a dream and then to re-issue as an influence on the character's daily life in the world. What Mrs. Radcliffe did for terror, Jane Austen parodied for comedy in *Northanger Abbey.* Later, in *Vilette,* not only is a nightmare integrated into the action, but there is an important episode in which the heroine, Lucy Snowe, wanders deliriously about the city at night, in a borderline state of awareness and somnambulism. Bierce, Wells, Cabell, and Sherwood Anderson have in various ways used daydream or vision under drugs, not alone for the wonder of imaginary occurrence, but as the region of it, for symbolic investigation. Conflict within consciousness, as an annex to the battleground of the world, has gone beyond mere episode in "Young Goodman Brown," "An Occurrence at Owl Creek

Bridge," "Markheim," "Dr. Jekyll and Mr. Hyde," and on the stage in Barrie's *Dear Brutus* and *A Kiss for Cinderella.* The agent as one entire person, whose consciousness is simply assumed, will not detain us long. The principal advantage of this presentation is for speed of movement. An additional one is that comment on or analysis of his character is made almost entirely by readers, whose participation and absorption in the fiction is thus considerably enhanced. The method is as old as story-telling. It is to be found in very ancient Egyptian wonder tales, in which a kind of animistic outlook simply includes human beings. It is nearly all that there is of characterization in mythology, in Aesop, in many of the Bible stories about historical persons of the Old Testament, such as Samson, and in the parables of the New Testament. In fact, it is used in any species of fiction in which character never rises above the condition of mere agency—in fairy tales, melodrama, farce, balladry, anecdotes of curious or exciting action, moral apologues (if they are very brief), detective stories, and the like. As Smollett implemented the humour, Scott the traditional formula, and Dickens the caricature, so the Arabian Nights, Voltaire, Samuel Johnson, Poe, Marryat, Lever, Mrs. Stowe, Dos Passos, and James Cain have exploited the assumed individuality of the agent for stories of wonder, philosophy, mystery, adventure, social reform, or capital entertainment. In any kind of fiction, even that which is markedly dedicated to presenting character in the principals, the method is used for minor agents not dealt with by indication or full treatment of individual consciousness. Here it approaches typicality, and at times merges with it, lending a kind of uniqueness to the type, especially in the types employed by Poe, Hawthorne, and O. Henry. The agent as a whole person whose consciousness is assumed is presented largely by his acts and words, with more or less information about his bodily perceptibility, and with such economy that he offers little resistance to a conflict or a thesis which operates about or upon him rather than within him. He is handled in the story pretty much as he might be in a synopsis of it. However, if his role is prominent, he is likely to develop details of personality in the hands of a Defoe or a Voltaire; nor does the fact that the method is appropriated for hackwork yarns like those about Nick Carter and Frenk Merriwell mean that it is beneath the dignity of good work. In the novel, it commonly tends to share at least a little with the method of indication of consciousness; but in shorter pieces, like some of those of Boccaccio, Chaucer, Sacchetti, Bret

Harte, and Stephen Leacock, it can be found without much, if any, mixture.

The discussion of the character as a consciousness has been so long and involved as perhaps to banish the memory of my remarks on him as a living body, and my intention to deal with him in his environmental phase. This last I have tried desperately, for the sake of simplification, to keep out of the section on his consciousness, not always successfully. The three are one. There is no compartmentation, save in theory. Take the scientist out of Tertius Lydgate, and the story turns tragic. Make Tom Jones Allworthy's nephew and Sophia's husband, and the errant foundling settles down into the respectable paterfamilias. Jane Eyre goes to school to be trained into a fierce independence. Marian Forrester is a lady who must have the style to which she is accustomed; remove the style, and she is a lost lady. Emma Woodhouse has been so conditioned into being Social Authority that she must refashion her mind in order to be a healthy, happy woman. In girlhood, Emma Bovary filled her head with erotic romances; they became her self and her ruin. Isabel Archer began as a mixture of high principle and youthful illusion; but not until disillusion, by stripping away the error, had disciplined the principle, could she sit for the portrait of a lady. With Dorothea Brooke she shared a certain conflict and a certain grievous victory. Jude Fawley was not permitted by circumstance to establish in his consciousness that aspect of his environment which alone he desired for happiness. Sister Carrie succeeded in becoming what she wished, but then could not be sure that she was happy. One need not go to the literature of political indoctrination only to prove that when the imagined agent is an entire person, his character is as truly a matter of the environment as of the mind or the body.

Is it not this triple organization that makes possible the integration of the imagined individual with the imagined setting, community, occurrence? The illusion of a story seems to have hidden nerves of relation, like buried telephone wires, running into and out of individualities, in a web of communication and continuity. That is why some prime motive of the action may be better personified in one agent than another, so that he is central and dominates. The neighborliness of Raveloe is best presented in Marner's adoption of Eppie, a development heightened by the wonder that his former apparent lack of sociability should have been only distortion of his bitter need of it. The heartless power of Egdon Heath is Eustacia Vye; she can suffer and be destroyed as Nature cannot; but otherwise, like mother, like daughter. I have never read a Russian novel in which each person was not something of Russia, and the more truly so, the more unforgettably individual. The Joads are the dust of the dust-bowl; the Forsytes have made a better thing of their property. Hans Castorp knows that he is in good health, learns that he is not, and is rehabilitated enough and in enough time to serve in a world war: he is his social generation in epitome.

Since certain lines of the action come together in the traits of the central character, it is not surprising to find that subordinate characters, with no manifest loss in individuality, may also be regarded as symbolic of aspects of him. Legree is Uncle Tom's slavery, and Little Eva his sweetness. There is hardly a personality in *Remembrance of Things Past* who does not reflect of some trait or stage in the character of the hero. The color harmony of a canvas, the thematic organization of counterpoint, are parallels to this matter of the network of relations in fiction whereby the many are gathered up in the one, and the one is dispersed into the many. Contrast, antipathy, and struggle are made into congruence. Symmetry is set in motion, and conflict is composed.

I have spoken of agents, like certain ones in George Eliot, who undergo marked change between the beginning and the end; a pressure from without is brought to bear upon some motive, which strengthens with resistance or is twisted in evasion; potentiality is made into cause of circumstance, and produces effect; the story makes the character, the character is the story. Again, Henry James presents a series of encounters between fallible intelligence and soluble mystery; each encounter is a bout, a training, and a development; out of the momentary adjustments of self to struggle, unsuspected resources are shaped into a clearer individuality. The sequence of the events of action by or upon character, granted enough minuteness for continuity, becomes the record of a life, for character is action. We have seen how Defoe, who had no more than this, nevertheless had enough. But when to the biography of clash and survival, there is joined a variety of approach and disclosure, then the complication of plot produces a complexity in the characterization, in imitation of the process of life. The imagined person need not grow or change in an outstanding way; but our knowledge of him increases with acquaintance, and the portrait rounds out and fills in.

This effect in a novel may be secured by brute mass of events and the impressiveness of elapsed time. However, even in a novel, the illusion of life may be achieved by the passage of time, not from decade to decade, or from year to year, but from moment to moment. Surely this method has advantages for the short story, better suited to illusion of change in the brief view than in the long. Here the writer must preparatorily survey all the events that cluster about the instant, whether they occur in the character's consciousness, body, or environment; must select now from one region, now from the next, out of the variety possible in each. Not only is monotony avoided, but the free motion in and out of consciousness makes the imagined individual seem to come to life at every point. Also, he seems alert with the shiftings of focal, peripheral, and disregardful animation. He notes some sound or sight in the enveloping scene, he responds with bodily sensation noted sharply or dimly, with a welter of feelings noted only as some dominance or other among them, with an idea he can barely apprehend until the private monologue of internal speech gives him the handle of a word, a phrase, a sentence with which to grasp it. He may check his idea either against the presences in consciousness or against others in body or world. To show what I mean, I will quote a paragraph from "A Little Cloud," one of the stories in *Dubliners*. After Joyce published these tales, he turned to a different, an untraditional technique, which he simply included as one of several in *Portrait of the Artist as a Young Man,* but then used very extensively in *Ulysses.* In "A Little Cloud," which appears to be one of the last pieces he wrote for *Dubliners,* he achieved a mastery of the older, orthodox procedures, so that the sample I take from it may serve to represent a conservative treatment of a specific artistic problem.

The central character of the story is called Little Chandler, a timid government clerk, who is married, and whose life is humdrum. From the past he nurses ambitions to be a poet, but these are no more than secret, inactive wishes. The dead level of his routine is therefore much agitated by encounter with an old chum named Ignatius Gallaher, now a London journalist, who is on a brief holiday in his former haunts in Dublin. They have made an appointment to meet for a drink after Chandler's day at the office; he can hardly work, for the stir of memory and of hope that his friend may somehow be able to help him to publication. As he strolls across the city to his rendezvous, he recalls how his friend had shown signs of "greatness" early. One recollection, of a supposedly adroit witticism, fills Chandler with vicarious pride, and tugs at and releases his repressed desires.

Little Chandler quickened his pace. For the first time in his life he felt himself superior to the people he passed. For the first time his soul revolted against the dull inelegance of Capel Street. There was no doubt about it: if you wanted to succeed you had to go away. You could do nothing in Dublin. As he crossed Grattan Bridge he looked down the river towards the lower quays and pitied the poor stunted houses. They seemed to him a band of tramps huddled together along the river-banks, covered with dust and soot, stupefied by the panorama of sunset and waiting for the first chill of night to bid them arise, shake themselves and begone. He wondered whether he could write a poem to express his idea. Perhaps Gallaher might be able to get it into some London paper for him. Could he write something original? He was not sure what idea he wished to express, but the thought that a poetic moment had touched him took life within him like an infant hope. He stepped onward bravely.*

The point of view is that of the limited third person, with the author saying "he" in order to confine himself as narrowly as possible to the agent's outlook, while nevertheless reporting it from his own. We are therefore directed to Little Chandler's conceptions, but objectively. The first sentence gives him to us in an external-internal ambiguity: we see him quicken his stride in whatever bodily appearance we imagine for him (a note which the last sentence of the paragraph picks up again) and we sense the muscular and nervous change of the quickening, as he must. The consciousness is indicated at once, then, and throughout the paragraph, so that his subjectivity is our object. In the second and third sentences, sensation blends more and more into mood as response to surroundings of place and people, or environment. Each alteration is an internal event; the action of the story has moved "indoors," but without losing contact with the surroundings. Since his past and the present environment are intimate—the text shows that—and since his response is novel to immediate momentary sense impression, he is mobile-body-mind-world, an exemplification of his concreteness as Man in the abstract. The fourth sentence shifts from apprehended mood to clear thought; this is rendered as though in the words of his interior monologue: note the substitution of "you" for "he." Then the crossing of Grattan Bridge indicates his progress amid the setting, and his pity of certain houses as stunted shows how unaware he is of any comparison that might be made between them and him. He compares them with tramps, an image of obviously vivid presence in

* Printed by permission of the Viking Press.

his consciousness. His inability to create a poem about his metaphor raises a doubt, and he mentally turns to the friend whose escape from Dublin and whose success symbolize two of Chandler's feeble desires. Thus the conflict between his weakness and his longings, delicately operative throughout the passage, comes to a minor climactic moment of frustration that promises little gratification in the story's outcome.

Joyce has transformed the fictional symbols—conflict, image, form, character, feeling, idea, word—into the semblance of a man's living and moving from moment to moment in a specific place, and has made all this into one episode of patterned illusion and of subtle conflict in the mount of a greater climax. If one will compare the expressions of the excerpt with my own in analyzing it, he will see that what I have said is an attempt at presenting the apparatus of a technical procedure, of which Joyce of course says nothing; what he presents is the illusion, the presence in his and our consciousness, of one certain man—Little Chandler—pursuing one certain route in the place known as Dublin, at one certain succession of moments in his life. He lives. He muses and remembers, observes familiar surroundings with unprecedented response of feeling, thought, and fancy, and with fresh hope of escape and of literary success. Occasionally he speaks words unhearable by another; or at moments his ideas are not verbal, but merely the mute postures of his active mind; or his awareness is simple sentience, or warm feeling.

It is this inherence of vital force which gives individuality to the creatures we imagine. And at the bottom, what we lend a character in creating or experiencing him is our own life. He moves about in the space of his world and co-exists, as we do, with men, the lower creatures, and mere things. Regardless of the point of view brought to bear on him, or the method of rendering him, he is himself by reason of that power to live which exists only in the concrete body, in the unique breath and pulse.

Chapter 6

Emotion

WHAT IS CALLED climate in the region of the world, is in consciousness called emotion. Its temperature alone is said to characterize the temper of whole races, and to comprise every variety of psychological weather. If we speak of Goldsmith's sunniness, the stormy restlessness of Melville, Butler's ironic coolness, or the fierce heat of Charlotte Brontë, we simply borrow back from our personifications of elemental nature some of the illuminating animism which on other occasions we confer upon weather.

When we read fiction we disregard the outside world, the better to concentrate on the world present in our consciousness. Consciousness has the power of attending to, of behaving towards its own illusions as though they were external. This process has been called, in one of the superb paradoxes of criticism, the willing suspension of disbelief; in its quality as willing, it is profoundly emotional. So are the products of this suspension: the engrossment of creation or of reading, the amused or grieved or otherwise absorbed attitude we address toward the imagined occurrence, the varied feelings of the agents as we apprehend them and respond to them. That is why I said earlier that fiction, like all art, is profoundly a mood.

The greater the art, the greater its saturation with the personal leanings of the artist, whether his name is known or not, and whether he tells us his feelings explicitly, by subtle means, conceals them entirely, or is even ignorant of them. One of the indispensables of creative vitality is the conviction that a thing is worth expressing. It is part of the recognition of value in "a subject"; the intuitive certainty is a property of whatever it is that we call "inspiration." This conviction, it is true, can be analyzed into rational principle and therefore into ideas; but in its instinctive action upon ideas, conviction is not only geminal, but is often born as the emotional twin before we suspect that there is to be any other. The vigorous disregard at work in creative action, by which a presence simply appears in consciousness, may be studied by the artist retrospectively before he sets to work on what has thus come to him; but the amazing speed with which artists have been known to leap from intimation to expression shows that no such analytical study is necessary. Regarded as impulse, art can certainly not be divorced from feeling. One can therefore understand why some commentators should regard emotion as basic and indispensable to art; and so I do—to the extent of declaring it one of the several invariable parts of the whole fiction.

There are differing degrees of intensity in consciousness. The brilliance of memories or dreams can sometimes occupy our whole attention, so that what we imagine we see leaves only enough of us to respond to it, without the power of breaking its hold. There are physical sensations with this same intense power of compulsion, as any one knows who has thrilled to a kiss, or has been reduced to whatever it is that sustains a frightful bodily blow. This tyrannical capture of consciousness seems most characteristic when the form or the state is that of emotion. Poe knew that if he could arouse fear in readers, or direct all their energies upon the regard of it, he had achieved unity in composition, whatever else might be lacking. His *Ms. Found in a Bottle* has atmospheric unity although the tale rambles, and is really nothing but a string of lightly connected anecdotes of rising intensity of terror.

When life has been stripped to a solitary biological feeling, and persists for a space as love or as rage, that, in the moment, is what there is of being, and therefore of mind. This is the secret of high lyric, in which the poet sings, not of or in but *as* one feeling. Lyric of such sort, in Herrick, Burns, or Blake, is quite distinct from that which celebrates emotions remembered in tranquillity, or broods attentive over them in the magnanimous introspection of Shakespeare's sonnets or the strange, cramp-chested songs of Donne and Hardy. A single mood can apparently supply the being of a poet almost for his lifetime, making the unmistakable note of a Housman or a Scott, a Dobson or a Frost. Literature of this sort, of which the composer seems to be not only such a man, but the voice of man's power to feel, I call romance, or rather, romance at its fullest and most typical. Wherever the dominant spirit of literature is lyricism, there we find romance, even in the shout of a laughing scorn whose butt of the moment is romance. In Peacock, in Hawtorne, in Poe, in Emile Brontë, in Zola, in Cabell, in Sherwood Anderson, in D. H. Lawrence, in Loti, in Leacock, in Faulkner, romance is that mood of fiction in which the element of feeling is raised to be the power of the whole. A story of such sort is one in which the fictional world is emotion, the characters moving about in it as in a medium, like submarine creatures observed in the depth of their element.

Romance, which is fiction seized by emotion, takes its emotion, obviously, from the author. It is his expression because it is his feeling. Accordingly, the author's feeling will in many instances be the attitude, the spirit, and the outlook of the characters, either the principal ones, or just the hero. One sees how this works out in Byron, and in the Brontës, who read and imitated Byron in their adolescence. This sympathy of author and agent is a veiled identity. Wordsworth is the hero of *The Prelude,* and something of him is discernibly the hero of *Michael.* So with Shelley and his Prometheus, and other impersonations and disguises. Scott's figures of physical adventure embody his love of athletic activity; his readers share it, or they are not his readers. His suspense is the see-saw of emotions reflecting the vicissitudes of combat; we must have a passion of our own in the game, or else reject it; there is no half way. The triple identification of author, character, and reader in the excitement of the moment is a mode of imaginative life which is glorious if—or while—one can enter into and live it. In his treatment of King Richard or Sir Walter, Scott began with a sense of kindred spirit. He did not have to project himself into their bosoms, but hit it off well with them because the likeness was really there.

On the other hand, with whom Bulwer-Lytton might have been properly sympathetic, I cannot pretend to say. The theatrical falseness of his characterization is a mark of his insincerity as a writer. As attempts by an author to project himself into imagined personalities to determine their feelings, his characters bear an astonishing resemblance to what journalists call printed matter. His sort of empathy is a literary short-circuit. The matter of plausibility in romance, granted the expression, must be taken care of by the author's contact with life. There is such a thing as the wish of the unimpassioned to be passionate, but when this is rendered as desire, it must be given its own quality, not that of the emotion it craves to be. Because Dickens was a genius, we know what the Mantalinis believe themselves to be, and we know what they are. Comic or serious, the true romantic lies somewhere midway between the reality from which realism takes its form, and the marvelous Cockaigne which is fantasy.

Hence sundry overlappings. In fantasy, characterization comes bathed in the light of wonder, whether in fairy lore, in myth, in fable, or in allegory. The characters are as truly symbols of the mood that gives birth to their world and permeates it, as they are of the natural forces they represent, or the ideas, or the human traits. The image or the occurrence is further bound up with the illusion of the impossible or supernatural. Romance, on the other hand, comes closer to life as we live it; it is one of the turns of everyday life when everyday life turns into something, if not better, then much more fascinating.

Also, romance is one of the ways everyday life is lived in

159

the privacy of consciousness. Our hopes or fears are likely to take the form of rehearsal of the coming event; in visionary anticipation people and occasions often take on a romantic cast, reflecting the engendering mood. Though these reveries are generally out of line with worldly fact, they are not false to desire or dread; they distort because they arise from distortion; and at times the business of art is to present, not to correct them. Dickens is inspired in his depictions of the excitement of a poor family preparing a festive dinner, or the arrival of a carriage at the door. No matter how ordinary a thing may be to others, if it is unaccustomed to us, it makes an occasion. If it takes us by surprise, we are flung into a chaos of feelings; if we have time to expect it, we savor and dramatize it over and over, till it delightfully or terribly or disappointingly occurs. Whatever plunges us out of peace or lifts us out of boredom stirs us in our importance. When such romance is conveyed in the spirit in which the character feels it, that is, with the fellow feeling of the writer, we have a sympathy that is not identity because it is so much more. Dickens sees more of the truth of Tiny Tim than the child does, but shares whole-heartedly in the poor little body's piping goodness. It is as though a traveler at night, passing a wretched hut, were to ignore the sordidness in order to warm to the laughter from the shining window. It is this hewing to some human truth amid the discordance of worldly facts which gives the romance of Dickens a blend of reality, as it does in the Brontës, in Katherine Mansfield, in Thomas Wolfe, in Erskine Caldwell.

Negatively, the critical absence of such championship makes the symbolism of de Maupassant seem realism. It is not so much that the hardness of the man's head cannot assume the mood of pity, as that unalloyed pity, of all the forms that sympathy can take, is the one quickest resented, since in its eye the recipient sees himself lessened. The fellow-feeling now flows from higher to lower; the interval marks a detachment; a plight has become a privacy less truly shared than stared at, though the glance be truly sorrowful. When emotion in the characters is rendered so, a realism of some sort has begun to elbow the romance. Championship or detestation has given way to contemplation, identity to observation, enough to make the key mood less one of a feeling that cries out, than of a form sensitively reflected. That is why George Eliot and Hardy, almost all of the great Russians, Flaubert, and Mark Twain are realists; their powerful humanity works out as a seeing of humanity plain. Dr. John Brown, who was no realist, nevertheless put the matter in a nutshell in his *Rab and his Friends,* when he said in defense of certain medical students who seemed to have become quite hardened to suffering, that in them sympathy had ceased to be an emotion in order to become a motive. In some writers the force of emotion is so irresistible as to break through and belie, or to warm and soften, an assumed exterior of other aspect, as with the bitter indignation of Swift, the needling probe of Voltaire, the mellowness of Anatole France, or the tenderness of Chekhov. Satire and philosophical balance are certainly no armor against emotion, for they are themselves moods, the one of antipathy, the other of harmony.

There are two principal emotional climates in aesthetics: comedy and tragedy; each sensitive to the extremes of ecstasy and sobriety, and with many degrees of intermediate condition. Either tragedy or comedy is a purge of emotional lethargy. The feelings are aroused, and their exercise is their discharge. In tragedy the catharsis comes from terror and tears: a human fault that calls for correction, perhaps even by punishment, is visited by an exaction disastrous beyond human conception of justice, and certainly beyond the power of human life to bear. The illusion of the suffering must equal our appraisal of what it must be like from such a cause, and the art of the expression must be adequate to convince experience up to the limit of the intolerable. Our observation of the hero's fate and our sense of kinship with him in fallibility stir in us the pity and fear which the tragedy carries off as a conduit. The excess of emotion is thus dissipated, not turned back or imprisoned destructively within us. Art thus is an aesthetic, if not a moral, equivalent for disaster.

The reader will see how I have adapted certain materials of Aristotle's *Poetics* to my immediate needs. I have not, for example, made a point of the hero's high place in the state, because so far as I can see, that has come to mean very little in the modern world. The downfall of a ruler is doubtless of widespread consequence and therefore import; but pity and fear over the tragedy of Oedipus or Medea were never heightened in more than a secondary way by the symbolism of lofty place. The most important point has always been that of human capacity to suffer: this will raise any one to a surpassing level of concern, since it wrings from the public world a full acknowledgement of the importance of private consciousness. It is true that the kings and the mighty of tragedy are enshrined in our corporate memory; yet many a monarch has died in the course of things and faded out of history. It is the tragedy itself that confers grandeur: Anna Karenina and Jude Fawley are elevated to a rank of dread and compassion beyond any they could have known in the world. In recent times the tragic model has been expanded by our increased concern with the conflict between the creative individual and the conduct of society. What was dim and feeble and even preposterous in *The London Merchant* and in so-called domestic or sentimental tragedy generally, broadened and strengthened into a powerful element in *Ghosts, The Emperor Jones,* and *Golden Boy,* and in the fiction of Balzac, Thomas Hardy, Dostoievsky, Hemingway, and Faulkner. The death of Robert Jordan in *For Whom the Bell Tolls* is lifted out of mere circumstance into spiritual triumph. The lonely anguish of his victory makes us aware of our own tragic failure as part of the unarticulated herd. In such works it is the hero who is cleansed, while we others remain, not what we were, but what he had made us in our own eyes, with grief a barb in the heart, and pity and lightning in the brain.

Since to acknowledge the fact of tragedy we must know both the cause and the outcome, tragedy is a mode no less than a mood. Its end is veiled in the beginning as foreboding. The chance of escape is slight; yet though there prove, as we dread, to be none, we may not flinch from watching the turns of the struggle, the downward fortune of the one doomed to torment. In the theatre, or in fiction, we are like neighbors incapable of helping the sufferer, yet morally bound to stand by. All along, we feel in our bones what it is we are sharing: a fate which, in befalling one of our kind, is our kind of fate. The impendence of the outcome, even at the start of the work, startles alive in us a deep unwillingness to credit the possibility of what we vaguely but all too certainly know to be inevitable; out of our own inner struggle tragedy builds the tightness of its structure, the unity of its action in which form and mood are fused, and in which emotion becomes less a presence in the illusion than an obsession replacing the very process of life. Poe, whose matter was terror or mystery, recognized the indispensability of determining the end of a piece, not at the end, but during the course of composition. It was an excellent schooling, from which we have all profited in the explicit lesson of his *Philosophy of Composition.* Nothing ever made a good tragedy except the reality in the author of the mood into which the work is destined to grow. That great skill is required to give this a fitting shape goes without saying. The ecstasy of grief can vanish in our ineptness of planning or phrasing; but no ecstasy of planning or phrasing is a substitute for a feeling which is vital and persistent enough to sustain the structure of the work. The whole underlying pattern, every word of the text, may be fixed and held only by inexhaustible reference to the final peak of intensity—an anguish lived out in place and time. Until the writer has reached the end, the end is a presence only in his imagination, in his consciousness; and to establish and keep it there, he must have a tireless apprehension of that closing note of supreme sorrow, of the pulse of life in tragedy, and the secret of its form.

Tragic fate may move the onlooker to give thanks that the victim was not he. This relief could never decently be happiness; in any condition above savagery, it could never be amusement. Aristotle said that tragedy and epic presented men as greater than they are, and satire as less. To Fielding, satire was the scourge of wrongdoing, at which one must not laugh any more than at privation or deformity. Laughter, he felt, should be reserved for affectation alone. As I see it, this would not make men appear less than they are, but only less than they presume to be, in the attempt to *seem* more than they are.

The truly tragic blemish marks the man in us as less than divine. It is a cancer of nemesis in the flesh of mortality. Comic blemish is the quality of whatever in us would make victims of others by snatching at rewards due to real merit we do not have, by aping the outward appearance of value. In so far as sham is merely vain, it is already punished by self-exposure; there remains no need of correction beyond ridicule, or boycott beyond laughter. It can readily be seen that this kind of comedy would be the natural coadjutor of satire, which is criticism by abuse. Such comedy is the sort practiced by Aristophanes, Juvenal, Rabelais, Swift, Smollett, Fanny Burney, Peacock, Thackeray, Samuel Butler, and Gogol. Also, it will be found in mixture with another sort (which I shall soon be discussing in Cervantes, Fielding, Sterne, Jane Austen, Meredith, Anatole France, and Arthur Schnitzler. The dominant note of corrective comedy is wit—a most graceful operation of the intellect which fashions absurdity into metaphor and organizes comment as epigram. It is adept at catching delusion or imposture in the act. Like lightning of the playfully freakish sort, it hurts and overturns and strips, but does not kill; and sometimes it does no more than flash an odd illumination. Not unexpectedly, this exposure of affectations may itself be affected, so that what in Butler is the genuine cold sparkle of the man's inner nature, is in Wilde a Life Work, and glistens by the sweat o' the brow.

I have alluded to another sort of comedy. Not all laughter is critical or corrective. Some laughter—much of it—is the natural expression of joy, or of less ecstatic pleasure. It may therefore be contrasted, not so much with mockery, as with tears. Babies, who are innocent of pedagogy or censorship, gurgle in this comic spirit and infect us with it; and it is the audible symbol of the mood of christening and birthday and wedding feasts, of carnivals, and barn dances. It, too, seizes upon the absurd and the ridiculous, yet less as a butt than as a benefaction. This attitude looks at comic blemish as part of common humanity; it is our insight, when we see others in a laughable pass, into our own pesky ridiculousness; so that what each of us has kept sheepishly secret, believing it to be a silly failing of himself alone, bursts from him with a roar of confessional relief when he observes it to be true of another. Goodnatured people join in this sort of laugh out of instinctive thanksgiving over fallibility as the tie that binds. Here is the sort of *common* comedy which I was referring to a little above, when I said that it was mingled with wit in Cervantes, Jane Austen, Schnitzler, and others. Without the added barb of wit, it warms the comic passages of George Eliot, Trollope, Hardy, Howells, Bret Harte, and Caldwell. It is the queer, uncertain sentiment of Sterne, and the grand fooling around of Artemus Ward, Daudet, Jerome K. Jerome, Leacock, Frank Sullivan, Thurber, Saki, and W. W. Jacobs. It is the heart of the laughter in Horace, Chaucer, Shakespeare, Goldsmith, Sheridan, Dickens, Heine, Mark Twain, Tarkington, and Harry Leon Wilson. It is the delight of smiling in *The Roger de Coverley Papers, The Legend of Sleepy Hollow, Our Village, Cranford, The Marriage of Loti, Sentimental Tommy, The Crock of Gold,* "Mademoiselle Olympe Zabriskie," *The Casting Away of Mrs. Lecks and Mrs. Aleshine, South Wind, Antic Hay, A High Wind in Jamaica, The Blind Bow-Boy, The Hard-Boiled Virgin,* and *Life with Father.*

What happiness is, I know no more than any other man who ever discoursed gravely about it. That there is such a thing as happiness, that it is no delusion, I know for a fact. Such misfortunes as grief and fear and pain, and the sorrow and the loss of dear ones, are the common lot: they are not to be subtracted from happiness, but must be suffered to stand beside it, for the fullness of an honest accounting. Joys may be marshalled into three grand classes—those of anticipation, those of exercise, and those of relaxation—appetite, function, fullness—dreaming, realization, reviewing—hope, accomplishment, composure. Each of these, it seems to me, could be a domain of one sort of comedy—of expectancy, of joy, of contentment: *The Midsummer Night's Dream, The Comedy of Errors, The Tempest; The Vicar of Wakefield, Tom Jones, Emma; Vathek, Pickwick Papers, Huckleberry Finn; Alice in Wonderland, Vanity Fair, Seventeen.* These are mere trials on my part. I am never satisfied, nor do I expect to satisfy others, with these categorizings. Somebody of a more severely scientific or scholarly turn, moved by my suggestion and my bungling, could perhaps classify comedies with finality as those of speculation, of actuality, of reflection: Romance (or Fantasy), Realism, Symbolism. Let me have one more trial: *The Misfortunes of Elphin, Humphrey Clinker, The Egoist.* Alas! one should never be tempted to do more with one's pleasures than give thanks for them.

Beauty, says Santayana, is pleasure objectified: and with this one dictum of his famous analysis, I heartily agree. Yet in agreeing, I hold out a modest reservation in favor of my triple classification, by which the subjectivity of happiness is multiplied by the recognition of what sorts of things call it out, and the complexity is further complicated by reference to time future, time present, and time past. On the question of what beauty is, then, the nature of fiction would make any agreement seem a charming loveliness in itself. Thus *Kubla Khan* has been awarded high praise for beauty as an object which gives pleasure not only for what it is, but for wonder at what it might have become if Coleridge had achieved the whole. But to say that the poem is a fragment seems from one point of view like a blunder, since it is wholly exquisite as it is, and even more than that, because we have no certain evidence that the poet ever really experienced any more of it than he wrote down. He may possibly have mistaken an unexpended momentum for continuing creative drive.

As against the forward-feeling joy of *Kubla Khan,* there are poems that are the very radiance of beauty in being, such as *The Ode on a Grecian Urn;* and there are others, like Wordsworth's *The Daffodils,* which by his express intention fills us with peace in the illusion of sharing a delight completely of the past. Now, *Wuthering Heights,* like *Klubla Khan,* has the form of passionate desire without end. What terminates is merely the recital; nothing else is concluded, because nothing else is gratified. The last words of the story are simply a leave-taking, as though the muse must at length bring to a close her pilgrimage to the shrine of an emotion; the story is an eagerness eternally suspended toward a gratification eternally deferred. In the lack of the object that ought to be the pleasure goal of the feeling, the feeling itself glows as an object of beauty. By contrast, the pleasure and the beauty of *Tristram Shandy* or *War and Peace* are lived out and achieved in the experience; while the pleasure and the beauty of *The Way of All Flesh* and *Remembrance of Things Past* lie in the illusion, neither of approach nor of capture, but of recapture.

Now I will turn to a consideration of how any one element of fiction may be a presence of beauty in embodying human pleasure. The image, for example, may be an illusion of something lovely in its own right. Scott's wild mountain scene or the sea in Conrad's page; the oasis in Gide, Hardy's heath, Stevenson's Samoa, Hudson's green mansions or Hamsun's northern acres; the charm of man-made loveliness in Beckford's palace of the Caliph, the art treasures visited by Corinne, or the hot-house refuge of the aesthete in *Against the Grain;* the appeal of Homer's Apollo or Helen, Thackeray's Beatrice descending the stair, James' exquisite Parisiennes— since such as these may fill us with a sense of beauty in the world, they not only may be beautiful in the experience of reading about them, but may illumine the whole story with their grace, making us exclaim that it is the *book* that is beautiful. As with the physical, so with the spiritual: the heroine of Gorki's *Mother,* Ma Joad, Uncle Tom, Sidney Carton in sacrifice, the dear Vicar of Wakefield, the Spanish peasant heroes of Ralph Bates and Hemingway, Isabel Archer and Maggie Theale, Jean Valjean, the grandmother of Proust's hero, Old Jolyon in his Indian Summer, and Dreiser's widower in "The Lost Phoebe." Again, there are creations in which the ideas of the author are a principal attraction because of their gleaming outline or pervading grandeur— *Everyman,* the *Utopia, Pilgrim's Progress,* "The Vision of Mirza," *Jonathan Wild, Rasselas,* "The Great Stone Face," *Erewhon,* "The Man Without a Country," *Crainquebille,* and *The Bridge of San Luis Ray.*

All three of the elements I have so far cited—image, character, idea—are, as we have seen elsewhere, varieties of pattern. But it is pattern as patterning, the formative principle in the artist as the inspired craftsman, that most often evokes a cry of homage—at the wonderful delineation of Flaubert or Turgenev, the amazingly supple characterization of Jane Austen and Henry James, or the illuminating exposition of principle or concept in George Eliot, Stendhal, Thomas Mann, or Aldous Huxley. There are, furthermore, in the formal aspect of conflict, opportunities for structural beauty which arise from the relations of action and time. The writer who can discipline the tensions of past, present, and future into a climax which rises harmoniously to a rounded satisfaction will be the envy and the model of others who wish to produce fictions of technical beauty: Poe, de Maupassant, Howells in *The Lady of the Aroostook,* Edith Wharton in *Ethan Frome,* Conan Doyle, Galsworthy, May Sinclair, Joyce in *Portrait of the Artist,* Mann in "Death in Venice," and "Mario and the Magician," and Proust in the central gift of his genius.

I take it that beauty of style is a reality which no observant reader would have to be argued into accepting, and that few if any of the writers I have named in the last two or three paragraphs would be denied credit for it; but I cannot fail to add a tribute, however brief, to the literary genius of Swift, Voltaire, Peacock, Thackeray, Meredith, Stevenson, Kipling, George Moore, Sarah Orne Jewett, Ellen Glasgow, Katherine Mansfield, Somerset Maugham, Sylvia Townsend Warner, and D. H. Lawrence in his more elevated moments, as in *The Virgin and the Gypsy.* Finally, since the question of beauty is properly one of feeling, there is the very great fictional art of creating the mood itself. Here the superb talent of Poe is bewildering in its riches. Not only do most of his finest tales proceed by stages of brooding, unease, premonition, foreboding, and terror to the climactic frenzy of panic; but the appeal to the eye in his work has the glow of color in lacquer, and the canvas magically sings through the lyricism of the language. He settled the question for all time of whether art can render even the ugly beautifully; his effect, as he boasted, is single, but with a singleness issuing from and triumphing over multiplicity. His name is deservedly the hall-mark of the fiction of mood; but he is not alone, and taking into consideration the varieties of mood due to differences in temperament, he is nobly companioned by some of those I have already mentioned in other connections: Bunyan, Voltaire, Sterne, Peacock, Meredith, Hawthorne, Turgenev, Dostoievsky, James, Conrad, Moore, Katherine Mansfield, and D. H. Lawrence.

Since it is beauty of mood we are thinking of, and therefore the mood that possesses us in the experience of beauty, the discussion can be appropriately rounded out by tribute to an artist who dedicated her life almost to beauty alone. In "Coming, Aphrodite!" in "Paul's Case," in the three tales of *Obscure Destinies,* in the short novels *A Lost Lady* and *My Mortal Enemy,* and in the longer ones, *My Antonia, One of*

*Ours, Death Comes to the Archbishop, Shadows on the Rock,
Lucy Gayheart,* and *Sapphira and the Slave Girl,* Willa Cather
has given the world a fiction which is beauty itself. What is
repeated until it is characteristic can hardly be accidental;
quite apart from her own declarations, the tendency of her
work must be regarded as the result of a deep urge; not the
sentimental silliness which proclaims that life is always beautiful, but the unshaken conviction that it often is, and that its
actualities so recognized have in themselves value and romance and drama. Since the beauty she presents is what she
found in this world, it has its material phase; no attentive
reader of "Coming, Aphrodite!" or *Death Comes to the Archbishop* will have to be informed that this author can select
and attend to a lovely object and render it in the full glory
of its being. To her pictorial power she often adds the auditory; "A Wagner Matinée," *The Song of the Lark,* and the
rehearsal scenes in *Lucy Gayheart* are flooded with imagined
tones of great music, an illusion fit to be mentioned with the
nameless air of Wordsworth's Highland girl. That Miss
Cather is intent upon the spiritually, no less than on the
physically, beautiful is clear in "The Sculptor's Funeral" and
"Old Mrs. Harris"; and in neither of these, nor in *The Professor's House* or *One of Ours,* is there any message of shal-
low blissfulness. Beauty, truth, goodness have their obstacles
and struggles; they are paid for with sacrifice and perhaps
heartbreak; but then sometimes they come. They have their
social significance, both for the aspiring and the unwitting; in
our time there have been more plainly explicit presentations
of the idea of liberty, but none profounder than the study
which is embodied in *Sapphira and the Slave Girl.* The beauty
of life when it is beautiful is a passion in Willa Cather, a passion romantically beating in the heart, but steadily observed
by the eyes, and conveyed with classic lucidity and ease. I am
not saying that the beauty of her art is the highest. The
streaming wildness of *Wuthering Heights* is raised to the
sublime, and the beauty of Conrad's illusion rises above delineation to inspired vision. What I am stressing in Miss
Cather's contribution is its singleness. This I believe to be her
originality—to achieve in story after story the high and august
mood of beauty by setting up before us the things that evoke
it. Moore attempts this too, and so does Lawrence; but they
do not unfailingly reach it, and what is to be subtracted from
their performances is that they too rarely purify themselves of
the presence of a beautiful Moore or a beautiful Lawrence.
By contrast, there has never been a technique more cunning

and trained in the detection and rooting out of exhibitionism, or more determinedly against obvious "style," than Miss Cather's assured patience in waiting for the word that is right because no one will even notice how unforced and simple it is. She has kept her consciousness, like a studio, bare of trash. Anyone who is spontaneously human can live in her books as in all lovely places, wonderfully, happily, and freely.

Without abating one jot of what I have said of my love of beauty or my veneration for those who can create it, I am no aesthete to set up beauty as the sole criterion of art. Besides, although the study of beauty is valuable and of deep interest, who can doubt that the obsession to make it the final standard and the invariable mark of great art has been one of the nightmare curses of criticism? This monomania is the very heart and brain and nerve of Philistinism, for it is the core of the Philistinism of the professing anti-Philistine. Not only criticism, but art itself, is hag-ridden with this one-eyed fixation. The artist creates what he wishes and needs to. The rest is the verdict of time. If his work gives his generation and succeeding ones any of the sorts of experience for which we go to art, he is acknowledged. That beauty is one of these experiences, and a very great one, is not arguable historically; but there *are* others. Discussion on this point is of value only for the uninformed. Otherwise the issue is about as fruitful as the debate between those who contend that propaganda cannot be art, and those who contend that, no propaganda, no art. On the one hand, sermons in stones are proscribed by fiat; on the other, nothing may be called a book unless one can first prove that it is a book—with the literary element literally explicit, as with alphabet noodles in soup. So with the issue over the indispensability of beauty. In nature we find both rainbow and gorilla. Art is a general creativity of which beauty is one department. In expressing this view, in subscribing to it and calling it mine, I am not claiming that is every one's, or should be. All that I assert is that I hold it, emphatically. As to the propriety of such hot affirmation, this is my chapter on emotion.

The bread-and-beans quality of Defoe *is* Defoe. He is not without moments of beauty, as a plain face may take on a light from within, but these exceptions prove the homeliness the rule. Whereas another writer might present the dull or the repellent by beautiful technical means, Defoe never lays himself out to do so. He will give a glimpse of a lovely land-and-sea-scape in *Robinson Crusoe*. Or he will permit himself

—briefly—an exquisiteness of feelings, as when Moll, who does not dare reveal herself to her son while he converses with her as a stranger, as soon as he has gone away flings herself down to kiss the spot of ground he was standing on. Generally, however, Defoe has as little time for such luxuries as his characters have. In our private lives we are occasionally amazed to learn that some person we have paid little attention to, because of no apparent promise of interest, was once the center of heroic or horrible or scandalous action. Defoe's people would be like that in the life, until confidence opened their lips in reminiscence. He conceived them so because, having no condescension toward them, he was relieved of any need to make them seem more than they were. It is therefore enough for us, in learning the facts about them, to realize, not what our average is like, but what it can be made to sustain. The relative lack of expressed emotion is no bar to our appreciating the strains and stresses of feeling that must have been the blurred accompaniment of the vicissitudes; we recollect the dumbness of our own responses to many crises; and we come away with a new respect for what men in the millions can take before death takes them off.

The emotional element is not the obvious one in Defoe; he is none the less grand, with a certain plain grandeur of the race. Perhaps this is beauty. Whatever he may say in so many words, his tone is matter-of-fact. This businesslike attitude of his characters, their unaffectedly behaving like ordinary men and women to whom extraordinary things have happened, makes our sense of the heroic in them all the stronger when at length it comes to us. Since his tone is much the same in narrating any episode, even one of lust, crime, or hideous suffering, it gives to the degraded aspect of life, so lurid when we romanticize it out of our ignorance, a mean sordidness. He interests us in the seamy, but leaves it unattractive; it has its ups and downs, like everything else; but as it actually works out, it is no more romantic than anything else. We come away from the reading with the common sense conclusion that there could hardly be any point in exchanging our fairly decent dullness for dullness only of another sort. In addition, we have the opportunity of observing how the actors of supposedly thrilling adventures not only soon sink to a jogging routine in them, but struggle, and often pitifully, to get back to some center of everyday averageness and peace. From this inference we may, if we are so minded, draw the further one that the Defoe of the *Essay on Projects* would have us draw: we manage life badly if people who at bottom are very much like ourselves are thrust down into misfortune until the harm of their fellows becomes their only trade of survival.

Again and again the history of fiction has proved that the man who writes about ugly and painful and disgusting things may have motives which, when we see them clearly, are perhaps not beautiful, but beyond doubt admirable. He writes for an ultimate happiness, though certainly not to give immediate pleasure. Unless fiction is to be cut off from existence except along only pleasant routes, indeed unless it is merely a trap-door escape from reality, there must be not only tolerance but encouragement of art that renders the fact of the repulsive in life by symbols of the presence of revulsion in the soul. In so far as the ugly thing is regarded as irremovable, imaginative literature can make our need to cope with it vivid, and provide a kind of rehearsal to live with it better than we might without hearsay acquaintance. In so far as it is regarded as corrigible or destructible, then art is an appeal as well as an instruction to our action. When the shocking thing reported in a story speaks the author's outrage that it should exist, he has already done his share; when it bespeaks a gloating foulness in him, we can see our duty. This could hardly stop at expunging a book from the context of society, granted that it should even begin with that. The text might better be allowed to stand as a clinical demonstration of something pathological, of so dreadful a disease in our values as to infect one sick fool with perverted glee.

When a Defoe or a Zola or a Dos Passos or a Farrell leads us to the site of the revolting, his motive, I repeat, may be simply a love of people showing itself at the moment as a blazing hate for what man has done to man. Without this love, the scholar is a pendant in perpetual flight from error, the statesman is the major-domo of a coterie, the priest is a termite in God's house, and the artist is the accomplished ape of better men. There are other ways in which human love of humanity can show itself, and I am sure I have explained how Dickens and James and Willa Cather have expressed some of these; but the love that cannot be silent in the presence of brother's or neighbor's misfortune is as true and as good as any. Beauty and ugliness, furthermore, are not always easy to discriminate. In life (as the matter or model for art) they often come not only together, but as one. A most insidious instinct in our shrinking from what is dreadful may be part of some fascination we feel for the thing that makes us recoil. On the other hand, doing good deeds for the glut-

171

tony of pride brings virtue down to the rating of temptation. Even for the senses the demarcation of beauty and ugliness is not necessarily obvious: a color as magnificent as eye ever saw may gush from the mouth and nose of a person terribly injured. The coward cries out or runs. The pervert slavers; for him there is art for art's sake even where there is no art. Sane health sustains the shock for kindness' sake, and though it cannot aid, gives at least what comfort the face of solicitude may offer.

As with life, so with art. If Dreiser, for example, could not be said to love his species, it certainly had his good will. In his eyes, it handled its affairs pretty badly. It muddled, and not through. Sometimes it was muddled, and got to suspect it, like Eugene Witla; sometimes it was muddled without ever suspecting it, like Carrie Meeber; sometimes it muddled dumbly into irretrievable tragedy, like Clyde Griffiths. To Dreiser who, whatever his faults, saw life steadily and earnestly, this was really too bad. No species that can help itself should ever become Jennie Gerhardt or Frank Cowperwood, and surely not again and again. The conclusion is so clearly right, and the instances Dreiser presents are so plainly the unvarnished truth, that to be finicking about the man's owlish philosophizings, or his *rus-in-urbe style* (it is often quite bad, but identifiably a style) is to exhibit a talent for lingering over irrelevancies. If a man shows me something real, as no one else has ever done, who am I to reject the service because the manner and the speech are uncultivated? In his revelation he is a better man than I, and I will learn from him what he can teach me. I will not make jokes about his grammar or his parroting what he has read, for the simple reason that to do so is too easy: the really hard trick is to refrain. As for his views on sex, which caused such a hullaballoo still echoed in some quarters, why, they have taken on, in the flow of time, a quaint primness, as of the sampler or Marie Stopes. But his depiction of the workings out of sex in certain lives is as faithful to reality today as when he wrote.

Those studies are solid ugliness as it lives and appears, all the truer in the presentation because the man who made them was really absorbed in the task of conveying something as he saw it. I would not exchange one of them for all the pretty-pretty of the magazines, the movies, and the radio. I would set all of them on a level with the beauties of Willa Cather. I would say that no American writing fiction in the contemporary world of either of these two equaled either of them in seeing and painting American life by the particular light of the artist's personal view. There are fine things in American life, and Miss Cather has recorded them—together with subordinate and scathing criticisms, as one may see in the superb quiet scorn of "A Sculptor's Funeral," and the even-handed justice of *Sapphira and the Slave Girl*. Then there is a contrasted phase, equally American, which by metaphor I will call the life lived out in the shadow and grime and discord of city El lines. That life is passing with the demolition of the overhead structures and the cleaning out of township junk-piles; it lingers in the juke-box honky-tonk and along Tobacco Road. When it goes altogether, *Twelve Men* and *Jennie Gerhardt* will be American primitives, not all of an era, but an aspect of an era which no later period will ever care to look like. If Dreiser comes to be dated, he himself will have done much to bring his own quaintness about; but perhaps the date will be a commemoration in literary history. His ugly theme and unlovely writing may prove no more a barrier to reading interest than Defoe's. Something in the man had a power to make things, and to make him an individuality. On the American literary landscape he stands like a gnarled old giant of a tree that thrust itself up out of our soil, unsymmetrical and unkempt, but towering.

When I spoke of emotion as the climate of consciousness, one of the things I had in mind was the climate of hatred. Some writers of fiction hate evil with a merciless blaze of the equator. The vision of suffering and injustice will not let them be. It seems to them needless and hideous to an extent beyond belief, so that no matter how often and how bitterly they paint it, they always feel that they have failed. As in some tropical countries an attempt seems to be made to match the torrid weather with a cookery that burns the insides, so these artists feed on a diet unbearable to the unaccustomed, and place it before their readers as their guests. Well advised or not, the hospitality is quite sincere. It is certainly consistent. Even when the ugliness presented is seasoned with satire, the mockery has a cayenne quality that withers the palate. It is altogether proper to decline such diet, and it is quite fair to say that the intensity is one-sided and disagreeable. It is another matter to say that it is not art. There are readers who go to Swift or Defoe or Zola for some reputed salaciousness or other sensationalism, but remain to think, and then to admire something other than the original lure. Not all of these share with the authors their fixity of gaze upon what they would like to see burned or blasted out of the world.

Some do; many others not only do not, but are people of catholic taste and of a judgment willing to hear all sides. There is a public of this strong-stomached sort. It is often comparatively large during the writer's lifetime, and sometimes persists long afterward, waning and waxing with circumstances, but persisting. This amounts to more than coterie; and although it is believable that there a cult of the ugly or the cruel exists, that fact alone cannot account for all the numerous faithful. Just as in painting there has persisted a sizable audience for Goya and Hogarth and Daumier, so there has always been an audience for Rabelais, Swift, Voltaire, Stendhal, Balzac, and Zola.

To equate this audience exactly with that of the pornographers is to collapse into abuse and bluster. True, there has never been any definition of pornography that has got itself universally agreed upon. But who needs any such definition? No adult really needs to have pornography defined. Its leer and cackle give it away at fifty feet. As for the challenge, "Would you put this book into the hands of a little girl of five?" it is never—in all the years of my life I have never once known it to be—an honest question, but only an especially nasty insult, the one little shred of vitality that keeps mental impotence alive. The question seems to triumph, very often, because the one at whom it is discharged is apt to be the kind of person to be suddenly disabled by pity for the helplessly mean face before him. How is one to instruct a man who cannot realize how often he is suffered in silence by the compassion of people who do not hurt those they can see through? There, in a nutshell, is the whole survival of the bore. Do not believe that there are bores who don't know it. I include the foul-minded with the prurient, and with them both the nonentities who cannot resist the safety of assuming a position morally unassailable—that is, while some hue and cry is on. It's as good, really, as trying to live a moral life. Meanwhile, above the controversy, there looms the assailed talent which has created a powerful illusion of reality that is hard and sour and unflattering, and, by the current *mores,* unpardonbale. This, too, is art. In our own times it has numbered among its representatives some of the most notable careers. There are differences according to whether the artist has expressed the ugly beautifully, tragically, comically, drably, or uglily—but scan a partial list: Gissing, Butler, Wells, Galsworthy, Conrad, May Sinclair, Lawrence, Huxley, Anatole France, Proust, Gide, Silone, Deledda, Gorki, Wasserman, Mann, Werfel, Feuchtwanger, the Zweigs, Kafka, Rolvaag, Hamsun, Undset, Norris, Dreiser, Cabell, Upton Sinclair, Dos Passos, Sinclair Lewis, Anderson, Wolfe, Hemingway, Faulkner, Farrell, Steinbeck, Callahan, Wright, and Weidman.

What has become of the character all black or all white? We take it for granted, do we not, that we are a mixture of good and bad? That, at any rate, is how we know ourselves in our heart of hearts. It is how we really expect to be regarded by others, though naturally we would all like a little more in the way of credit than our heart of hearts would grant to be our just due. So the person who seems an angel or a devil evokes suspicion long before he does any other response. The way we regard people is the way we regard characters in stories. It is enjoyable for some people, and for all people some of the time, to meet and identify themselves with heroes and heroines of whom nothing appears that is not admirable; but when there is a mixture of qualities, we know very well that that is how life really is. This tacit agreement of imperfection represents a high standard of civilization, and is therefore not easy for a reader to maintain—or an author. Moreover, it leaves the reservoir of human cussedness, which must be drained by Aristotelian catharsis, at times somewhat full. We perhaps effect a sort of discharge in our light reading and our movies, which have with cathartics the common quality of not needing to be true. Of course, if there were enough good books for constant reading, we could get the relief from them; for the honestly varied character, who is by turns noble, detestable, weak, wise, intelligent, and foolish, really gives us a workout. In calling forth so many contrasted feelings, he exercises our emotional nature in his own way. To observe him is as strenuous as swimming steadily along, keeping the entire musculature constantly at work.

In establishing and continuing a conflict, even the naturalistic novel derives its seeming truth to life from what we know about ourselves and this determines our changing feelings towards the characters and their fate, their emotions, their lives and their unique natures. If a character is courageous, we may share his courage. In the same way, we may identify ourselves with suffering, or pity it; or we may regard it impatiently if we believe that it comes from a silly, unreal standard, rather than from a veritable cause. While we are lost in the illusion, we are kept too busy in the experience to be analytical about it; in retrospect we recognize how true to life the author has been. In Proust, for example, the action proceeds by presentation and analysis of impressions, a dissection in which reason is the scalpel, laying feeling bare for appraisal. From this analysis judgments emerge, as we gradually realize, for example, that the only person presented by the narrator for our unqualified affection is his grandmother, who is also the only person devoted to him with utter self-sacrifice. Whether this self-betrayal of a brilliantly perceptive intellect is the central triumph of Proust's art or the Achilles' heel of his skepticism, I do not pretend to know. As for the other personages, each is good and bad. The Verdurins, who are certainly keen discoverers of talented people, are otherwise paltry souls; the Guermantes are by no means ideal, though in general superior; Swann's powers end disappointingly; and Charlus, in view of his helplessness as one cursed, has many moments of undeniable magnificence. By the time we come to the last volume, good and bad have not so much disappeared as been flattened to one unimportance. One feels that they drew their earlier significance from the youthful greenness of the hero in his acceptance of what he was told and in his romanticizing of it. In time, the conclusion seems to imply, all cats are grey; that is, all selves are ego.

Whereas Proust's masterpiece rounds itself out with self-hypnosis, Joyce's work tends increasingly as it goes along to speak in terms of self-rejection. In a letter to a friend he once wrote that his purpose in *Dubliners*, his fictional first-born, was to damn existence in his native Dublin as "paralysis." There is not a story in the book that does not do this, so that to deny that Joyce is a writer of strenuous social views is all the more amusing. (Was there ever a critic who demanded that art teach something, who did not have in mind precisely what the lesson should be, so that he could deny that any other was a lesson at all.) Considering that there are only fifteen short stories in *Dubliners*, the reader will find the coverage of human activities surprisingly extensive and varied, and since in every story some cherished human desire is indirectly disclosed as based on illusion, the effect of the little book is progressively, though subtly, devastating. People are shown as prizing what really does not exist, or else they become painfully aware of how their trust has deceived them. In "The Dead," Gabriel Conroy, after an evening of almost solid happiness, symbolic of his acceptance of life as good, discovers that he can never give his lovely wife, nor have from her, the intensity of love that lies buried with her girlhood suitor. "Eveline" is the story of a girl so conditioned to the life she thinks she wishes to leave that not even love can tear her roots out of it; what she assumes without examination to be her mature womanhood simply does not exist, but she has no way of knowing that. Perhaps the most typical of all the tales, and certainly the most explicit on the theme of disillusion, is "Araby." A half-grown boy throws his heart into a romantic little pilgrimage, only to find that what he has prized so confidently is trash. The closing words are confession and protest: ". . . I saw myself as a creature driven and derided by vanity; and my eyes burned with anguish and anger." Values that are imaginary, or that break like reeds when experience leans on them, are the thematic material of the book; and Joyce's attitude toward standards and their relevance for emotion is therefore like Proust's in taking the form of critical attack. Since Joyce's art is to give only obliquely what Proust details with minute particularity, the little tales read as though innocent of purpose, and their ostensible tone is that of aloof, reserved irony. Yet the better acquainted with them the reader becomes, the more he grows aware of a quality of sentiment like a faint perfume—the author's regret for a Dublin lost to him, the city of his young illusions, all vanished. The nostalgia lingers over the precise naming of streets and shops, in small details of evidently preserved recollection, and especially in the nice identification of each of the touching faiths represented as infallibly doomed. There is a melancholy that pervades the volume, as real and as reticent as Hawthorne's, but inherent in the object and no longer stirring the author's heart except as a farewell tribute to the past.

In *Portrait of the Artist as a Young Man* the theme gives the book its structure: a young life grows up amid standards alien to it, which must all be tragically stripped away at the end. The nameless boy of "Araby" has advanced to the stripling Stephen, who little by little is forced back on himself by his environment. He suspects and hates his cultural pattern, and resolves to battle it with "silence, exile, and cunning," and "to forge in the smithy of my soul the uncreated conscience of my race." When we meet him again in *Ulysses*, the heart has gone out of the struggle. The exile has returned to dreary, insecure scratching for bare and unclean subsistence. His "cunning" makes witticisms and critical sophistries for the bewildered amusement of those it scorns. The "silence" is a sickening drift of consciousness, troubled by erudite speculations, and the plain fact of failure. A young man understands that the achievement of his boyhood dreams lay altogether in the dreaming of them, that he can no longer dream of achieving them. His day, as the novel reports it, is a steady break up and dissolution of a superb awareness under the relentless analysis of self-contempt and drunkenness.

The companion picture of Bloom as the "scientific" or at any rate "practical" mind is equally a presentation of dissolving patterns: an incorrigible optimism that cannot gull itself long; an inventive practicality too practical not to discard each invention quickly as unpracticable; a survival by the desire to go on without satisfactio nof desire. Finally there is Molly, a presentation of the self at the moment of disintegration into sleep, a consciousness dissolving into its component forms, like a city broken down into a mob in the terrible equality of devolution, a symbol of the earth's crust compacted of seeds and death and warmed with the will of driving pointlessness. She is the consciousness when it is reduced almost to the flesh, so that her shapeless and sodden awareness is the last stage of Stephen's futile reasoning, tumbled out of heaven by a witless sun which both melts the Daedalian wings and indifferently lights the fall. Thus at last the distrust of patterns turns on the patterer, the consciousness which deceives itself as to the very form of its skepticism. One may regard *Ulysses* as Joyce's agreement with a certain age-old criticism of fiction, namely, that it romanticizes and falsifies life. But he seems to find the indictment true only in so far as it holds even more strongly against life; and his novel reads like a titanic effort to expose the double falsification at one great stroke.

In *Finnegans Wake*, under the protective rationalization that what is presented is the state of the mind in sleep, the consciousness whirls anonymously in the rain of its own atoms, all its fragmentary powers gaping with the empty suggestions of what they cannot actually become. The blade of night, cutting the knotted mystery of sentience, has precipitated the flying fibres into a hurricane, and there they dart and circle and circle. Life and death merge namelessly. The body teems with purgative and restorative powers. The mind is dispersed and driven matter. In the morning, a self-cleansed personality will again take on the delusion of self, and by that act will reconstitute space and time and all their resident phantoms. Joyce and Proust are as like as the poles, a world apart. The epicurean Frenchman built the ego into a richly elaborate design, as though of a king's garden viewed from the highest window of the palace; the Irish stoic starved consciousness to the bare grinning skull. The one devoted a career to making his meaning as clear as possible, the other to a relentless pursuit of the possibility that there is no such thing as meaning, at any rate in the sense that meaning has always been used. Neither of the two can, by the conditions of his art, have any readers save those capable of applying an unusually exercised strength to the reformulation of their own views.

Perhaps it is because Mann is more orthodox than Proust or Joyce in his faith that he is the most old-fashioned in his technical art. By every sign a deeply religious man and a stalwart democrat, he is a shining instance of what novelties can be made out of familiar values by the gifts and the exertions of the creative soul. The artist must withdraw to privacy while he works, to his work-room and to his consciousness. To Mann this necessity is cause for neither snobbery nor self-pity. Since it is a need, it is an honorable obligation, though in some ways a matter for regret. A literary man is a man like any one else, but differs in the respect of his craft; he has to maintain a balance between the resemblance and the difference. Above all, it is bad for him to get out of touch with his kind; and Mann keeps in touch, both in his disposition and in his expression. No matter how far afield he may guide his readers, he starts them from the general headquarters, and periodically returns them there for the comforts of home. His inclusiveness, and his harmonizing of elements ordinarily considered opposed he practices as a matter of philosophical and religious principle, but also more profoundly by nature, as a matter of course. His standing as one of the most cultivated men in the contemporary world therefore rests on the cultivation of his heart; the light and wealth of his mind and the supple beauty of his art are outgrowths of that sound affection and reinforce its development in others as in himself. He has enjoyed world-wide popularity in addition to fame, and has merited both. A man who starts with the love of life and truth is a spirit cleared of the lumber of prejudice. His consciousness is like a virgin continent whose hospitality is its capaciousness. I find this magnanimity basic in Mann, accounting for everything else in him, even for certain shortcomings. If, for example, one is to be so clear that readers of no great brain or culture may find one's teaching not too hard to follow, then not only must every *i* be dotted, and every *t* be crossed, but the lesson must be periodically re-stated, so that what is new in spite of all its clearness may be made to sink into the mind's confidence about it. The teacher is a little the drillmaster; but there are always pupils in the class who feel that some of the difficulties have been somewhat over-appraised, who wish that the pace might be smarter, who wonder whether the teacher may not be enjoying the routine as such simply because he knows how adept he is at it. Furthermore, although this Macaulay-like pedagogics has a most gracious humaneness of motive, the graciousness itself is conscious. It too is practiced. It is tender, it is genial, it is playful—and it is condescending. It does not jibe, or turn sarcastic, but it might as well. For whether it is the reader who is elaborately worked over, or the character who is patted on the head to show how goodnaturedly a low grade may be announced, what is really being polished off is the beaming smile of benevolence. If only the kindness were not rubbed in so!

Without these faults, Mann would be superhuman. Also, the faults are not vicious, but only a little vain. They represent an excess of virtue doubling on itself. Indeed, they may not be personal at all, but national, or perhaps more fairly, European. The meek outlander is a little touched to note that a certain condescension, observed of old in the address of visiting foreigners, may actually be no more than something they practice at home upon each other. Yet one must regret that charity, the aristocrat of the virtues, should (like everything else, of course) have gone class-conscious. When Proust over-elaborates some detail of exegesis, his mistake lies in believing that the lesson is too hard; when Mann does it, he seems to go on the principle that the pupil may be expected to be a little dull. Joyce, in refusing to abate one jot of the difficulty, in fact by screwing any difficulty a little tighter, implies a high valuation of our native powers, if only we could be roused from parasitic sloth to develop them further. He is, of course, contemptuous; but far less of our attainments than of our smugness in being less than we can.

I hope that my exceptions to the manner of Mann's mind will not be regarded as my whole view of him. The faults I have noted I consider a very small price to pay for the far more numerous and characteristic benefits of true wisdom and kindness. There has been no greater, truer heart in contemporary literature; and whatever the lapses of his manner, his vision is almost unbelievably perceptive, penetrating, and retentive. In whatever he sees, he sees all of the aspects, and not as a conceptual pattern, but in organic oneness. His characters are rendered in the attributes of good, evil, beauty, ugliness, perception, dullness, modesty, conceit—briefly, in the life. The confusion which Proust re-patterns into an explorable maze, and which Joyce presents as raw dominance, Mann simply includes, as the average man finds it puzzlingly included in his world, but not to the point of making the world seem paralyzing in its obscurity. There is a great deal more in our universe than meets the eye; but much of it does meet the eye, and the eye gets much of that pretty plainly, and recognizes it for what it is. Mann, as I say, penetrates the ordinary to its extraordinary core; but he does not omit the familiar. Rather, he holds to it, and thus allows us the comfort of its familiarity even while he disturbs us with intimations of our dreadful doubt and ignorance, as in *The Magic Mountain,* or of foul obscenities bordering our loveliest feelings, as in "Siegmund and Sieglinde" or "Death in Venice." When the evil is plain, when it divides man from man, he attacks it vehemently, as he does in his pieces dealing with the relation of art to living people. Emotions as the average man knows them, the peaceful and the beautiful as well as the painful and the terrifying, are alive on his every page. They vibrate in his colorful painting of the illusion of scenic background, buildings, people, even animals; they animate his intelligence; they are the music and rhythm of his superb prose. His condescension and banter are hearty with them, his justice is impassioned. Of all the intellectuals of this portion of the twentieth century, he is the warmest, not only with the heat of controversy, but with the natural temperature of the human blood.

The subtlest aspect of feeling in fiction or in any art lies in the mystery of what makes a good subject for writing, or a good book to read. The story sense, as it is sometimes called, is an instantaneous apprisal in which the writer recognizes or at least suspects) certain material to be *his* the moment it presents itself to him. Depending on his way of working, he may know it to be sufficient at it comes, and may be right or wrong about that; or he may realize that what has come is clay that must be shaped. One way or the other, what is touched off in him is intuition, the electricity in the brain doing its own thinking, cognition stripped to its speed and flash like miniature lightning. Afterward, this may in the best sense of the term be rationalized into reasons and reasoning; indeed, for purposes that demand analytical construction, it must be. But what makes possible the elicitation of such intuition is that, in all common sense, it is "there."

One of the troubles with people who declare that they do not believe in intuition is their failure to take into account that, like everything in nature, it may evolve; that there is,

I mean, such a thing as trained or even sophisticated intuition. A writer's native sentience may be enhanced by what it acquires in the way of learning. As the great specialist in medicine is envied by colleagues for his clinical eye without any denigration of his erudition, so the artist may grow in his power to size up his inspiration. Any responses of the adept artist not pertinent to, and therefore tending to operate against, the production of the one desired effect would tend simply and quickly to fall away, and the surviving single sharpened apprehension would give off the glow of a signal. In a tale by Poe, accordingly, the story progresses from nervous exhaustion at the beginning, through stages of aroused agitation and shuddering, to the frenzy of the last outcry. The character would be stripped to such specialized aspects as would promote the fulfillment of the more dominant fictional elements by offering them a cooperation of the least possible resistance; while on the other hand, the literary element, in lyric language and rhythm, would announce emotion by secret contagion.

I have used Poe as a first example in this exposition of the role of emotion in determining the choice of subject, only because it seemed sensible to pave the way with an instance in which emotion is pervasive and obvious—as of course it is, though in such varied ways, in Hawthorne, Peacock, D. H. Lawrence, and Katherine Mansfield. Yet the role is equally ascertainable in fiction where emotion is subordinated as satire or tenderness to other purposes, as in Anatole France, Mann, Galsworthy, "Saki," and Ring Lardner. In still others, it is the less evident but still detectable temper of the author's drive toward an effect not immediately one of feeling: the well-bred but avid curiosity of James, the steady joy in beauty of Willa Cather, in Turgenev the brooding that has survived heartbreak, the ironic hate in Swift's heart, the easier irony in Butler's mind. Even in two samples from an author with only one characteristic mood in which emotion is not the principal presentation, this story will be marked off from that story if only by the quality of an additional feeling mixed in with the basic one; distinguishing, for example, *The Isle of Penguins* from *Crainquebille*. The presence of emotion of some sort in the inspiration, that is, in the original choice of subject, is an influence which, when it is not definitive, is never less than contributive. This is true of fiction which is markedly of ideas, as I have just hinted. Ideas, as we conceive them abstractly in a sort of timeless absoluteness, seem as unmoved as statuary, and may actually be of this impersonal unfeelingness of which our concepts of them would then be appropriately symbolic; nevertheless, in our experience of them they often appear with the complexion and tone of live being, a complexion and a tone not changeless, but modulated with the season and the very moment. Let them but enter our flux, and they are flooded with it. Quixote charges the windmill, Crusoe sees the footprint, Eliza flees across the ice, and Ahab pursues the white whale—amid the words of monologue and text but not *as* words—no, as illusion by imagery in motion, as ideas powerfully and irrationally *felt*.

Chapter 7

Idea

IT HAS AT TIMES occurred to me that ideas are difficult to describe not only because they lack physical appearance as people and houses have it, but because in their physical imperceptibility they take on a variety of forms, so that any notion of ours as to what an idea is, would necessarily take on this protean character of the original. For example, triangularity and ugliness are ideas. In our experience of them, they produce concepts of themselves, or (as one prefers) are so constructed by our conception. In other words, what are called ideas are also called concepts, and they have also been called qualities, properties, essences, eternal objects, and so on. The verbal symbols are important as attempts at accurate designation; they are not the thing itself. That reality, correspondent to the name, is plainly not the name, but what makes some name necessary, simply by being, and by being experienced. Of course, if its being were outside our experience, we should not need to call it anything. For example, horses and whales and worms, so far as we have evidence, do not call the idea anything, and therefore may be presumed to have no need. The necessity appears to be human, and so the idea of idea survives from century to century. It has engaged some of the most famous thinkers of our race in the effort to determine its nature, and has been used with confidence and ordinary practicality by millions. Ideas are also regarded as abstractions and logical propositions; they are named not only by abstract nouns (sovereignty, statehood, sweetness), but implied by modifiers (sweet, loud, round), or by verbs (declare, linger, be), or by phrases, as in definition by synonyms, or by whole sentences, as in the imperatives of religion, the terms of the syllogism, the equations of mathematics, the hypotheses and laws of science. As guides to other ideas, conceived or acted upon, they are principles; as orientations of thought and behavior, principles are associated into attitudes of mind. An attitude persisting in any one or any group or society is habit or custom or typicality. In fact, the type, as we have seen, is an idea; and a type regarded as desirable or perfect or lying entirely in the future is an ideal. So that whether all these protean forms of the idea are real or delusory, they are recognizable ingredients or aspects of fiction, constituting one element of it beyond the permissibility of omission from any study of the whole fiction.

In this chapter I behave toward an idea as most other people do; that is, I treat it as something directly apprehensible by the intellect alone. Negatively, that would mean that ideas are not directly apprehensible by the senses or the emotions. To me, *idea* means that which is entertained directly by the intellect as concern of focus, with relegation of sensation and feeling into disregard. Unless I have been deluded, I commonly entertain ideas just so, and with or without entertaining them, act upon them. I do both in the whole fiction. Stories like *Rasselas, Nightmare Abbey, U. S. A.,* and *The Grapes of Wrath* give ideas explicitly. Any story, to be read at all, as a text and as a private monologue, requires implementation of the meanings of words. Since any element of the fictional medium may be so far the least ostensible as to escape focal attention, certain stories may seem to be utterly without ideas. Yet if there were actually such a species of the art, what unfortunate person could be trusted to make the identification? At one extreme there is the fiction *of* ideas, like *Utopia,* or *The Way of All Flesh;* at the other, there is fiction only *by* ideas; that is, by literary signification and comprehension, as in *Alice in Wonderland,* or any fairy tale that requires only such understanding as is necessary for enjoyment.

When I say that fiction is aquiver with ideas, I have in mind not only the story as an instrument of controversy in so many declarations, nor the story which would present some truth obliquely to win it a welcome of the Trojan horse, but also, and in view of what art is, the kind of novel or tale which has no commerce at all with ideas in their own right, but employs or unwittingly obeys them as a formative element of technique. Such fiction might indeed, by a few scattered epithets of approval or pity or condemnation of some point of view, include the ideational element it appears to omit; but the seeming omission results from the fact that any mentionings of them are lost in the more absorbing shuffle and disregarded by the reader because the preoccupied author has so relegated them himself. That is the way we get the Toryism of Scott (when we do get it), by indirection and secondary inspection and searching review. Does the average reader, especially in childhood, know anything of this? And of course, why should he? Yet Scott's ideas are apprehensible in the alignment of his agents, in their characters as laid down upon either side of the line of controversy; for though *he* is characteristically no doctrinaire in his discourse, *they* most assuredly are doctrinaires by the sword and the bow. They are the controversialists of ambuscade and battlefield and race against time. Their swarming rivalries are the shock of issues meeting in the armed flesh; and so the large, loose story forms and rages, and its conclusion hangs upon that turn of fortune in which tragedy or triumph marks the championed principle. Scott's sportsmanship acknowledges in the antagonist whose stand he disagrees with such incidental virtues as courage, intelligence, and even sincerity; but these virtues, beyond their service to the conflict in making its thrill more breath-taking, are simply exceptions lighting the basic villainy of the agent's being on the wrong side. The ideas of right and wrong are not deeply examined; they are assumed by inheritance as patrimony and survival, just as, in controversialists of other sorts, the ethical stand is merely espoused. If Scott has lost out among mature readers, it is largely because of this rationalization of an attitude of mere will to mastery, a position we find not only capable of villainy and barbarism on its own, but utterly and pathetically inadequate to the adult-sized problems of a civilization anxious for a future that shall be better than our own age. Whatever it is that will settle the strifes which threaten our posterity, it will be no mere rooting for the home team. So much for the criticism of the ideas embodied by the Waverley novels. The point is that they are there to be criticized or applauded.

In Poe's fantastic romance in which, most readers of him would say, the ideas, if present at all, are not important, they are nevertheless influential in so many ways that one hardly knows where to begin to discuss them. There is, first of all, his aesthetic credo, fortunately formulated in a number of critical essays quite clear in their expression. In these essays he enunciated principles which the inquisitive reader will find operating in the tales. If Poe does not follow them down to the last sub-tenet, he surely does in the large outline. The doctrine of the need to determine the end at some time prior to final composition is exemplified in all his first-class fiction; and its rigid application to the doctrine of the single effect would alone have been enough to make Poe the very classicist of romanticism. The single effect is whatever effect on the reader one wishes to produce; and an indispensable instrument toward the attainment is the idea of what that effect must be. This idea, perhaps of a certain very special pitch and intensity of one discriminated emotion, will determine the selection of the terminal event and image, and they in turn will dominate every antecedent fictional element, including the choice of words. This program, which the detective stories alone indicate was Poe's actual procedure, will be found to apply also to his cunning tales of the grotesque and the arabesque. Behind the horror of "The Pit and the Pendulum," the ratiocinative author (to use his own word) adeptly manipulates the effect so that the reader shall be entirely in its grip, unaware of the careful choice and graduation of the steps of the action.

Not always in his wielding of ideas does Poe confine himself to suppressing them into implementation. When he can strengthen his effect by enunciating ideas, he does not hesitate to do so. "The Descent into the Maelstrom" includes a statement of the nature and action of whirlpools, to the extent of about one-third of the piece. There is an exposition in "The Fall of the House of Usher" of a theory of the sentience of inanimate things, to add to the dread of the collapse of the building. The Inquisition comes in for comment in "The Pit and the Pendulum." Survival after death and transmigration of the soul is dealt with in "Ligeia," where it is the whole point of the horrible climax. There is an explicit treatment of the evils of alcoholism in "The Black Cat." Poe's adroitness in the use of the fictional narrator enables him to shift the responsibility for such ideas to his characters; and the ideas themselves are generally put in as brief substantiation of the narrator's endorsement of some theory difficult to believe, so that the intellectual content is merely one aspect of the emotional content, and is swiftly blotted out of attention by it. Yet, as I say, ideas there are, and they are given in so many words. Poe detested the didacticism that divides interest with the tale, or overpowers it, because to him the supreme effect *was* the tale; but ideas in themselves fictional, because part of the illusion of reasoning on the agent's part, he exploited as he would any other element of the fictional medium. By comparison, Hawthorne, who in many instances had in mind an audience of children as well as adults, seems comparatively unwilling to state ideas that may be beyond his readers' comprehension. I have attempted no statistical count, but after many examinations of the two, I come away with the strong impression that in intellectual content the moralizing allegorist and the "pure" romanticist are about equal.

Granting that this is so, it is interesting to see how in the one man ideas seem to be almost totally absent, and in the other, inescapably prominent. Fiction employs the illusion of physical perceptibility, the characteristic mode of imaginative literature. It does not exclude presentation of ideas; it does not exclude their presentation by directly expository discourse—witness the essay passages, sometimes quite long, in novels by Fielding, George Eliot, Tolstoy, Proust, and Mann. Such sections of discursive prose has been made to stand side by side with those of imaginative narration; for the whole fiction, being the comprehensive reality that it is and not being rigidly comparmented from other literary forms like the essay or the drama or the lyric, has included what it has included, and the rhetoricians have had to make the best of it. On the other hand, no one would assert that it is the essay content of a novel that makes it a novel. Fiction seems most itself as the creation of illusion for experience, least itself as analytical or expository disquisition. With reference to ideas in fiction, we therefore have, not a right method and a wrong one, but one generally preferable and one generally less preferable. So long as direct statement of ideas does not jostle the story constantly out of the limelight, so long as it somehow enhances the illusion, it is all right. But ideas may be conveyed indirectly, by situations that are either plainly illustrative or seemingly independent of the concept which, in fact, they convey. That is why certain episodes in any story have meaning though there is no direct word of it on the page. Now, the point of Poe's fictional art is that it is to be experienced *as fact;* that is, credited as actually occurring, though the assurance rests only on the slightest basis that can support a tendency not to disbelieve. We are in the same case with our superstitions, obsessions, premonitions, and fixations when, instead of reading about them, we really live them. It is this engrossment in the illusion, and not, as we have seen, an absence of ideas, that makes Poe's art the ecstatic thing it is, communicating its intensity of absorption to the accommodated imagery and even to the piercing lyricism of the literary style. The ideas are not apprehended, because they are hidden; the suppression converts their energies into fuel for drive, and their pressure tightens the dramatic tension.

Hawthorne's gentler pensiveness, though usually enveloped in melancholy, is an effect arising from a treatment of illusion quite opposed to Poe's. He enjoins us again and again, not so much against experiencing his inventive illusion, as against making too much of it, lingering over it. He intends it only as an exquisitely diverting preparation; in the simpler tales like "The Great Stone Face" for some explicit moral, and in the subtler ones like "Young Goodman Brown" for some delving on our own part into the psychology of sin. The experience of "The Tell-tale Heart" as provided by Poe is the story; the experience of "Ethan Brand" is provided partly by the story, but also and importantly *by means of* the story. What we do with it and with "Rappaccini's Daughter" in plumbing depth after depth of an implied significance for man as a social being, is what Hawthorne is after. Poe hypnotizes our will to believe; Hawthorne challenges our will to question. In some of his finest pieces, therefore, he deliberately deceives us with an obvious message, in the hope that its very triviality will arouse our impatience to seek out, according to his own phrase, "a more subtile" one. He was the sort of man who could not take his mind off the human sickness in which man is divided from man. He behaved as though to cure this would be to minister to human misery as to a mind diseased. But the medicament must come from within that mind, captivated at first by glow-worm fantasies, then enticed by them into dark recesses of its own anti-social impulse, and so apprised of humanity's need of pity and love. At times the work of this fantasist seems like something halfway between the confessional of the church and the confessional of the psychoanalyst, and there is an episode in *The Marble Faun* which reflects this suggestion most oddly. Hawthorne's symbolism, then, is a reference from his image, not directly to his idea, but, vaguely, to *some* idea, that is, to our own active and uneasy reflection. If one will compare his "Wakefield" and Poe's "The Man in the Crowd," he will find the same theme in both: a study of the psychopathic solitary. Hawthorne's attitude is more unobtrusively sympathetic, and Poe's more brilliantly objective; but Poe makes the type no more attractive than Hawthorne does, and Hawthorne actually offers less of moralizing pronouncement than Poe! Both of them, at any rate, are here symbolists. Apparently, as Dodgson the mathematician sometimes twinkles at us through the mask of Carroll the fantasist, so in the terrible fantasy of Poe there is an occasional gleam of the intellect we meet face to face in the critical and social essays, and in the metaphysical *Eureka*.

I have made Scott and Poe my examples to prove that ideas are actual and influential even in fictions where one might at first hasty reflection deny them importance, if not existence, because it seems to me that once the demonstration concerning them is accepted, it must be presumed to have application elsewhere or anywhere. During the past century and a half, there has grown up an entire social literature of interpretation of ancient myth, fairy-tale, and folklore. One of the general findings has been that tales seemingly expressive of wonder and nothing else are developments out of older materials marked by some such clearly held conceptions as that of the fertility ritual of primitive animism. The gradual and complete obliteration of this initial intellectual content produced the wonder-yarn without ideas from the salvaged and altered imagery which had originally dressed it up, so that the operation of disregard in fiction seems to have social as well as individual aspects. The rediscovery of folklore has resulted in its publication in the original tongue or in translation: and there has also been adaptation of the form and manner for contemporary purposes. Much of the work of the Celtic renascence was along these lines. Cabell and Wilder have done something similar on this side of the water; and Mann's recent work has availed itself of Hindu and Biblical materials. Once again, as in the days of Montesquieu and Voltaire, a troubled age has put a fantastic costume upon its serious symbols. To the international scope of the movement (the names of Maeterlinck, France, Kafka, and Silone belong to it) must be added its invasion of many arts, represented by Rostand, Shaw, Capek, Dali, and Disney. Joyce's nightmare fables of "The Ondt and the Gracehoper" and "The Mokse and the Gripes" in *Finnegans Wake* are only the most bizarre outcroppings of this modern rationalizing of fantasy by extreme indirection. We renew the purposefulness of our forebears in the quaint styles they bequeathed to us.

Before I leave the topic of the kind of fiction in which the idea is least ostensible and so most disregarded, I would like briefly to emphasize certain matters which I have only touched on in passing, but which deserve to be at least singled out for their relevance. For example, although in fictional illusion we may experience conflict without a distinct idea of it, there can be no doubt that one of the things consciousness is responding to is that idea. Children who after a number of years of reading stories hear the word *conflict* explained for the first time have no great difficulty in showing that they know what is meant by it. They have had practice in the idea long before learning that it exists. Dean Woodbridge, in his *Nature,* offers a capital anecdote which may be used in this connection. He says that when a certain little lad saw a dog gnawing a bone, and asked, "What is he doing?" he knew very well what the animal was doing—what he wanted was rather the words which name it. In the same muted way, if at no other level, we know that conflict among characters is to some extent, somehow, conflict about ideas, and therefore conflict *of* ideas. What I am here referring to is not only the struggle that occurs when the agents are ideas personified, as in *The Faerie Queene,* but also the battles and single combats of epic, and the conversational duels to be found, say, in *La Princesse de Clèves* or *The Spoils of Poynton.* That is, certain opposed ideas confront each other in the acts and words of the characters, and the emotional accompaniment to the see-saw of that struggle registers our awareness of the contrasted significances. Human right and tyranny may be Uncle Tom and Simon Legree; human will and natural force, Ahab and Moby Dick; the abstract greater and abstract lesser are the Bull and the Frog, or Gulliver in Lilliput and Gulliver in Brobdingnag.

Ideas may also assist in the illusion of fiction by an incidental appearance as part of the reader's reaction. Of this sort are all aesthetic feelings arising in us as we read with bearing on the story in hand. Books that survive as historical curiosities will often have a quaintness for us that was no part of their composition, when their authors thought of themselves as very radical innovators indeed, in the forefront of progress. In Brooke's *The Fool of Quality* there are pronouncements plainly intended to rout an evil tradition; they come to our ears in pathetic flourishes of naive enthusiasm, yet no less lovably for that. There are moments of Smollett's when his colossal amusement at cruel horseplay makes him an especially nasty brute, fit for one of Hogarth's pillorying portrayals, and lending credibility unaware to Sterne's Smelfungus. There are effects in Dickens intended to be heartrending, and others in Zola intended to be eloquent, and still others in Dreiser intended to be very deep, which have embarrassed their admirers considerably. Maybe I am wrong, but Pearl Buck's earnest love of her kind at times cloys with a little too much of her own meek sisterliness, just as Steinbeck's affection for common men occasionally condescends to make them too damned uncommon. I wonder how much first-hand acquaintance, over how long a period, his picture of the Joads actually represents. They stagger under a hefty dirt-gilding of lyric, applied by a brush frequently blissful with its own rhythms. As for *The Moon Is Down*, I do not enjoy calendar art for themes that can be made bearable only by real feeling. If aesthetic sins such as the few I note can produce such response in me even against those whom I esteem for principle, it is easy to see how a disagreement on the ground of principle itself may give fiction a tension not supplied by the author in his conflict. Pamela's debatable virtue, Kipling on imperialism, de Maupassant or George Eliot on sex, Booth Tarkington or Faulkner on the nature of the American Way—these are matters of controversy in the illusion and the characterization, understood with or without a single didactic sentence.

The accord of views between author and reader may rest on direct expression, but not necessarily. Two people of about the same stamp, who have never met before, may witness something together, and then share a glance. Also there are situations to which the overwhelming majority of people everywhere respond in pretty much the same way, so that only a marked deviation in behavior would call out any expression of attitude. Not to blunder into explicitness about things of this sort is one of the accomplished author's nicest feats of mature tact. Although this is a matter of the man rather than of the technical point of view, it is not hard to understand that the frankly first-personal lends itself to the inclusion of bits of commentative essay. Yet the veiled first person, that is, without the *I*, may confine the creative omniscience to the matter in hand, so that the author refrains from stating his views as such; and the limited third-personal, and the fictitious first-personal of the substitute narrator, will increase the tendency to suppression. They have in fact been used as devices for so doing. Whereas one learns to expect that Feilding or Stendhal, George Eliot, Tolstoy, Proust, or Mann will take a position and enunciate it quite clearly, he also knows that if he wishes to find out how Poe and Flaubert and James and Joyce regard any situation of their creation, he must have a sharp eye about him, and might even have to turn detective or researcher. Between these extremes, there is the large middle ground of every degree of indication, from some mild hint in an adjective or an adverb, as in Howells, to the jocular poke in the ribs of an O. Henry wisecrack. In so far as we read fiction at all to test or to reassure or to improve our standards, or only to exercise them (without knowing it) in diversion, we are bound to respond to the action and characters with some reference to the standards in the book, expressed or implied.

How we do respond, and what we prefer, is a matter of degree. Powerful conviction may be gratified at hearing its outlook spoken, or be irritated by obviousness. Inexperience may be grateful for precise prescription, or wish simply to be included in the superior company without being lectured at. The modulation of ideas in the fictional medium, all the way from downrightness to guarded secrecy, is one of the most important steps an author can take in prefiguring an audience. Besides, there are snobbery and hypocrisy. The author's awareness of social standards is one of his privishings. Most generally, I suppose, he wishes to accord with them, or not to run afoul of them, but either way, he wants to express himself by fresh means. Here is another instance of the Aristotelian dictum on mingling the familiar with the unfamiliar. Sometimes the author wishes to change public opinion. If so, his approach is as important as his attitude, not only with regard to the kind and size of his public, but equally with regard to his originality in creation and in craft. If he is a man of great power in evoking illusion, he may rely instinctively on that, and let his ideas take care of themselves in the story as best they may. If his talent for direct exposition, his eloquence, or charm is unusually winning, his ideas will come to the fore along with the story he is telling about them. Regardless of the style, of course, his convictions are present; his fictions wear them like identification badges. They are his self-expression, or in failure, his unexpressed self. No one ever attacks a thoroughly unprincipled writer (although many people claim they do), because a thoroughly unprincipled writer is lucky if he can get into print on his way to speedy oblivion. Principles may be hateful; they may be ludicrous; but the term *unprincipled* will not serve to define even a hack. If I were to call a writer a great artist only because his ideas were very close to mine, what sort of windbag would that make *me*?

One of the chief expedients of the novelist who does not wish to intrude his ideas upon the text, but who nevertheless intends that they shall be conveyed, is to limit *explicitness* to the illusion in such a way as to arouse our private comment as we read. The author can count on producing certain reflections along lines of certain social beliefs as held by certain kinds of people. Other readers will reject his implication, and others will miss it entirely. He writes for those who are like himself or are capable of coming close to his attitude when they guess what it is. He may resist opponents, he may scorn the unsusceptible; but he writes for agreement, if only to set his ideas out and let people react to them in their own way, especially if he believes that he must make a new or an enlarged public for the new conception or technique that has persuaded him. Even when his ideas differ from those of the past only in a revelation of how those ideas should be symbolized in an illusion which will present life accurately, he certainly wishes to make his point. Then if he makes us concentrate on the illusion by providing no other immediate concern, he will try to supply it with a power of suggesting what he chooses not to say outright. Since we are bound to respond to the illusion in some personal way, his problem is one of adroitness in insinuating his response into us apparently as our own, by making us draw certain inferences difficult to detect as his, and yet difficult to avoid. A shrewd prefiguring of his public would therefore, as I have said, be at least half the battle. For the rest, the more pronouncedly each element in the illusion affects us as being an identity, and the less inclined we are to question the truth of the various elements as being no more than themselves, the more subtly powerful will his tactics prove: for the obvious contrasts and other relationships among the elements of the fiction will evoke equivalent associations in our own minds, and we are lined up before we know it. That is why the writers of "objective" realism and naturalism are the most cunning of controversialists, frequently infiltrating the position they would capture with such success that they need not attack at all.

Since natural contrast carries no announcement in life, it need have none in fiction; but subtler contrasts may pass unnoticed because the reader might think it laughable to suspect any such thing. There would, for example, seem to be no figure in *Robinson Crusoe* to be contrasted with the solitary castaway. Yet there is a contrast, between Crusoe as man and the island as his environment. The vegetation, the goats and fish and fowl, the weather, the seasons, the very days and nights, and the unremitted dumbness, are the wild contestants he must one by one domesticate into clothing, shelter, larder, granary, cultivated acres, barnyard, journal,

193

and communion with Heaven. His resolve not to succumb or be destroyed is his story, as it is his survival. We are moved to sympathy, to admiration, to reflection. There are passages of outcry and piety, but these would be thin, familiar stuff without the narration. Its stages climb to a symbolism of considerable grandeur; if there are sermons in stones, we decide, here is one in the flesh. It is not the thoughts put by Defoe into Robinson's mouth that speak the most exalted meaning we find in the book, but our own ineluctable thoughtfulness as observant humanity. Given the contrasts of Crusoe's consciousness, body, world, and possible fates, and the actual fortitude and resourcefulness of the lonely wrecked sailor, as against our possible fatalism were we in his place, we people his island with the invisible presences of our own inferring. Whether or not Defoe intended these contrasts which we perceive, clearly he knew them as part of the struggle.

Fielding, more expressive if not more conscious about fiction as an art of rhetorical practice, used the word *contrast* himself in declaring his employment of the device: Allworthy is set against Western, Molly against Sophia, Jones against Blifil, and Thwackum against Square, so that the alignment gives the book the classic quality of balance. Less simple, less easy to make out, is Sterne's contrast of the idiosyncrasies of Shandyism within the family likeness of eccentricity, his gorgeous demonstration of the characters' union in sentiment despite their constant failure to convey to each other the thoughts each takes for granted as so precise and definite. The dialogue is complex with contrast, for to the differences of ideas and verbal usage there are added the different postures of mind in speaker and listener. James turns matter of the same sort to infinitely subtle account in his dialogue, whenever he makes someone who is speaking the observer and even listener to another's betrayal by response, or makes the listener a silent speaker in his significant failure to say something the occasion should really prompt him to. The double employment of dialogue as speech and screen not only can make a certain silence into innocence or delicacy, and another silence into deceit, but can also provide sudden, overwhelming insight into character and so into amiable or detestable principle.

Howells, less sophisticated than James in his technique, is as sure in his effects of characterization. Silas Lapham is sounder in character than the opportunist Bartley Hubbard, and provincial by comparison with the Coreys; yet all that Howells does when he brings his agents together is to let

194

them speak for themselves, while he casually reports the response each feels or otherwise silently shows to whatever touches him. Howells' method suits his art, which is not rich, like James', but candid, like the type of American he loved to draw. Because, like such people, he was loath to talk about sex, a freer generation declared him emasculate and forgot him; but he was a man if there ever was one, and when he is restored to his place in our reading, he will be cherished as much for his affectionate portraiture of what is good in American life, as for his clear comprehension of the ideal standard by which that goodness judges its loyalty and its shortcomings. To consult one's conscience and genially to let the other fellow do the same, to mind one's own business in the very act of helping one's neighbor, to be good or brave without affecting to, to make shrewd appraisals of reality good-humoredly, to sustain one's emotion with decent self-respect, and to hold up one's end in all things—these articles of his creed might be written all over the page, for all his cultivated disinclination to exhibit them. Thus, the ideas entertained by his agents, spoken by them outright or obliquely indicated by what they say of something or in what they do as response to emergency or routine, need only the qualifications of his equally indirect asides to show us where he stands. He will have one character say something, and another answer him, and then tell only *how* the first reacted—not *why,* as George Eliot does, and certainly not why in terms of right or wrong, in the fashion of Fielding, Horatio Alger, Dreiser, or D. H. Lawrence. Howells felt that for most people life kept to a certain averageness—perhaps normality—most of the time. This consistency he emphasized. He did not leave out the seamier side. It will be found in every one of his works, but in its place, or what he certainly believed to be its place. Since this even tenor of life is a kind of good in itself, the account of it and of its value is taken by many of the public to be necessarily uninteresting. Howells, in his impulse to present not the ideal, but the admirable, as a kind of working model, lost out in the short view of an era impatient for Dreiser, Sinclair Lewis, reform, and debunking; but when the times again call for clarification of standards not too heroic for plain you and me, his modest strength of civilized conviction will have its day once more. His pages offer a world in which people get along as people. We could use him now, if we were ready for him. Our children may be luckier.

Writers who feel that they can do most good by exposing

evil expose themselves to trouble if they hint their ideas instead of speaking them bluntly. Our age has its superstitions: there is a wide social area in which it is held to be self-evident that anyone who writes a foul thing on paper believes in it. Witnesses under oath have been known to balk at repeating obscenities spoken in their hearing. This animism pays an unwitting compliment to the power of the written or spoken word, and with equal unawareness sets it above the heart's lust for malignant efficacy. The existence of such an attitude is what makes it possible for the censor to get a conviction for one dirty word torn from context. For one Judge Woolsey whose cultivated intelligence can relate the alleged offense of a *Ulysses* to the total intent, there are thousands to battle their way into the court room at the least promise that dirt is to be shoveled out. Also, it appeals to their sense of fair play, as a good-natured crowd, that somebody ought to pay for all the fun.

In all my years in this vale of sin, I have met not one single adult who really needed to have indecency defined for him. Since the vast and overwhelming majority of the population of the most civilized countries cannot be got to open one book a year, much less to read it, the source of their inerrant ability to laugh at or denounce a dirty story is elsewhere to seek. Granting, then, that the general uncultivated and unlettered state is one of corruption, is this what *Madame Bovary* corrupts, or *Ulysses,* or *God's Little Acre,* or even *Lady Chatterley's Lover?* Alas, if the art of fiction really had such power of good or ill, it would have the antecedent power of getting itself understood! But then, what would happen to the censor?

Regardless of the public influence of ideas in novels or tales, nobody really believes that ideas are not there. Indeed, because of a hold on the few millions who are actually readers, the power of books is overestimated by them, with a parallel estimate quite as exaggerated on the part of those who cannot cope with books at all. It is extremely doubtful that any entire schools of publicists ever exerted a small fraction of the change brought about by acute, widespread human misery. It is because literature floats on the surface of life that it is so valuable in revealing the secret currents that run deep; in this sense it does exercise a prophetic function and does enter into the creative social experimentation out of which it has emerged.

In classic epic and tragedy there is a characteristic type of scene, so curiously emotional that we drain its feeling with an experience like a thirst, not daring to take our lips from it even to surmise why it should shake us so, a scene in which it slowly dawns upon two persons who are or have been strangers who must meet and get to know each other, that in reality they have a prior bond, long mislaid, of blood, or country, or any of those relations that seem primordial in underlying experience and giving it birth. These ordeals of recognition, by mother and son, sister and brother, lord and vassal, master and hound, transform the reason of the two who recognize, by disarming it down to the naked knowing. This stripping of intellect to its emotional self is shared by the imagined bystanders, and by audience and reader. There is a thrill in the air, a resonance beyond hearing but vibrant in blood and bone, a reduction of each of us out of unique personality, somehow made up for by an elated wisdom. This apparition of truth in the midst of the humdrum traffic of merely ordinary meaning, this realization that our usual signs and conceptions are not in themselves significance, but only the counters of that value now suffering us one thrilled glimpse of its awful might, is symbolism in the life. A consanguinity is uncovered between us and the stars; time is experience, with all things in its, and we are the knower and the known. Poetry is this mood singing. The common quality of the *Œdipus Rex,* of *Hamlet,* of *Don Quixote,* of *Tristram Shandy,* of *Wuthering Heights,* of *Madame Bovary,* of *Crime and Punishment,* of *The Way of All Flesh,* of *Ulysses,* of *The Castle* is this quality of the universal experience and not of an individual provenience; of composition not alone by a dreamer or a thinker, but by the imagining reason.

Fiction, as we have seen, is a domain bordering on others. Where they meet, they impinge, in travel and intermarriage over the border. Hence the infiltration into fiction of the migrant poem, drama, letter, and essay. Since the essay opens communication with regions of human knowledge not classified as arts, novels and tales are often fitted out with explicit ideas, as with imported furniture, from theology, ethics, and the social studies. Sometimes all of this suits the spirit or taste of the characters; they are people who collect such things and live among them in alert awareness of their appeal, sharing the author's relish in discussing them analytically and suggestively. Lawrence's Freudianism and Wells's science are examples, as were in earlier times the intellectualist convictions of Fielding, George Eliot, George Meredith, Zola, Charles Reade, Hardy, and Butler. It is the sort of thing practised in the theatre by Ibsen, Shaw, Hauptmann, Bernstein, Pirandello, and O'Neill. I have left this matter of the open declaration of convictions and principles to the end of the chapter, believing that there can be very little about such obviousness that needs to be divulged, and feeling that most of that little would have been taken care of by this time anyway. As we saw previously, other elements of fiction, such as conflict and imagery, may be modulated by any of the processes of relegation into background, passing indication, or forthright expression. So ideas also may be present in fiction as silent partners, as inconspicuous servants, or as guests joining in the conversation. Their susceptibility to management gives them their place, but also keeps them in it. That the place is at times not only a prominent but an honored one does not dispose of the fact of cooperation.

On the other hand, common action sometimes throws single performance into high relief. When the wedding procession starts down the aisle to the altar, the minister has no more guarantee of attention than anyone else; but once he begins to read the lines, we regard his office almost as the sacrament. When in fiction what we experience at a given moment is the illusion of an environment with people in it and things happening, we are witnesses; when the illusion is one of the author speaking his mind, we are jurors. Focal attention has a familiar characteristic, namely, that two things cannot occupy it at the same time. Therein lies the peculiar nature of explicitness. It presents what it presents; and if we take it that way (and we usually do), then what it presents is what we get, that and no more. The sight of Scott's mountains, or of Conrad's sailors battling the storm, the sound of Wassermann's disputants or of James' polite conversational fencers, may be the all-in-all of some interval of reading. So may Fielding's little lecture on what love is, or Tolstoy's plea for peace. When ideas are the ostensibles of fiction, that is because for the reader nothing in the universe is being mentioned except them; for explicitness, no matter what else may be involved in its use, is always characteristically and doggedly so-many-words.

Chapter 8

The Word

WHETHER OR NOT Heaven especially lies about us in our infancy, the world certainly does. I was born into an existence of precedent actualities, many of which were words. These were uttered in the air about my inattentive head and were spoken throughout the earth in my native tongue and in many others. They appeared to eyes opened for them as script and print; they were piled solid and high on library and shop and warehouse shelves like all substantial commodities that have their use and price. Therefore, regardless of the manner of their origin in prehistoric times, they were of the awful primitiveness of Nature when I met them. I was a little later admitted to my patrimony in speech, on the simple title of human being, and not only did the administrators of community give all this to me free, but they encouraged my every first acceptance with celebration.

As fast as I could, I acquired the verbal means to do hundreds and hundreds of things by saying. At my mother's knee I had my prayers and baby rhymes, and afterward with small fingers and a big pencil I mimicked letters. In school I was soon learning by speech and writing; as a city child, I joined a library, and practiced a way of living by print. Soon I knew that I had a vocabulary; and several high school teachers urged me to "develop my style," to mold the great public propriety into my private property. In my professional turn I have urged the same course on trusting youths of other generations, and from their efforts I have observed that this is no easy thing to do. It seems that words always retain something of their physical character, for even in our minds they are no more readily malleable than iron is in the physical world. One learns to stand in awe of Shelley's meteoric fire, Pope's hunchbacked sinew. Ah, words are hard things, even the easiest of them. In a context they flow—but to get them there! Either they come, unbidden and barely noted, with the speed of thought or hot feeling; or they are all square pegs to the round holes of our intent. Furthermore, although each is fixed in the dictionary definition, our ancestors were sometimes better able to agree on what to call a thing than on what the thing itself was. They named the babes, but took no fingerprints, with the result of occasional transfer in the cradle, and subsequent litigation. Again, like all substantial realities, words have their vicissitudes. Some are as old as the hills; others have no more span of life than the amoeba; and to make matters worse, the survivors often have a long and complex history, sometimes losing the early signification or growing unrecognizably fat from a rich diet of usage. Finally, any one of them may, by the accident of bystanding at some terrible or ludicrous or otherwise unusual association, take on for someone or some group a connotation which is no part of its antecedence, yet which sticks, and may spread.

Like any physical thing, the written or the spoken word is charged with the mystifying fact of its existing at all. In ordinary currency this passes notice, so that it is those who take words most for granted who know them least, and those best informed of their nature who often seem little adept in their function. We live in relation toward words as we do toward other things and each other, that is, symbolically, suspecting in them no character beyond their utility for us; yet when we think or speak of them, we gravely assert their independence, their unalterable selves, plain to any dolt, if he will only take heed. It means what it says, don't it? Here I am tempted to take a cue from Bacon: we often read the way we eat, with more energy than taste, and so find writing as mystifying as cookery. When words are reduced to the general function, they almost vanish out of attention in the moment of their use; that is, the meaning of any one of them is disregarded, because the total intent of what we are saying is the focal concern. We then behave toward what we say or hear as though it were not there, as though thought were meeting thought directly in the world. This illusion is one of the subtle persuasions of the talkies: when the sound stops or fades, and before we realize that something has gone wrong with the mechanism, we have a fleeting incredulity, as though we were faced with the possibility that something has gone wrong with the characters, an epidemic speechlessness. So, in deeply interested reading, an encounter with some kraken of a word will remind us of what we are really doing, just as a stumble while we walk will remind us of our indispensable feet. Even the most logical reader, as Dewey says, commonly goes by the feel of the thought, not by perpetual syllogistic analysis.

The self-effacement of language is one of its greatest uses and, equally one of its greatest abuses, for it may produce either intense vividness of meaning, or only defacement. As an achievement of skill for free emotion, it is one thing; quite another as mechanized expediency. There are millions of literate robots, and they have an enormous intake of sub-literary "reading matter." What this amounts to is a linguistic equivalent of the rush-hour, one of the heartrending failures of an education administered too much after the routine of animal training. Fortunately, neither our speech nor our schooling is all of our selves. There is the substantial core which is still human; and no triumph of consciousness over frustration is more moving to pride of race than this quite modern evidence of power to survive in the teeth of advantages.

The materiality of language, its accessibility to our organic presence, or its inert, moulding massiveness upon our habits, preserves for it its place as the greatest common denominator of communication. Words are substantial. Their perceptibility by the senses is one manifestation of their energy. When written down, words are spatial—the line, the page, the volume. Words also involve time, both the time of composition and the time of reading of the private monologue. The art of writing unites the dimensions of space and time; what we contribute is the form which this union takes—that is, our formative power to convert physical things outside ourselves into the emblems of what is in us, though imperceptible to sense. Thus art is the taming of wild matter, for in its essence art is the self-liberation of consciousness giving its presences to the world. It is the invisible creator of visions. It is blind Homer seeing with words.

Some conveying instrument is essential to the unspoken word, but it does not convey all of it. In one of his most perceptive epigrams, Justice Holmes declared that language was not the clothing of thought, but its skin. As the outermost layer of tissue the word contains the meaning still naked within it; it is available for perception as itself, and at the same time reveals and explains what it covers. Wordless thought, whether in the mind, or in codes and formulae, is less nude than skinned, like the manikin of the anatomy lecture.

Just as speech tends to lose its substance with familiarity, so when we regard it for itself, it takes on an obtrusive solidness. This is true of unfamiliar words in our own idiom; in a language we do not know, the dermal aspect seems to differ from ours in kind, with a rhinoceros effect of monstrous drapery. Living symbolically as we do, we are likely to take the clothes for the man. But whenever we look at his head and hands, we respond to their surface as if it were the man himself, since that is all we have to go by. The cut of his hair and beard, if he has one, and of his mustaches give us, we like to believe, an insight that brings the hidden to the surface.

One can see, then, why the literary aspect of fiction is still taken, not as an aspect at all, but as the whole reality, and why all of the other elements of the medium are generally considered parts of the verbal texture. In this older-fashioned view, some little exception, it is true, is always allowed for the fanciful behavior of a mysterious thing called the imagination; there will be a brief introductory concession of it as a "gift," midway between an innate talent for affairs and a gypsy's way with cards, but nothing to keep one long from the solider and jollier business of definitions and rules. In fact, in putting the word at the end of my pageant of parts I was moved in measure by a confidence that the prevailing attitude could be counted on to take care of itself while I was redressing the balance in justice to the other elements, and also in measure by a wish to use the word, as the common receptacle and conveyance, to round out my book with a retrospect on fiction as a whole.

The most concentrated state in which a thing is found in nature may be neither the commonest nor the most valuable, yet it may be considered a kind of maximum, an extreme of a theoretical scale, and so a standard of purity. There is fiction of this all-fictional sort, which I shall call *pure* fiction. It has no more than a trace of any other kind of discourse— no noticeable description, exposition, or persuasion as a passage apart. I do not hold such fiction to be any *greater* than a more mixed or dilute sort; certainly it is not encountered nearly so often. In all frankness, on the other hand, I must confess a personal preference for it. There are stories that can be read with deep enjoyment just for the experience of the illusion, and then reread and reread in marvel at the skill which put them together. Other stories which are wonderfully interesting in the first instance do not bear up so well under examination. They are like houses that are made to charm visitors, but are not very good to live in. When their fashion is superseded, builders will be found to do equally hasty work in the new mode. But the sort of fictions which we are considering, since they are the product of art as well as of ready gifts, will, I repeat, hold a public that respects conscious craftsmanship, especially if that craftsmanship has created novelty in its own way.

Given time, that public will react about as follows: Here is a newly published work. Does it convey imagined presence with novelty? Does it do so with a rich consistency subordinate to the intense concentration of the first reading and defiant of any later analysis except a trained and tireless one? The fact that people unsophisticated in reading deny the book any such surplus of substance is, of course, no matter. If some readers suspect that much more has gone into the work than lies on the surface, and if others can turn the suspicion into knowledge by producing internal evidence, the public I have in mind is apprised of a new excellence. Like other publics, this one includes people who prize a novel exemplification of reality in the world, and the expression of great emotion and thought. If, in addition, a newly published work is recognized as having enlarged the standard applied to it, or as having illuminated the standard afresh (a contribution of the highest nature in view of the essence of the art), then the standard is itself proved to be an exceptionally reliable map for exploration. If I were to reduce it to its simplest terms as I conceive them, with a lively sense of the dangers of omitting much that is relevant, I would say that the experience of an imagined occurrence should be as nearly as possible *itself* as any experience I might have in the world.

This means that the occurrence must be actual to me at the time I experience it in reading, and also whenever I think about it afterwards. Thus the memory of an incident in a story is like the memory of any experience, and rereading a story is like reliving an occurrence in memory. To the extent that a work does this, it is a triumph of art, for then the created experience is real in the sense that itself, and nothing but itself, is evidence of its reality. In other words, the illusion of identity is perfect, as in life. The imaginary incident can be analyzed, as all experience can, but not analyzed out of existence. This, of course, is the ideal. No story has attained it; perhaps none ever will. Yet some fiction has been thought, by the very special public I have been talking about, to have come closer to this ideal than most other efforts. Achievement of this high level defies analysis to an extraordinary degree; in fact, it promotes the superstition that art cannot be examined at all, that it is unfathomable throughout, that those who say they can add technical understanding to enjoyment are imposters or cranks.

Actually, even at the first reading we make a provisional analysis. With the very first words of a fiction, a form begins to take shape. Since the first words cannot convey everything, and since they contain innumerable possibilities of thought and action, the form supplies its due share of the suspense simply by lying in the future. The potential form—one among many other possibilities—is being realized, and before long it is firmly established, and we are confident that it will be maintained and developed. By this time a glance backward will show whether the work, by design or shrewd intuition, really has form. The text itself says nothing about this, for the fictional text does not normally discuss fictional form, but simply expresses it. Our own rearward glance, however, is enough to inform us as to whether the author knows what he is about—whether the form is there, or whether there have been regrettable omissions, redundancies, gropings, wanderings, and returnings. If the experience is occurring to the author exactly as it is occurring to us—if he is improvising haphazardly as he goes along—we may rejoice in the fertility of his fancy and join him in the lark, but our sense of the form itself is gone. Somewhere in the middle of the story it must be possible to turn back to the opening words and see that they were deliberately chosen, and that no others could have been more fitting.

The interrelationship of word and form can be illustrated in other ways. Let us consider the illusion, for example. As an imaged presence, the illusion is some fictional world, perhaps fantastic, perhaps realistic, existing in the author's consciousness. This subjective world is then evoked in the consciousness of the reader by means of the word. The words have the task of naming what is in the illusion, so that we know what it is and what happens in it. If they do that well, they do everything, for then the story, as an illusion of perceptible places, people, and speech, is not merely presented, but is accepted by the reader as the focal concern, so that the experience of words and form is relegated into periphery or disregard. The manifest presence is now everything; the fiction, in being itself strictly, is its own form.

Unfortunately, to say what is there is a task easier to prescribe than to do. Not everything in a story can be named, or the description will seem a mere inventory, and the illusion will be broken. There must be some selection of material. The selection may be inspired, in the sense that the author cannot account for it, but it cannot be random. For the part of the illusion which is chosen must be representative of the whole, and must also convey the author's feelings toward it, his conception of it, his mood, his point of view. None of the author's feelings, let me repeat, need be explicitly discussed. In choosing the presence to be named, and the name to call it, the author puts his trace on the paper as clearly as if he were a little animal running across the snow to escape pursuit. Ironically, the cunning with which a writer withholds all evidence of himself from the text is inevitably a trait of his work. It is the task of analysis to recognize this cunning and account for it, but in our first experience of the story we are not aware of it.

Selection of detail is dictated by organic consistency of form. The detail which is named suggests unnamed details appropriate to it, and such selection is economical in implying so much. The author must provide a sufficient number of details; otherwise the reader has to supply more than his share of the response, and under the strain the illusion snaps. When the detail is really suitable for the moment, then it also fits into the larger scheme of imagery of the entire story, and so becomes part of the background of what follows. The problem is how much or how little is to be named. Some of the decision is made for the author by the inspiration which brings him the occurrence he is to relate, and his world as that seems to him; and inspiration may provide wording, too, as a baby is said to bring its own food. On the other hand, he may have to revise, if only by ear. He may go further, and be his own best friend in becoming his severest critic. Treating what has come to him as in no danger of going away, he will scrutinize detail or wording with an eye to true economy by removal of excess, addition of what is lacking, and exquisite fitting of things into places. Above all, as I have said, he will remove every trace of his hand, leaving his illusion and language neither artful nor artless, but, bafflingly, art. The better he succeeds, the less the division of our attention between the story and the telling, and the purer the "purity." I believe it was Renan who declared that the last great quality of the writer is ease. This is something to be achieved, not just a gift—easier in the look than in the getting. It is not mere fluency; it is never glib.

The harmonizing of word, form, and illusion in fiction necessarily involves the action. Events are details; conflict is a pattern. Climax—where has it ever been tightened by a discourse on climax? When the fiction is pure, events register directly as success, disaster, threat, suspicion, change of feeling, or whatever may betide, but not necessarily labeled as *success, disaster, threat, suspicion,* or *whatever may betide.* Something is doing. Someone is speaking, acting, feeling, thinking. Mr. Collins is proposing persistently and Elizabeth Bennett is persistently declining. Maître d'Hauchecorne is seen by his enemy to pick up and pocket something; later, a man reports the loss of a wallet. The time required for the reading of the text from start to finish is passed in reading unit by unit. When the text is relegated into disregard, the duration of the reading is experienced, not as reading time, but as illusion of time in the imagined occurrence. When this is adjusted to events in sequence, we have narration proper. Pure fiction will exploit this illusion to the limit. That means that there will be as little time out for descriptive, expository, or persuasive writing as can be managed with effective economy; better, that such passages will be infiltrated with events; best, that the material for such passages will not be localized in separate paragraphs, but deftly scattered and spread through the running narrative of the happenings, in shreds and wisps of commentative asides, expressed preferably in subordinate grammatical elements (clauses, phrases, modifiers, connectives) dependent on principal grammatical elements presenting events. When the asides are turned over to the characters, for their casual mention with reference to something much more interesting in the course of the events, the method attains its closest approach to absolute unobtrusiveness.

Henry James mastered this art of uniting non-narrative to narrative matter, by cutting the former down to a minimum, so that the latter could include those other functions in the performance of its own. He did this in his plan and in his language—more and more so as his career progressed. His action is therefore packed too tight for readers who are used to a looser rictal and a more readily comprehensible division of labor, and who find themselves further puzzled and irritated by the strangeness of the use of events in the mind as clues to events in the world. Hence his impenetrability for the uninitiated; but those who accustom themselves to his dense swiftness naturally rate him high among the creators of pure fiction. Since, in addition, his procedure aims at a final, rather than a distributed, delivery of intent, his sentences and paragraphs tend to be periodic in the rhetorical sense for their minor climaxes, with much painstaking postponement uncommon in everyday speech. All this perfection of means has, of course, its faults as an addiction: in his poorer works of the later years, like "In the Cage," and *The Outcry,* the narrative is overstrained with an expository function, and gives an effect of an only apparent movement, almost empty of occurrence. Such writing cannot help seeming thin, wordy, tedious; the subject seems to lie talked to death. However, when his method is put to work on material charged with events, as in *The Ambassadors* and "The Turn of the Screw," he achieves a purity of fictional illusion unequalled before his time. Jane Austen, in her *Emma* and *Persuasion,* has greater ease than he, but not nearly so much matter to the page; and Joyce has more complexity, but a slower pace; James, at any rate for the purposes of our age, surpasses them both in the accommodation of substance to time.

It stands to reason, since the creative artist intent upon producing the fictional concentrate must first and last be true to himself in order to be a creative artist at all, that fiction must to some irreducible degree be contaminated by the artist's personality. On the other hand, the fact that performance has very little likelihood of ever being the ideal cannot possibly mean that a certain performance need be at a very far remove from that ideal. The closeness of the approximation, despite a remarkable individuality in the artist, is what we who are enthusiasts for the ideal applaud, not lessening our appreciation one whit in crying out over the narrow interval. It would never do, for example, to say that the writer of wood-pulp fiction is the true ideal. Since he produces nothing but action, he gives far less than enough for the sort of readers we are considering here; for they see quickly enough that he really gives his readers no action at all, except what he mechanically contrives out of a reshuffling of the materials of his own reading. He no more creates than a manufacturer of dolls begets a living article. He is simply a drillmaster for people who have a set of pat imaginative calisthenics they cannot be put through too often; and he exercises them, like a masseur, while they sit still in a chair.

Pure fiction is never the result of avoiding the exactions of really creating experience. Any art worthy of the name, even when imperfect or downright bad, affirms something. The aim of the artist is of course to provide an experience for the reader; but, more than that, he wants to guarantee a reader of a certain sort one experience precisely and no other. By "a reader of a certain sort" I mean a reader willing to submit himself to the minutely close guidance necessary for the enjoyment of an experience requiring such tight alertness. The extent of the reader's willing suspension of his right to imagine freely within some large loose sketch provided by the author is the measure of the author's control of the art as a medium. Conversely, the author's sacrifice of happy spontaneity in composition, his subordination of his own joy in creation to the demands of craftsmanship for truly economical effectiveness in the experience, is the very thing his sort of reader reads him for! Even though the public I refer to is relatively small, it has proved big enough to support a surprisingly large number of reputations. In addition to the three great novelists I have already mentioned, I would for myself add the following, if only with respect to their best achievement: the Abbé Prévost, Sterne, Poe, Flaubert, Emily Brontë, Galdos, Trollope, Turgenev, Howells, Gide, Kafka, Willa Cather, and Isak Dinesen. I have no doubt that Dostoievski is greater than most of them, or that Defoe is far more widely known than any; but that is not what I have been talking about.

To continue the discussion by turning attention to still another of the elements of the fictional symbol or medium, let us consider how imagined character fits into the scheme of the concentrated form. There must be, plainly, such treatment of character as will generate the illusion of uniqueness in the agent, without letting the reader's awareness come to rest on that treatment, or in it. Thus, during the reading, the reader must at times actually believe that what he notes and admires as individuality of character, in spite of the fact that not one word on that individuality is being spoken, is a matter of his own perception, a private discovery very few other readers have hit upon. The effect should be one of a little secret shared with that other brilliant mind, the author's; and it should be shared telepathically, as by two onlookers exchanging not so much as a glance with each other, since the words themselves say nothing directly about character or characterization. In such fiction, a character is revealed only through events, and revealed not only in external acts and words, but in his inner thoughts and feelings and responses of every sort. Though characterized indirectly, he is presented directly, as part of a pattern of complex occurrences; as part, indeed, of the whole imaginary physical and social environment that makes up his world. Consequently, he can be made an object for study by social criticism, as an instance of what is right or wrong in the world of which he is both a product and a presence; and so he invariably is in Turgenev's novels, or the tales of Ralph Bates. As a symbol, he can express the mood and point of view of the story. Yet though he clearly performs this service, not a word about it, let me repeat, need be said. The language reveals him in his many acts; in expressing them, though it refrains from comment, it allows for comment. It allows, too, for *his* language— that is, his participation by speech in the dialogue. The author provides the material and the occasion for our inference repeatedly, and, at specific moments, strikingly.

The incidental triumph of this inferential mode of characterization is that your two invisible onlookers of the story, the author and the reader, are also characterized in their own individualities: the one, because his procedure, illustrative of the sort of man he is, is ultimately impressed upon the public mind with great incisiveness; and the other, because he stands revealed in his own eyes as a person of unsuspected potentialities for understanding human nature so displayed. True, certain, and perhaps many, readers may fail to draw the proffered inference, may be incapable of it; but there are others who are equipped and who will get the design, and it is these whom the writer of pure fiction has chosen to be his audience. Such an audience may at the outset be small. Yet happily it can grow. What begins not through snobbery, but necessity, as a handful, may multiply into the cultivated many.

Having thus sketched the integration of the word with the other elements of the fictional medium for the conveyance of what I call pure fiction, I would like now to consider its integration with itself. This paradox, I hasten to explain, means simply that the word must be regarded as a complex of many phases—spelling, tone, rhythm, denotation, and availability for adjustment with other words in large patterns of meaning. Any one of these aspects, according to the particular modulation and our reponse to it, may be the apparent soloist of a performance actually rich in harmony. Now, in pure fiction, the literary element would be wholly in the meaning, and the meaning wholly the presence of the illusion. Hence the verbal element must be unobtrusive; it must seem to be what it conveys; it must vanish into, and therefore become, the place and the people and the occurrence. This effect can be produced only by such accuracy of expression as will both make a focal concern of what it names and at the same time efface every mark of the care exerted in making it do so. Here Jane Austen easily surpasses James and Joyce (at least, by the standards of our time), as she does every other writer of fiction in English. The inevitability of her phrasing sets her beside Flaubert and Turgenev for this literary excellence, and it is worth noting that all three were patient to revise and slow to publish. In none of them does the writing attract the attention from the story at first reading; in none does the writing ulimately fail to be admired as superb style. Equal celebrity has been achieved by stylists with the gift of brilliant ornament, like George Meredith and Marcel Proust, but it is significant for the theme I am pursuing that Jane Austen, Flaubert, and Turgenev (if we may take the word of compatriots of the latter two) wrote in such a way as to make language indispensable and yet utterly unapparent, like the air. The illusion breathes with it, and this rarity makes it the purest of all the cooperating forces of pure fiction.

The case I have been trying to make for the existence of one kind of standard for the art of fiction has been presented. There remains only my personal obligation to make restitution to the great practitioners for one willful injustice in the appraisal. In order to express their ideal in terms worthy of their vaulting aspiration, I made the casual actualness of experience in the world the touchstone test of their achievement. By this measure, as we can see, they must absolutely fail, since infallibly we recognize the other man's presented presence apart from ourselves as presences. Even our own reverie, vagrant and disorderly as it generally is, has an immediacy for our awareness that an effective fiction may snatch, but never hold. Yet though the attempts at pure fiction must fail in this absolute sense, they triumph comparatively. In terms of performance, therefore, their admittedly no more than comparative success in coping with hopeless odds becomes itself a standard, and a mark to shoot at. We may despair of agreement as to which one of them historically is *the* measure. In the same spirit, I have no hope that all of the few I have named would be included in every roll of honor, or that other people will say that I have named all of the few who should be on that roll. The fact would the more surely remain that since the thought of such a roll excites such vigor of disagreement, not only must some names beyond question belong on it, but the conception must be real, however elusive. Even if it could be established with a very close approximation, it would still not, I suppose, be the whole fiction. Yet it might be the nucleus of the whole fiction; and that, even in my uncertain apprehension of it, I suspect and believe and take it to be.

Now I may return to the consideration of the word at large. As a letter of the alphabet, or a number of letters in single file, it is the unit of the text line by line and page by page. That is the principal use of its spelling for fiction—to be, to be taken for granted, to be disregarded. We do not read by the method of the spelling-bee, but, as the mathematicians say, by inspection. Apparently we take hold of a group of words at a time, according to our facility or lack of it. The mind uses its optic power in sweeping movements forward and a little backward, brushing the row of deposited ink marks as though with imperceptible touch, a species of Braille for the seeing. Actually we read as much by convention as by sight, picking up what we conceive to be part of a general pattern of meaning, and trusting that details, such as letters and marks of punctuation, will be as they should. Only very observant readers consistently take note of errors, and even they make mistakes.

Also, we unwittingly change the text: if the pattern of a sentence, as we apprehend it in the opening words, promises a continuance of a certain familiar phrasing, we may read that for what the author has actually written. Later, this is somehow taken care of, as though we had fallen out of step and back into it without noticing. If we never chanced to read aloud, perhaps we should never know we did this sort of thing, sometimes to the point of making a field day for the Freudians. So trained are we in combinations of words rather than in words singly, that if a term like *condign* or *impervious* appears in a familiar pattern of setting, we improvise an understanding of it from the way its associates behave toward it; and in spite of never looking it up in the dictionary, we learn to spell it correctly, and feel that we use it so. Our use may never be in conversation or in our own writing, but only in the response of hearing and reading for which our vocabulary is so much larger in this practical, uninformed way, than it is for full communication. The enlargement and the habituation of our verbal stock are two benefits of literary reception generally, and therefore of fiction, which gratify the impulses of certain readers more than of others.

The linguistic phase of the whole fiction plays its part in determining the writer's public. If his resources are extensive and he uses them to the full, there will be tens of thousands of readers excluded as effectively by the physical barrier of the printed text as by a Chinese wall under an armed guard. Some critics, of whom we might expect better, inveigh against the exclusion, assuming that what in fact excludes must be exclusive by motive, and thereby fall prey to the fallacy that what is human power to-day is all that there is of mankind, including its potentialities for growth. The existence of an understanding audience, no matter how small, should be proof that the aristocratic creator has a higher opinion of his kind in the long view than those who would peg our standard at the level of a contemporary average, and knows better than they what people can understand. Let journalism, even in book form, give the public what it wants, and let genius do the same for posterity. Since that seems to be what will happen anyway, what could be more reasonable than to yield gracefully to the development we cannot possibly prevent?

In the unique whole fiction, the word is a short division of the tonal flow of private monologue. Lip-reading is the obvious manifestation when we are still learning to speak from print. An illiterate person cannot do even that little, yet in conversation he does not utter each word by itself—the flow of his speech may seem not to pause for breath. The varying index, the span of words seized in the larger unit, will again create a class-system amid the democracy of reading to oneself. Those who are unequal to Sterne's pace, or the grasp of Meredith's or James' scope in the period, will sincerely complain that the book is too slow, unable to suspect that it is they who have been left at the post, or suspecting it too dimly to do more than rationalize their inequality into the other fellow's defect. Also, in many persons the monologue is demonstrably a monotone. Unless people may be presumed to read aloud to themselves better than they do to others, a large number are kept out of all reading except the most necessary by self-inflicted boredom. What wit or profundity, subtlety or erudition, do to limit any contemporary public, this lack of variety in silent reading does in its own way, without the slightest blame to the author; for, in addition to the fact that some tonally dull readers work their own frustration, others who persist and survive miss much of the rich provision. A flat hum can hardly bring out the stress of emphasis or the rhythmic flow of the text as it was projected; varieties of pitch, rate, quality in the dialogue of characters or in the writer's changing moods are held down to a flat level. The envious surprise, the grateful pleasure of certain educated people listening to an accomplished reader, one who does justice to the text, is a reality no teacher of language can have failed to observe. Doubtless this is one reason for the delight of being read to, and of course for the hold of the actor upon our admiration. It is certainly one of the causes of the flourishing of fiction as literary art, that it can not only conceive and order a reverie better than we, but put it better, as well—more clearly, steadily, agreeably for the inner ear. When

212

someone who is reading to us shows his gift or acquired ability for conveying differences of feeling, rate, characterization, we see that his actor's knack contributes greatly to his relish when he reads within his consciousness; and even when his power seems generally about equal to our own, we are interested in whatever makes a difference within the equality.

As with readers, so with writers: some pens have antennae to catch the very accent of speech in the world; yes, even in the character's consciousness as self-address. These authors, when they wish, can render every man in the signature of his idiom. This ability becomes the chief, if not the only, means of characterization; so that readers who cannot reproduce the variation in private monologue lose the nice identification of the imagined people, perhaps a leading excellence of the work. Richardson and Smollett performed this miracle in the style of letters by divers hands, Jane Austen and Dickens and Mark Twain caught the very breath of individual talk, and Browning and Joyce were no less than magicians at recording to the life the finest shadings of secret self-expression in the thought of imagined persons. Some writers, like Sherwood Anderson, are very good at this in one specialized connection. Anderson is superb at the mute inglorious yokel, as Meredith is at the wit. But Meredith seems to make almost all his people wits and Merediths, as Shaw seems to make them all irrepressible and therefore Shavians, or James seems to confine himself to multiplying himself as a host of adepts at balancing lighted intuitions and sharp scalpels in a towering rhetoric of phrases and clauses on the very tip of one nosey surmise. Other novelists, notably George Eliot, Trollope, and Hardy, deal with people, dialect aside, whose speech is that of some social average, so that the sameness comes from the imagined society. But whether the character bites off and chews his piece of the common idiom, as in Dreiser, or produces his unique variation of it, as in Willa Cather, he is marked as a representative of some fictional community. Even in Meredith and James, he is a member of at least the author's society, in the sense that to belong, the character must exhibit skill in the difficult complexity of a certain way of speaking. Since the monotonous reader misses this conformity quite as much as Dreiser's uniformity or Joyce's variegation, what he says about style as well as about characterization is likely to be more curious than helpful. Without evident power to stand in the presence of pitch, quality, or rhythm in such a way as to note them by his response, his conception of literary form and of literary beauty can be at best a handicapped sensitiveness. In addition, he may be an imageless thinker, so that when (and it happens) he lays down the critical law, he presumably speaks in the sacred name of free speech as trespass. To discuss art with him is to debate justice with a poacher who knows his statutes.

The significance of this for what, a little while back, I was calling the "pure fiction" is that one of the ways the writer of such high aspiration promotes his atttempt and at the same time guarantees his failure is that in phrasing his creations for a public equal to the interpretation, he loses other publics in advance. Now, although much of the world's great fiction, when read aloud to the quite illiterate, produces a clear, instant effect on them, some of it, obviously, does nothing of the sort. Furthermore, even the kind that is easy to penetrate is not equally penetrated by everyone; but, finally, it is hard to see why greatness should derive its basic identification from a widespread handicap. Are we committed to nurturing a class of illiterates *in perpetuo* as a touchstone of excellence? Or is it to be our fate that when men and women everywhere are, in the process of things, cultivated people, the race will have lost its power to understand the fine simplicities and take pleasure from them? No human being is out of mankind; and I can only wonder at the partisanship of those whose solicitude for the underprivileged takes the form of damning any effort to augment the privileges of their descendants.

Spelling and speaking cannot, of course, be considered apart from meaning. The appearance of a word is the material expression of its intent, and when the living word thus takes its place in the world of physical objects, it becomes fixed and rigid like them. The definiteness of its outline, we are prone to forget, is *rigor mortis*. From the live flux of language we have anatomized the verbal organ, which thus dies. We mistake the shape for the form, and the dictionary pickling and bottling for the habitat. A word in its separateness is dehydrated food; for consumption, it must have restored to it the fluid life. The meaning of a word is its participation in meaning. Its definition is not that, but a formula of it. In the same way, we make wooden posts and rails to fence in the woods. Like every abstraction, then, the word as we have come to conceive it is an enormously useful localization, an invention whose utility is priceless until it gets in the way of import. That is why a dictionary may be a glory of the printer's art, but never of the literary.

Fiction harnesses the power of language to express meaning as it courses through human existence, to turn the wheels of illusion. What we call the text is a contact for a current of power, like an electrical outlet; the words are not even the meeting, but only its place. To change metaphors, they are the footlights to the scene, escaping a notice they would delicately direct to everything but themselves. When, however, in producing some effect so wonderful that they raise in consciousness the outcry of applause, our private expression, directed to theirs in tribute, surprises their nimble participation in the act. In a moment's illumination we who have been staring at an illusion now stare at an apt phrase, or a paragraph magically producing some climactic novelty out of its demure simplicity.

What we think of as "modern" writing is a transparent substance fitted indistinguishably to the contour of thought and the color of feeling and imagery. It is not different from the everyday speech of people who speak well unaffectedly. The sentence, without uniformity of length, is commonly short, or each of its clauses is. It has just enough variation from the word order of its neighbors to lull suspicion that there is any word order at all. It is intended to pass observation as a sentence, though if it should be noticed, to be remarked for correct effectiveness. In grammar and rhetoric it uses the devices of more ornate eras, but sparingly, with less piling up and more parceling out. Instead of bold rhythms, soaring out of the horizontal or plunging deep below it, it ripples closer to a level, subtly. Since our language has absorbed its materials into one English, contemporary writers do not usually make a feature of Anglo-Saxon or Norman French derivatives, or of latinity, but keep themselves to the thoroughly blended mixture. By avoiding eccentricity, sensationalism, and parade, they earn a right to occasional unfamiliar usage when nothing else will serve for precision. The exactness of the diction is therefore in accord with the practice of educated people to-day, and not imitated from great writing of the past. As a result the style is in most cases a little more the society than the man; but authors who are too emphatically individual not to take infinite pains stand out from the mass because of what they make of the social convention in fitting it to what they are, to what they have to say. Without attempting to declare who are the best stylists who have published in our century, I have no hesitancy about naming some of the very good ones in fiction: Samuel Butler, Joseph Conrad, George Moore, the Joyce of *Dubliners* and *Portrait of the Artist*, Ellen Glasgow, Willa Cather, Sylvia

Townsend Warner, Aldous Huxley, and Ralph Bates. Stylistic superiority in a foreign language must be left to those who can determine it; but it is hard to believe that Anatole France, Maeterlinck, Proust, Gide, Schnitzler, Sigrid Undset, Thomas Mann, and Ignazio Silone are not writers of such excellence.

If style is the expression of meaning exactly as the meaning is and is valued, then style for fiction must be the conveyance of presences in consciousness as imagined occurrences. This means that the illusion must convince, the narration must move. Then fiction is the writing of imagined events; and the event, created by the imagination, is the immediate meaning which the style expresses. Whatever the events for their part convey obliquely in the way of thought or feeling, they themselves are conveyed by the words, directly. What the words do, therefore, is to take over into themselves something already expressed in the writer's consciousness as the events, in which meaning has already taken one expression. This is translation of the dumb show of imagery into the audibility of speech, and thence into the manual inscription; and what makes these transpositions possible is that meaning is polyglot, and can assume the varying idioms of fancy, of tongue, and of hand.

All of the literary arts employ this complex instrument for purposes of human self-discernment. Since fiction is hypothetical in its nature, temporal in its operation, and private in its distribution, it is a device for laying up in the individual consciousness a large and varied store of imaginary human experience. Through the dual nature of the word as matter and meaning, we modulate what is physically present in the worldly environment for bodily experience into mental experience of what thus becomes a presence in consciousness— a presence appreciable as environment, persons, and occurrence. Progressive development by artists in the skill to use language self-effacingly, so that it says whatever they wish without calling attention to itself, has produced in our time an effectiveness which is believable only when we respond to it in the disregard of taking it for granted.

Has that absent-minded contempt become complacency? Apparently some writers have thought so. Sterne took the convenient form of the novel and broke it to pieces, large and small; he fractured the chapter, the paragraph, the sentence; and with maddening smile and mock obeisance he handed the reader a bagful of the odds and ends to experience as best he might. Browning's form is form to the life, the spontaneous informality of speech-as-it-is. Meredith moulded words into

216

life masks of the passions. James' ciliary sentence groped as by touch through mazes of nuance to clear conclusions. Gertrude Stein blew words onto paper through a stippling pipe. Proust laid out a pattern of Gallic definiteness in the detail and in the whole, but on such a scale that the reader, at any one moment until the last, may know where he is, but not be sure where *that* is; one has a little less sense of direction than a midge on a revolving globe; in fact, anywhere in the midst of *Remembrance of Things Past* one might as well be a person in the incomprehensible world, as an intelligent reader, not to say an intellectual. In Kafka the words and the sentences are precise to punctilio—what do they pattern? But all of these men at least let the word alone. Then *Finnegans Wake* shattered the atomy. That might not have been so bad if the piecelets had been left unassembled for the philologist to sort out and reconstitute; but a nightmaie chemist has done that job, too, alas! with a thorough piecing together of bits from different words into brand-new what-is-its. Can it be that with one book this Irish scorner of the ground thrust the entire race into a state of cultural lag? Or is it that he has revealed us there, as history has never dared to? Sterne hinted that we are all Shandys in the actual inability of our language to convey the thoughts we fondly believe we exchange. Perhaps Joyce undertook to prove it.

Each of the writers I have just finished listing has been rated high by a public of the sort of readers who keep reputations alive. Each is notable for the attitude that old established simplifications of literary expression are inadequate to say some things well. Each has had some followers or adapters, but not many. What they did (who knows?) may be as hard to do as to read. It is not even easy to parody. The profits of pioneering are long to come by, and anyone willing and able to undertake such ardors is likely to go off on his own expedition. The follower of the geographical discoverer may be another explorer, but he is more frequently the trader or the settler or the tourist; for once the region is found, what is the service of finding it again? The area which the exceptionally original artist, in the sense in which I am now using the term, actually opens up, is not simply a place where a few primitivists can go native, but an extension of civilization to new possibilities. An established perfection in art may spell immortality for particular forms and for those who produce them; but its very finish as tradition is its death-warrant: it will be degraded by lesser hands into an inferior routine; it may not be superseded, but it will certainly be

217

succeeded. Yet whether or not language and art go to the extreme of novelty and stay there, they do change, and often the man whose contemporaries denounce him as an extremist is the arch-changer. When, after generations, he is remarked for many disciples, their names are likely to be Smith, Jones, and Brown, while his is still a synonym for fame.

I have left to the end of my discussion the curious phenomenon of dialogue, which has already been partially discussed under the headings of auditory imagery and of the scene as structural unit. Since the self-spoken thought of the character is a process very much like the private monologue of reading which it exploits, the reader enjoys two contradictory advantages. The first is the very real intimacy of the experience, since it is within himself. The second is the equally real objectivity of observation, since the words, no matter whose they are, the writer's or the agent's, are of course *not* his own. This detachment absolves the reader from any complicity or responsibility. That the agent is thinking, for example, in language of criminal or obscene intent is certainly no charge against the reader, a mere bystander. The same reasoning holds true for the illusion of dialogue as speech aloud. It should equally, I am sure, hold true in the case of the author. What he reports as the speech or thought of a villainous or depraved character, he may report out of utter loathing for it, as part of the quality of villainy or depravity, as he himself sees and detests it, and would rid the world of it. He has witnessed it as a presence in his creative consciousness, to his own bystanding attention. In view of the scruples of certain authors against intruding upon the illusion, in their attempt to produce pure fiction, one can see that the aesthetic scruple and the moral one might very well merge into single idealism.

In the rendition of dialogue, I would say that there are two main principles: the intent of the character in speaking, and the event of his speaking. Though each is recognizable as itself, they not only may be combined, but usually are. What makes the emphasis, then, is the extent to which the force of the one is superior to the force of the other. When dialogue, at the one extreme, is baldly devoted to meaning, the situation is this: there is some point of view or set of facts which may be considered privy to the agent's knowledge, as Greek epic and drama: a course of action is discussed, or a messenger reports an action completed away from the present scene. The speech is long and formal; the art of the rhetorician is as manifest as the fact of speaking. The use, furthermore, of indirect discourse in classical oratory, history, and so on, emphasized the gist of what was reported as having been said, and therefore in some degree depersonalized it. Naturally, if Cicero or Plutarch reports a man's view with accuracy, even in a summary, something of the man comes along, and this may be very much to the point. Yet the individuality is rendered in a general way, as what is typical of the person, in accord with the spirit of formal classical rhetoric to pose the sitter in an attitude that is consistent, rather than to catch him in some unique moment of being. This classic kind of dialogue, as I will call it, was not only revived by continuators of the classic in the renaissance and later, but also made its way into the Greek romances, the picaresque fiction of Romance countries, and hence into English imitations. It is the dialogue, for example, of Defoe, whenever he uses dialogue: everyone who speaks or thinks, does so in the set, conscious way of oral composition, dressing his thought carefully in Sunday clothes. In Addison's narrative sketches, the persons are evidently accustomed to elegant verbal clothing throughout the week; they are easy in the mode, ill at ease without it. The characters of *Rasselas* all talk Johnsonese; the lesser novelists of the end of the eighteenth century—Godwin, Holcroft, Moore, Mrs. Radcliffe, Walpole—obviously regarded this as the right model.

With Miss Edgeworth and Scott the classical tradition, never rigidly followed by Richardson, Fielding, and Smollett, and unceremoniously tossed in a blanket by Sterne, gave way much more to naturalness. Miss Edgeworth used the tradition for some of her characters who were not Irish, and therefore with some predominance in her starchier tales, such as *Leonora, Harrington,* and *Patronage.* In *Castle Rackrent,* and in the Irish portions of *The Absentee* and *Ormond,* where dialect made art give way to nature, she is intent on the living note of speech. As for Scott, he too is naturalistic in delivering the language of his peasants; but his heroes and heroines enjoy every advantage of education—if not theirs, then at least his. With Fanny Burney, and triumphantly with Jane Austen in her maturity, the stylized address not only goes out, but is teased and made into a burlesque of itself. By "goes out," I mean that the mode is reduced to a lower standing. It continues in varying extent in Bulwer and Disraeli, Wilkie Collins, Mrs. Gaskell, and others, but the bigger writers either discard or disguise it. Dickens used a travesty of it for some purposes of his comedy, and George Eliot, Thackeray, and Meredith made the dialogue faithful to the character. There are lapses, or exceptions: Gissing, Dreiser, Moore, and Lawrence in his uninspired moments are all capable of falling in the Horatio Alger deadness in dialogue. (I would add, among contemporaries of ours, Pearl Buck, and the "serious" works of Steinbeck, she out of rapture with the eyes closed, and he from bending over the little people. Is it better to be gracious, like Wilde, and pretend that everyone is as fascinating as oneself; or to acknowledge sensibly, like Moore, that no one is?)

For the sort of dialogue that treats every remark or thought as a unique event of character, we must acknowledge a powerful nineteenth century impetus outside of fiction, in Browning. In his astounding empathy he was able to make his imaginary characters seem to speak their nature, their idiosyncrasy, their momentaneous framing of expression, even their aberrant stammering in confusion. He had many high talents, but this was their stamp. If at times his hunter's instinct for rarity seems to overindulge itself in the bizarre, his greatest personations are full and round to the life. Not one of the principals of *The Ring and the Book* is bizarre essentially; and Pompilia, Caponsacchi, and the Pope are realizations of truly noble natures, more human, and not less, for living their ideals. In their speeches and in Guido's, it is hard to find a phrase not apparently born on the lips of the moment, yet saturated with the whole lifetime from which it is delivered. Perhaps Chaucer equals Browning in this production of the only words that could have been spoken, at a time and place, by a certain person, and perhaps Shakespeare excels him. Few others approach him. In English fiction I can be sure of no more than Sterne, Jane Austen, and Joyce. James catches the avidity of the moment, but not its accent. Thomas Wolfe has many exquisite recordings, but also so often the needle sticks in the groove. I am well aware that there are other means of creating illusion of unique speech and thought, and that there are readers who need no such particularity as Browning's for the effect. Yet for those who wish to give themselves over wholly to a writer, in order that the credit for every detail of the illusion may be his, this gift of patience for character in the minute occurrence, and for the inevitable word on the character's part to substantiate it, amounts to the very illusion of illusion, the ultimate in created experience. One feels that if the future can go higher than this attainment, it will be only by building up from it.

Among the many resemblances and differences of speech

in the world and dialogue in a book, it is curious to note this: that what characters, as distinct from people, say, is fatally fixed, in being written down. The only parallel we have in life is the phonographic recording of conversation when the speakers do not dream that they are being overheard. Our power, therefore, to turn back to the printed passage and to repeat the concrete words is, alas! a subtraction from *their* uniqueness, though, no doubt, not from our experience of them. Here, of course, is only one of the ways in which fiction is distinguishable from life, in being history. The stories of a past age are period pieces, like its surviving furniture and bric-a-brac. Even historical and Utopian fiction has this quality—the retrospect, the wistfulness, of a certain time. In addition, there is written into novels and tales in which the time and place of the illusion are those of the writing or a little before, many a contemporary feature of topography, custom, and the like, introduced into the narrative as a matter of course, but later sought out by the professional historian as evidence of old landmarks and vanished manners. Defoe's circumstantial care in giving place names and other facts, and Fanny Burney's or Thackeray's delight in public gatherings, give their works documentary value for the student of times bygone. Who can doubt that Wells, Galsworthy, Proust, Mann, Farrell, Thomas Wolfe, Ellen Glasgow, and others will serve future historians similarly as remains and monuments of the generation we regard simply as our world and ourselves?

Most writing, fiction included, sooner or later drifts into this status of mere indication of what was. Lodged in cellars, attics, or on the shelves of great libraries, it serves by preserving. The pages once fresh for experience are cemetery directions for scholarly footnotes; the words are coral trinket antiques for the showcases of quotation. I am speaking now of books no one any longer reads, but only consults, like letters whose unknown writers and recipients are at peace in the oblivion of death, or like characters and covenants no longer in force. Rarely, some name, like Melville's, that seems to be doomed to the museum quiet, is returned to the current of time by enthusiastic re-discoverers. The many forgotten remain where time has left them, if indeed they are so lucky as to remain at all. Paper burns, mildews, or simply crumbles; and once the material word has returned to diffuse, anonymous destructibility, it takes away with it every last trace of the wrought meaning.

At the other extreme, enduring works enjoy a phoenix immortality, shedding one consumed edition for a shining new print. Textual corruption, and later restoration, are the obvious proofs of what the reality is. At any rate, the great tales of all ages are the circulating library of eternity. For any present, they are. Theirs is the present of humanity, of which they are one category of presence. In grammar there is a phenomenon known as the historical present, in which yesterday's doings are rendered in today's tense. This is paralleled, in criticism, by what we should dignify with mortality by the calendar. All the external facts about a masterpiece—the dates of composition, publication, republication down to this year—are dated by itself. It endures, it survives, as I say, because continuously it really is. *The Iliad, The Canterbury Tales, Robinson Crusoe, War and Peace, Tom Sawyer, Remembrance of Things Past,* are contemporaries of a more numerous host. The fact is given physical demonstration in series of reprinted texts: "Everyman's," "The World's Classics of Literature," "The Modern Library."

These, however, are volumes of pages of words of print, ink on paper again. The actual words, the words that activate and anoint the dead matter on which they impress their transfiguring succession, are timeless and placeless in the reality of meaning, in the fact of experience, in the significance that invisibly signs itself with perceptible symbols. They are the quickness of what I call "the whole word," a quintessence of the universal importance, a concentering of what lies sprawled abroad as diffusion of experience, like the gathering of much heat and light into the sun.

Then the word of the whole fiction is of course the word of our hard, substantial world. Yet it is material not as the key, but as the keyhole, through which we squint at life on the other side of the door of organism. Its shape is physical, but its form is conscious, so that it and we may function in knowing *together.* Therefore the word of the fictional medium is whatever is communicated in the conjoint operation of the image of illusion, the conflict powering all occurrence, the characters peopling the action as its presences, the thoughts and the moods, and the forms of all the elements as the ostensible satisfactions of creative surmise. All these together, in togetherness and togethering, are the whole fiction as it flourishes in our day, as it tends toward growth, as it lies behind us in the superb works which are its past and ours.